DAVE STONE NEW HOME SALES

 REAL ESTATE EDUCATION COMPANY / CHICAGO

While a great deal of care has been taken to provide accurate and current information, the ideas, suggestions, general principles, and conclusions presented in this book are subject to local, state, and federal laws and regulations, court cases, and any revisions of same. The reader is thus urged to consult legal counsel regarding any points of law—this publication should not be used as a substitute for competent legal advice.

Library of Congress Cataloging in Publication Data

Stone, Dave.
   New home sales.

   1. House selling.   2. Real estate business.
I. Title.
HD1375.S749   1982   333.33'8'0688   82-15084
ISBN 0-88462-418-8

Copyright © 1982 by Development Systems Corporation

Published by Real Estate Education Company/Chicago,
a subsidiary company of Longman Group Limited

All rights reserved.

The text of this publication, or any part thereof, may not be reproduced in any manner whatsoever without written permission from the publisher.

Printed in the United States of America

10   9   8   7   6   5   4

To the memory of my father, Ernest Marshall Stone, who died in 1978 at the age of 92. His inspiration as a father, master builder, Realtor ®, and friend added a very special dimension to my own appreciation of the challenges of the real estate profession and of life in general.

Contents

Preface		ix
1:	**The Opportunities and Challenges of New Home Sales**	1
	The Unique Challenges of New Home Sales	3
	Motivation: The Key to Meeting the Challenges	7
	Preparation	8
	First Impressions Are Important	16
	Making Customers Feel Comfortable	17
	Organize Your Personal Sales Environment	19
	Requirements for Success	19
	Making the Most of the Opportunities	25
	Conclusion	34
2:	**Using Well-Planned Presentations**	37
	The Importance of Selling Skills	38
	The Objectives of an Organized Sales Presentation	39
	How to Build a Presentation	44
	Address Yourself to Your Buyers' Motives	73
	Guidelines for Management of Sales Exhibits	76
	The Credibility of the Presentation	82
3:	**Qualifying and Counseling Prospects**	83
	Beginning the Qualifying Process	83
	Qualifying Categories	86
	Questioning Techniques	99
	Self-Evaluation	101

4:	**Demonstrating New Home Values**	105
	The Importance of New Home Demonstrations	105
	Planning a Demonstration	111
	Competitive Research	119
	Using a Value Index System	119
	The Walk-Through and Rehearsal	120
	The Do's and Don't's of Showing a New Home	120
	Achieving the Purpose of the Demonstration	121
5:	**Converting Objections Into Closing Opportunities**	123
	The Nature of the Homebuying Decision	123
	Avoid Jumping to Conclusions	124
	Types of Objections	124
	When to Be Hard of Hearing	128
	Avoid Defensiveness	128
	Stay on the Prospect's Side	129
	The Seven Steps to Handling Objections	130
	Anticipate Major Objections	135
	Third-Party Stories	136
	The Principle of Reduction	137
	Documentation	140
	Prepare a Working Plan for Dealing with Objections	141
	Commonly Heard Objections	142
	Summary	144
6:	**Creating Urgency to Induce Action**	145
	Everything in the Sales Arena Should Convey the Message of Urgency	146
	Teamwork	157
	Phasing and Marketing Strategy	157
	Summary	159
7:	**Generating Sales with Be-Backs**	167
	The Importance of Be-Back Business	167
	Getting Be-Backs by Generating Emotional Involvement	168
	Maintaining Good Prospect Records and Profile Data	177
	Selling against Competition	180
	Follow-up	181
	The Importance of High-Yield Opportunities	183
	Conclusion	184

8: Closing the Sale — 185

- The Relationship between Qualifying and Closing — 185
- Handling the Difficult Decision-Making Process — 189
- The Four Steps to a Sale — 192
- Closing Techniques — 193
- Avoid Introducing Too Many Decision-Making Subjects — 197
- The Closing Question — 201
- Types of Closes — 202
- Body Language and Buying Signals — 208
- Relieving Buyer Tension — 209
- The Salesperson's Approach — 211
- Initiating the Close — 215
- Confirm and Reinforce the Buyer's Decision — 216

9: Opportunities Through After-Sales Service — 219

- General Forms of After-Sales Service — 219
- Keeping Buyers Informed — 220
- The Purpose of After-Sales Service — 221
- Specific Ways to Provide After-Sales Service — 221
- Maintain Good Customer and Sales Records — 230
- Buyer Involvement — 231
- Help with the Transition to a New Home — 232
- New Resident Activities — 254
- Welcoming Buyers to the Community — 255
- Summary — 256

10: Managing and Marketing New Homes for Builders — 259

- The Role of the Broker in Builder Sales Management — 260
- How to Effectively List Builders' Homes — 265
- Commission Arrangements in New Home Sales Programs — 271
- On-Site Versus Off-Site Representations — 276
- Models and Demonstration Homes — 277
- Selection and Recruitment of Personnel — 280
- Educating New Home Sales Agents — 289
- Motivating Salespeople to Achieve Optimum Results — 290
- The Responsibilities of On-Site Personnel or Listing Salespeople — 294
- Communicating and Reporting to Builders and Managers — 294
- Creating Cooperative Broker Programs — 296
- Responsibilities of Listing Agents or Builder's Sales Managers — 300

	Policies and Procedures Manuals for New Home Sales	305
	Summary	308
11:	**Improving Communication Skills**	309
	The Importance of Listening	310
	Major Rules for Communicating	310
	Natural Communication Tools	315
	Props and Visual Aids	324
	Cooperative Response	325
	Conclusion	325
12:	**Creativity in Selling and Financing**	327
	The Need to Understand Creative Financing in Today's Housing Markets	327
	Creative Financing Checklists	328
	An Application of Creative Financing Techniques	340
	Some Creative Mortgage Alternatives	351
	Contracts for Deed or Land Contracts	353
	Wraparound Mortgages	356
	Conclusion	357
Glossary		359

Preface

The need for professionalism in marketing and selling new homes, condominiums, vacation homes, and new residential communities of all types is obvious to those associated with the homebuilding industry. As a student of the real estate profession and consultant to hundreds of builders, brokers, and developers, I have dedicated myself to improving the quality of the educational programs for the salespeople and managers who represent the housing opportunities created by the building industry.

This manual on new home sales techniques is based on years of practical experience and the research that comes from sharing results with other professionals. This book is the most comprehensive work on the subject I have attempted. I sincerely hope it will give readers a better understanding of the basic principles involved in this highly specialized field.

It is not enough merely to build a good home or develop a fine master plan for a new residential project and expect that the public will automatically perceive its value. The presentation of these housing opportunities justifies a professional sales approach that can effectively translate features into benefits and motivate potential homebuyers to purchase a home.

The housing industry suffers from many external forces that we cannot control and that have a tendency to affect the confidence of prospective buyers. It is our responsibility to see that those who need homes are given the information and necessary reinforcement to help them buy.

The author wishes to acknowledge the following individuals and organizations for their support, assistance and contributions made to this book:

Lee Anderson
Gary Elliott
Lester Goodman
Tom Hopkins
John Lumbleau
David Olsen
Thomas R. Richey
Gary Ryness
George P. Shafran
David Wolfe

American Salesmasters, Inc.
National Association of Homebuilders
National Association of Realtors®
National Sales & Marketing Council
Realtors® National Marketing Institute
Urban Land Institute

1: The Opportunities and Challenges of New Home Sales

A story is told about a young applicant for a position in real estate sales who commented to a seasoned veteran:

"I think I would like to try real estate."

to which the older man replied:

"You don't try real estate, it tries you!"

There is a great deal of truth in that observation. Selling real estate, although profitable and exciting, is trying in many ways. Literally hundreds of things can go wrong in the process of developing land, building homes, and selling and financing them. Buyers, too, usually have problems that must be resolved before final settlement and delivery. The mortgage market, the lumber supply, the labor unions, local politics, the subcontractors, the national economy, the weather, and numerous other factors can and often do adversely affect homebuilding programs.

This book discusses ways to overcome the frustrations and challenges of real estate sales in general and new home sales in particular. More important, the book presents positive steps you can take to use your time and talents to the best advantage and to sell new homes skillfully.

The art of selling is learned the hard way, by acquiring and practicing the basic skills every day. Skill comes when habit frees you from the need to concern yourself with the mechanics of your actions. Webster defines a habit as a "constant, often unconscious inclination to perform some act, acquired through its frequent repetition." By forming the proper habits, you increase your potential for success. Horace Mann once wrote:

> *"Habit is a cable. We weave a thread of it every day, and at last we cannot break it."*

Most of the things we want are really in the hands of others. To the degree that you give others what they want, they will give you what you want. The whole purpose of sales training and self-development is to get better at *human engineering,* so that you know how to give others what they really want. Human engineering is the art of communicating with people for the attainment of meaningful objectives. It is based on knowledge of human behavior and the skills of positive interpersonal relationships.

Today's housing market has little need for real estate salespeople who are order-takers or clerks, just standing behind counters and accepting what prospects already have made up their minds to do. The need is for people who understand how to qualify, how to resolve problems, and how to help people over the potentially difficult situations involved in purchasing new homes and relocating to new environments.

This book can assist you, but please do not accept everything it says as being final or the concepts as being totally applicable to you. Test what you read and learn, and apply it on a day-to-day basis, knowing that everything changes and that you must therefore change as well.

This first chapter provides a description of the challenges specific to new home sales. Along with these challenges go opportunities. The rewards that you will receive depend upon the goals you set and your willingness to achieve them. To this end, the chapter discusses goal setting, time management, and personal motivation. These might be considered aspects of the most important sales tool: the salesperson him- or herself. Along those lines, this chapter continues by addressing ways to work with customers and make the most of sales opportunities.

Chapters 2 through 9 concern the specific steps of the sales process, providing suggestions for each step. Chapter 2 discusses preparation for selling, an important step without which the others are likely to fail. Chapter 3 concerns qualification and control of prospects. Chapter 4 supplies ideas on how to demonstrate new home values. Chapters 5 and 6 have to do with bringing about a close—Chapter 5 in terms of handling objections, and Chapter 6 in terms of creating a sense of urgency. In Chapter 7 are suggestions of ways to generate more sales with prospects known as be-backs. Chapter 8 discusses the closing process itself. The sales process does not end with a closed sale, but is a continuing process of serving customers. Chapter 9 is concerned with after-sales service and its importance to new home sales. Chapter 10 addresses the responsibilities of real estate brokers and new home sales managers.

The last two chapters of the book concern more general issues, issues that are important throughout the sales process. Chapter 11 discusses communication skills. Chapter 12 concerns financing a home—an issue of ever-increasing relevance to today's homebuying market.

While many of the principles presented in these chapters may seem to apply to real estate sales in general, the focus of this book is on selling new homes, including condominiums, planned unit developments, resorts, and individual home sites. A need exists for such a focus, because new home sales presents unique challenges to the salesperson and to sales management. These special challenges are the focus of the next section of this chapter.

THE UNIQUE CHALLENGES OF NEW HOME SALES

Many resale specialists are ineffective in representing new builder products, and the reasons are normally related to the selling concepts they have developed to meet the specific demands of their business. The following paragraphs define the major differences between selling new homes and resale properties.

Customer Versus Product

The typical resale agent is not married to his or her merchandise, because he or she has the freedom to work on a large variety of listings in the market area. If customers do not like one section of town, the resale agent can show them homes in another section. If the first few offerings are unacceptable, there are always more to show.

In contrast, a merchant builder's sales representative is normally married to the builder's products. He or she seldom has the freedom of showing or selling competitive properties. The merchant builder's philosophy must be built on the concept that *you have to sell what you have to sell.*

It might then be said that a resale specialist is married more to customers than to merchandise, while the reverse is true of the new home salesperson. That is why a new home salesperson must know more about his or her products than a resale agent normally does. If a resale agent spent too much time studying a single home, it probably would be sold by someone else before the agent could profit from the knowledge.

Many resale agents successfully represent and sell both pre-owned homes and new construction. Those that do so usually adjust their roles to meet the specific criteria of new versus older properties.

Negotiation Versus Price

The very nature of the general brokerage business requires a resale agent to learn to negotiate prices, terms, offers, and counteroffers. In most cases, homes are listed within a negotiable price range, and then offers that are somewhat less than the original asking prices are presented to the owners.

The opposite is true in new home selling. Prices are almost invariably fixed by the builder, and they are seldom negotiated. Thus, new home agents must develop selling approaches that are distinctly different from those of resale specialists. The manufacturer's price and terms must be presented from a position of strength, not weakness.

Agent Versus Customer Control

The resale salesperson obtains a measure of control over the buyer through counseling the buyer, selecting limited offerings, driving buyers in his or her own automobile, and determining what will be seen and in what order. The resale agent even controls the amount of time available for inspection, as a result of this direct involvement with the prospective homebuyer.

The salesperson assigned to a subdivision or new home sales office seldom has as much control over a customer as a resale salesperson enjoys. The prospects normally arrive and leave in their own cars. They are free to inspect property at their leisure, often without the presence of a sales representative. They tend to be more independent and less involved with any single sales agent or product.

These distinctions mean that totally different methods of selling are required. The on-site new home salesperson has to learn how to qualify more quickly, obtain psychological control through skillful use of involvement tools, and to cultivate relaxed relationships on which to build be-back business. The resale agent has more control, more time, and usually more offerings with which to work.

Discovering Versus Demonstration

Successful resale agents have learned that they cannot safely defend or justify a pre-owned home. First of all, it is used—and that means the present owners have probably made some modifications. A salesperson who defends the home risks losing buyers. Also, few if any warranties are given with an older residence, and the used-home buyer knows and understands this.

A new home, in contrast, has new appliances, innovations, and materials that are worthy of demonstration. Thus, the salesperson learns to use these features to reinforce buyer interest. This means he or she must know everything there is to know about the builder's merchandise, including manufacturers' warranties, because the new home buyer wants and expects them.

In sum, whereas a resale specialist *discovers* a used home with a prospect, a new home specialist *demonstrates* his or her products. The approaches are justifiably different and equally successful when used by professionals who have really mastered their roles.

Reality Versus Dreams

There is another difference between selling new versus resale homes. Existing homes are part of an environment that has been influenced by many factors over the years. Sometimes these are positive factors; other times they are negative ones. New homes, in contrast, are generally part of a new way of life in a new environment. The difference in selling these two kinds of homes is the difference between selling reality and selling a dream.

A progressive builder is probably offering buyers a better environment than they had before. The project will have recreational facilities, common green areas, parks, walking paths, and natural beauty. From the beginning, the sales associates can market the dream of what will be, and involve the prospective buyer's imagination in the benefits of living in a new community that will not be marred by unpleasant architecture, adverse neighborhood influences, or limited amenities. Any new home has a romantic aspect about what it will become when the new owners bring it to life. Thus, while both resale and new home specialists use marketing environments, the first is working with existing conditions, while the other has the advantage of newer development concepts and the dream with which to stir buyers' imaginations. The challenge is to successfully portray the dream while construction is in its initial phases and conditions are less than optimal.

Buyers Versus Lookers

Another difference between new and resale selling is that resale customers are more often buyers than lookers. Shoppers do sometimes call brokers, but the majority of people who take the aggressive action of picking up a telephone to call an agent are more likely to be in the market to buy a home. They have already decided to buy something and usually do so within a relatively short period of time. The average sale in resale operations is made within the first week of contact.

In contrast, a high percentage of new home buyers start out as lookers who have not really decided to buy now. They may begin with just a Sunday drive to a new model complex—an impulsive action without specific objective.

The freedom of visiting new home sales centers without pressure or the necessity for personal involvement with an agent encourages the impulse prospect to inspect new merchandise. This is one of the primary reasons for going to the expense of producing quality model home centers. In these environments, people see, feel, and experience our products under the most relaxed conditions, and become excited about them because of what the salesperson does to stimulate emotional appeal.

The difference here is similar to comparing window shopping to going to an old-fashioned delicatessen where everything is behind the counter and must be specifically ordered. A resale broker depends upon specific requests, while a new home salesperson usually has a supermarket of products open for free and uninvolved inspection. Also, a large percentage of sales of new housing are made to people who return more than once before making a final decision to purchase. In the trade vernacular, these prospects are known as *be-backs*.

It is important to understand this difference in order to take advantage of the showcase the builder/developer has created. Visitors should never feel under pressure to buy, for relaxed lookers can become excited buyers when they do not feel the anxiety of decision making.

Service After Sale

Another difference between selling new homes and pre-owned properties is the matter of service after sale. A resale transaction normally is consummated in a relatively short span of time, while a new home sale takes considerable time, especially if the house still has to be constructed, and delivery is three to six months away. There is also a myriad of details involved in new housing such as selecting colors, options, changes, and other variations.

Once a buyer takes possession, there are usually many call-back items that must be serviced by the building team. These may involve some coordination with the sales department and the settlement of potential disputes when they occur. A greater degree of responsibility is involved in servicing new home sales than is true for the majority of resales. Attention to detail can make a substantial difference in your success in this profession!

MOTIVATION: THE KEY TO MEETING THE CHALLENGES

This book emphasizes that the psychological climate in which one does business determines success or failure. The human tendency is to react to negative factors with certain patterns of response. It is natural, for example, to become defensive when constantly challenged by others. If buyers come screaming into the sales office each day demanding explanations and complaining about things you cannot seem to resolve, your instinct is to fight back, even though this builds barriers to effective communication. To remain poised, polite, and positive under such circumstances requires patience and understanding.

The strain and frustration of trying to cope with daily irritations can make it easy for a salesperson to lose perspective. Some become so depressed by the pressure of their problems that they treat with apathy each new prospect who walks into their offices. Such an approach, in the eyes of a prospect, is like saying, "What are you doing here? We have enough problems without you." You cannot sell real estate effectively with negative attitudes. The buyer has enough fears and uncertainties. He or she does not need yours. To sell effectively, you must keep yourself *motivated*.

You are not born with all the attributes necessary for survival and progress in the field of human relations. They are acquired skills. It takes discipline and consistent mental and emotional conditioning to become master of your own psychological environment.

Change Your Life by Changing Your Attitudes

Attitudes, more than any other factor, control the direction and quality of life. It is easy to say: "Be enthusiastic!" or "Think positive thoughts!" Indeed, such an approach may sound too easy to be effective. But you cannot appreciate how much strength you can gather from the application of such maxims until you have tried them.

It is one thing to tell a person to think positively, and it is another to explain how to do it. This book does not pretend to be a guide to positive thinking or a substitute for the outstanding works of such experts as Harry Overstreet, Norman Vincent Peale, Earl Nightingale, Dale Carnegie, and Maxwell Maltz. Instead, this book aims to bring into focus what the practical aspects of personal attitude control mean with regard to the salesperson's role in representing new housing.

Selling is an art. It depends upon the ability to communicate with people in positive ways. People are responsive to people. Everyone is influenced by others' attitudes and actions. Selling new homes is a profession that pays well when you are a positive force for the good of others and yourself.

Success at influencing other people's attitudes and actions begins by understanding how to control your own behavior. The quality of your personal presentation is directly related to your own mental and psychological approach to life and your career.

It is equally important to recognize that the environment you create and maintain throughout the selling process has a direct impact on the attitudes of prospective homebuyers. This is the subject of a later part of the chapter. Your effectiveness will be determined in no small measure by how well you handle the environmental factors that influence your customers. Always be concerned with the little things that visually and emotionally affect prospects' attitudes. Take into consideration the total sales climate, including your interaction with others in the sales organization. Negative feelings produce negative results; conversely, positive feelings tend to produce positive results.

PREPARATION

Prepare Yourself for Success

Mental and emotional preparation each day helps you to cultivate and sustain positive attitudes needed for success. Exercising the mind and body adds energy and enthusiasm to your life. Each person must learn how to conserve his or her energies and establish physical programs that are appropriate. What one person might work into a daily regimen may not be wise for someone else. To lack a plan for each day and a method of stimulating mind and body is to risk failure, however. A runner who does not prepare for the race has little chance of winning.

There is a direct relationship between the activities in one's private life and one's success in business. Every thought and attitude establishes a pattern of thinking that becomes a real part of your daily existence. That is why it is so important to cultivate good habits that strengthen physical and mental powers. It is a matter of self-renewal. Remember, *each day is the very first day of the rest of your life.*

Before you begin any of your daily assignments, take a measure of yourself. Are you in a positive frame of mind? Are you ready for the challenges and opportunities that the day may bring? It is important to establish your priorities for the day and to find ways to recharge your own emotional attitudes with positive thoughts. The only way to warm up the engine is to start the motor running. Begin your day by doing those things that will stimulate your mind and body. Here are a few of the types of activities that many successful salespeople practice:

Exercise and Recreation

Calisthenics
Cycling
Jogging
Yoga
Handball
Golf
Jumping rope
Walking
Stretching
Tennis
Bowling
Other competitive sports

Meditation

Prayer
Quiet relaxation
Reading
Listening to music
Listening to tapes
Attending church

Creative Activities

Gardening
Painting
Ceramics
Studying
 educational subjects
Pursuing other
 hobbies
Needlepoint
Writing
Photography
Playing musical
 instruments
Singing

Personal Organization

Reviewing prospects
Planning objectives and goals for the day
Practicing selling skills
Reading or listening to training programs
Scheduling activities

Participating in Social Events

Social clubs	School activities
Toastmasters	Public speaking
Charitable causes	Political causes
Neighborhood improvement programs	

Your Attitude Toward Failure

Too many salespeople crumble at the first sign of adversity. Why do they fail or give up when persistence would have brought results? I have frequently asked that question in seminars, and the responses have typically included the following:

- People are lazy.
- They lack self-confidence.
- They do not believe in their products.
- They cannot stand rejection.
- They need excuses for their lack of performance.
- They listen to the negative thoughts of others.
- They have competing interests.

All of these may be valid, but perhaps most valid of all is the fear of failure itself. One of the major reasons so many salespeople give up or retreat from difficult sales situations is that they cannot stand the possibility of failing, and so they are unwilling even to try. The first sign that things may not work out justifies their fears, and they no longer need to be persistent or exert themselves.

Yet look at the magnificent achievements of mankind. How many people succeeded on the first try? Thomas Edison reportedly tried ten thousand filaments for his light bulb before he found one that worked. And when someone asked him why he wasn't discouraged because he had failed so many times, he said:

> *"I haven't failed ten thousand times; I have discovered ten thousand elements that won't work."*

You may see setbacks as self-defeat or personal failure. If so, you will destroy all that you have to offer others, for you will project a lack of confidence in everything you do. Instead, think of a setback as a learning opportunity. If you try something that doesn't work, make adjustments and try again. Experimentation is a good way to learn, especially in sales.

Merely overcoming something that is difficult is a source of strength. Success in life is not so much a matter of talent—or, for that matter, opportunity—as it is personal concentration, self-motivation and perseverance. As Abraham Lincoln once said:

> *"Your own resolution to succeed is more important than any other single thing."*

Your Attitude Toward Achievement and Praise

You achieve what you expect to achieve, whether or not you are conscious of the impact of your thoughts on your actions. If you expect to fail, or you expect others to fail you, it probably will happen. If you expect things to work out, they probably will. In the first instance, the fear of failure results in a lack of confidence. In the second, mental conditioning gives you the enthusiasm to persevere when the situation requires endurance and skill. That is the power of self-fulfilling prophecy.

This view of expectations is similar to a definition of luck:

> *"Luck is opportunity meeting preparedness."*

Your mind, like your car, works best in forward gear. If you are in reverse or coasting in neutral, there is little chance you can switch gears fast enough to respond to unexpected conditions. The mental conditioning that gets you into forward is important to your readiness and responsiveness when prospective homebuyers enter your sales office. Your anticipation and expectation of positive results can be the force that moves others to take positive action now.

A good illustration of this is a story told to me by one of my real estate broker friends. The story is about my friend's most successful salesman. One day the salesman came to work and immediately went the the sales-activity board and wrote the word *SOLD!* When the others asked him what he had sold so early in the morning, he replied, "I don't know yet. The day isn't over." And, true to his expectations, by the time the day was over he had sold a home.

Learn to sustain yourself on less praise than you feel you deserve. Some salespeople become upset when their accomplishments are not recognized to the degree they feel they should be. It is true that personal recognition by others is an important source of image reinforcement, and everyone seeks it in one way or another. But as you mature in being able to handle a variety of situations, you should be able to sustain yourself on less praise than you really feel you deserve. That means not expecting praise from others every time you work hard to put a sale together, solve a problem, or do something behind the scenes that makes the builder or someone else look good.

You know what you have done. That is the important thing, and it is its own source of strength. Give yourself credit for your achievements. Keep your own personal scorecard. If you understand your own value, it will be like charging your own battery each day. No one else can really do it for you. If you need a hypodermic needle from someone else, you will have lessened your control over your own life.

Your Attitude Toward Yourself

The mental picture you have of yourself is transmitted to others by your attitudes and actions. A positive self-image is the result of depositing positive thoughts in a mental bank over the years. When you need them, they are there to withdraw. If all you put away are negative thoughts, they will be all you have to draw upon when you seek reinforcement. Therefore, maintain a positive self-image.

The subconscious mind can be programmed for positive results. If, every day when you get out of bed, you thank God that you are alive, that you have something worthwhile to do, and that you want to do it, you contribute positively to motivating your subconscious level and thus reinforce yourself. This helps build the reserves you need, and gives you cheerfulness and a contentment that will make others happy to be with you.

It is easy to see things that need improvement and to deprecate yourself when you do not succeed. At the same time, you should also set up a positive inventory of your talents and abilities. List those positive attributes you know you have, and then make a decision to strengthen and use them. If you harness your assets and compensate for your liabilities, it will be far easier to keep things in perspective, moving forward each day and attaining the desired results. Spend some time each day improving your weaknesses, but use most of your time to develop your strengths.

Emotional Stamina

Emotional stamina is vital in new home sales. You are, and will be, the emotional "punching bag" for many other people, at times even for your builder. Emotional stamina is possible even in such circumstances if you have yourself in focus each day.

Accept People as They Are. Recognize that you must deal with people as they are, and do not try to change them. If you are disappointed with them, you will show it. If you accept people as normal human beings who have reasons for getting upset, then your attitude will remain in balance, and you will have the emotional stamina to sustain your position.

Keep a Good Sense of Humor. Another way to maintain emotional stamina is to avoid taking yourself too seriously. A good sense of humor, keeping yourself and others in perspective, tends to provide emotional balance and can remove some of the sting of what otherwise might be highly charged emotional events.

Live in Day-Tight Compartments

Many years ago, Dale Carnegie wrote a famous book entitled *How to Stop Worrying and Start Living.* In it, he identified the value of bringing larger problems and goals down to controllable periods of time, specifically, the span of one day, or 24 hours. He used an expression that carries a great deal of meaning:

"Live in day-tight compartments."

Phrased differently, we might say: Today is what is happening while you are planning for tomorrow.

By living one day at a time, fully alive to the opportunities and challenges at hand, you can experience immediate rewards and retain your perspective about the things you are not yet able to resolve. There is real strength in the knowledge that you can live for and handle the next 24 hours. The objectives you set for yourself within that time frame can become guideposts toward larger goals. Because you keep today in perspective, you are better prepared for tomorrow.

Each day, you set the stage for your responses to the opportunities presented. You do it by the way you put yourself into motion each morning, and by the way you look, talk, listen, think, and feel. An important part of your job is to cultivate positive attitudes and to make a habit out of productive actions. The following paragraphs describe some ways to achieve this:

Start Each Day Properly. Every thought and attitude establishes the patterns of one's existence in small but significant ways and gives one's life meaning and purpose. That is why it is so important to cultivate the right habits for mental self-renewal upon beginning a new day.

There is a powerful saying that is well worth adopting as a private motto for greeting every sunrise:

Start every day as though it were the very first day of your life —because it is the first day of the rest of your life.

Before beginning your daily assignments, take stock of where you are and where you want to go. Find personal ways to recharge your mental and emotional batteries with the fuel of positive thought and personal self-motivation. Since each of us is distinctly different, what works for one may not work for others. Some people have found it helpful to start the day with quiet time for prayer or meditation; others have found that physical exercise helps to put them in a positive frame of mind. You must individually find your own private reserves of strength and then draw upon them every day.

Operate on VHF. Professional salespeople learn the value of operating on VHF—"very high frequency." To communicate with your buyers in ways that will motivate them to action, you must be able to transmit and receive at the highest possible level of efficiency, and on a clear channel that is not obstructed by mental and emotional barriers.

You are least effective when you are upset, frustrated, worried or unenthusiastic about your selling role. It is difficult, if not impossible, to change your thoughts and attitudes from negative to positive in an instant. Therefore, you cannot afford the luxury of frustration, anger, and worry. Your whole future, and probably that of your builder or broker, lies in your capacity to rise above the little things that can adversely affect your attitudes and actions.

You know the motto, "The show must go on!" Those words are true for everyone; always be mentally prepared to go on stage, on cue. While waiting for the unknown prospect, your thoughts, actions, and emotions are conditioning you for the reactions you will display when your opportunities appear. While waiting, do things that will keep your mind active and alert. Follow up the business of the previous days—and quietly prepare yourself for today's game. Remember, every event is a prelude to the next one.

This chapter already has observed the human tendency to transfer the emotions, attitudes, and thoughts of one experience to the next one, and that allowing oneself the luxury of negative thoughts probably leads to carrying them over into the sales arena. That is true of your prospect too. When he or she walks through the door of your office or model home, that customer brings the background of previous experiences, emotions, attitudes, and thoughts. Whatever they may be, it is your job to turn them into as positive a force as you can as quickly as possible. Burdening yourself with your own negative thoughts complicates the assignment.

Buy Your Product Fresh Each Day. When you have been selling the same housing designs and products for weeks or months, it is often difficult to become excited about what you are doing each day. You drive to your model sales area in the morning, open the doors, shuffle some papers, and wait for an unknown prospect to arrive. Maybe it is three or four in the afternoon before the first one appears. In the meantime, you have handled several complaints and difficult problems. How can you greet this late arriving prospect with warmth and enthusiasm? How can you rise to the mental and emotional demands of a new opportunity?

This can be difficult if you are mentally subdued from the pressure or lethargy of preceding events. A solution is to start with a fresh approach to your merchandise each day and to play mental games to prepare yourself for the opportunities that may be just around the corner.

One way to do this is to mentally repurchase your remaining properties each morning. Imagine, for example, that you are staffing a subdivision that has four model homes and a hundred remaining homesites or units to sell. You have been on this project for a full year, and the models seem somewhat shopworn and stale to you. How do you put yourself in the right frame of mind to do your best to sell these homes?

First of all, remember that even if you do have one hundred sites to sell, you do not have that many today. You cannot possibly do justice to one hundred homesites or inventory units in one day. You can only sell one at a time. Thus, you should first determine which ones you will concentrate on for the day's objectives.

As you start the sales day, mentally review your products. Walk your models and your key lots. Decide which are the best values available today and which ones you would most like to sell. Picture homes on them, if they are not already there, and review their benefits in terms of price, view, trees, or other amenities.

Playing this game will prepare you for the prospect who walks in a few hours later and indicates a potential interest in a particular model. You can quickly respond, "We have a choice site left that will give you some unique benefits. May I show it to you?" Then you can zero in on those one or two properties you have already mentally prepared yourself to sell that day.

It is best to select at least two lots or inventory units for each model or type of home you have remaining for sale and to determine the reasons for choosing one over the other in terms of price, possession, amenities, or other differences. This gives you the advantage of helping the prospect to make a choice and thus reach a decision.

When you are making your selections from the available inventory, try to pick alternative sites or units that offer a real comparison. If you have two locations for the same plan, take the two that are most dissimilar in benefits. Then, when starting the selection process with the buyers, begin by concentrating on the least likely of the two. If it fits and they buy it, you will still have the other one with its benefits available for the next buyer. If it is not all they have in mind, you can easily upgrade to the other one.

This procedure has another advantage as well. It prevents you from being left with only the difficult homesites to sell when the project is almost sold out. No buyer can really select from a hundred properties, or even from ten. The choice must be narrowed down to two or three and then to one as quickly as possible. Failure to do this will confuse the issue, giving your customers a reason to think it over and possibly not buy at all. You can give a buyer house-indigestion by offering too many choices.

The first person to make a decision must be the salesperson. If you do not know which properties to show, demonstrate, and sell, your customers will not be able to make a decision either. Your freshness each day, and your personal enthusiasm for what you have to sell, will make the difference in helping your prospects reach the right decisions.

FIRST IMPRESSIONS ARE IMPORTANT

It has been said that first impressions can be last impressions if they are not favorable experiences. You may never get a second chance if the first one was lost. How will your customers react when they first meet you? Will their interest be sparked and enhanced by what they see, hear, and feel? Will the psychological climate be one that is conducive to relaxed communication? Will there be a pyramiding of positive emotions that can lead to positive results?

How you look, act, and sound are all part of the total sales environment you create for yourself. As a professional new home sales specialist, you want everything working for you physically and psychologically. Good grooming habits are not expensive. They simply entail taking time each day, as you prepare yourself for the sales arena, to pay attention to the little things in your personal appearance that show you care about how you look and feel.

Always represent yourself in a professional manner. Your company is judged by the people it keeps. When people meet you, they will be forming impressions of you—and thus of your company as well. In managing your personal grooming habits, be conscientious about such items as clean, well-trimmed fingernails, polished shoes, neat hair, clean teeth, and fresh breath. As for dress code, be appropriately attired for the business environment your company has created. Neither overdress nor dress so casually that it might appear as though you do not respect the role you play as a new home sales counselor. If you are in doubt as to what is considered appropriate for your particular assignment, discuss it with your manager or your associates in sales.

If you do not demonstrate pride in yourself, you will not reflect confidence in your relationships with others. The two go hand-in-hand. Before you leave home in the morning, take a second look in the mirror to be certain you are ready for your role as an ambassador for your builder and your profession. Upon arrival at the sales center, double check your appearance—particularly on hot or uncomfortable days. While you may look good at the beginning of the day, this can quickly change as you pursue your activities of showing homes, reviewing models, and walking construction sites. There is a direct relationship between how you dress and how you feel about yourself. *Good grooming increases your own self-esteem.*

Whether or not you are aware of it, your first actions do have an impact on the people you meet. Your intent should be to always make those initial impressions so positive that they help to overcome the basic resistance many people have toward getting involved with others they do not yet know. Most people have their guard up when they encounter strangers, especially salespeople. They do not necessarily want to become involved until they feel comfortable with the new situation. They tend to keep their "emotional screens" in place as a protective shield from the unwanted and the unknown. This is a natural survival technique people have developed in life to safeguard themselves from unpleasant events. They can't get hurt if they don't allow other people to get close.

MAKING CUSTOMERS FEEL COMFORTABLE

Most individuals use defensive mechanisms to protect themselves from the potential adverse consequences of premature involvement. For example, they will enter your sales office and begin asking you questions like:

> *"Where are your models?"*
> *"What are your prices?"*
> *"How much is the interest rate on your homes?"*
> *"What's the square footage of your homes?"*
> *"Do you have a brochure and price list?"*

Such questions are designed to keep you on the defensive and the buyer in control. They can prevent you from getting close to the prospect if you allow that to happen.

Since you do not know the motives behind prospects' questions, nor how they really feel, you are at a distinct disadvantage. You never know what has transpired before they arrived or what they are thinking about at that moment. Perhaps they are trying to make a quick comparison between your homes and those featured by your competition. They may be looking for excuses to avoid seriously investigating buying a home now. Not infrequently, the issue is between spouses —one wanting to explore housing opportunities, and the other resisting the idea. In any case, you are helpless until you can break the ice and establish common ground where open communication can flourish.

To make others feel comfortable, begin by helping your prospects to feel at home. Home is a place where a person does not feel threatened or insecure. It is warm, friendly, and cheerful. It is a place where people like to stay because it usually brings out all the secure inner feelings of their basic human nature. That is how customers should feel when they enter your sales facility. The initial greeting and opening comments quickly set the stage for a positive interchange. Do nothing to put the customer under psychological pressure. Just the opposite should occur. The environment should radiate pleasing, unthreatening messages—and your own presence should add to the transmission of those feelings to everyone you greet.

Body Language. Body language is an unspoken aspect of the communication process. People receive nonverbal messages from others by the way they physically act and visually portray themselves. If you build barriers to communication with your body language, you will defeat your objectives. For example, if you approach people with defensive postures—such as folded arms across the chest—you are saying to them that you are not very friendly or interested in getting to know them.

One of the most effective symbols of goodwill is the smile. Someone once defined the smile as *the light in the window that proclaims our heart is at home.* The human smile is the shortest distance between two people! A polite smile makes the other person feel good and also important. It is difficult to smile and not be friendly. The two go together. Smiling relieves tension and opens the doors to communication. *Practice smiling, and with this physical response maintain an open attitude of positive goodwill toward others.* You will find that it tends to produce similar expressions from other people toward you.

ORGANIZE YOUR PERSONAL SALES ENVIRONMENT

It is your responsibility to maintain the area of the office that has been assigned to you and to have it organized for business at all times. Your desk (if one has been assigned) should be neat and orderly. The reference materials you use throughout the day should be kept where you have ready access to them. Sales brochures and other literature must be where you can obtain them as needed. Everything with which you work should be well organized, accessible, and in presentable condition. Untidy desks and tattered sales aids do not add to your image or to that of the company you represent. If you use your automobile in any way to escort customers, consider it an extension of your office. Keep it clean, uncluttered, and ready to transport clients. Remember that it is the little things that often make the big difference.

You are like a doctor who has a kit with all kinds of valuable equipment. If a doctor's working instruments are not ready for patients when they are needed, the doctor would hardly be considered a professional doctor. The same applies to you. If your tools are not ready for use, you are unprepared to serve your customers with the professional attention they deserve. When several sales associates are working together in the same environment, there is a mutual responsibility to see that everything is working together for the benefit of the entire staff. Get into the habit of going through your own checklist each day to be sure you and everything you need are ready to take advantage of the sales opportunities you are presented that day.

REQUIREMENTS FOR SUCCESS

Practice

All your selling skills, including imagination, become sharper when you use them every day. Don't take your talents for granted. Continually practice, stretch your mind, and get out of the ruts of laziness you can so easily fall into when you lack specific challenges or a disciplined program to keep active.

The only thing better than positive thinking is positive action. When mentally subdued and uninspired, try doing something that will put you into motion physically. At the same time, stimulate your mind with such questions as:

- Why do we do it that way?
- How can we get more buyers?
- How can I close another prospect in this situation?
- What is the best approach for handling that objection?

If you are fortunate enough to have others working with you, do some role-playing of imagined scenes with prospects. Let each salesperson take the role of the prospect and challenge the other's ability to control a certain situation, such as handling an objection or overcoming a financial obstacle.

Flexibility

Working conditions in which to show homes to prospective buyers are not always ideal. At times, you must operate with less than optimum circumstances. The stage of construction, the weather conditions, the status of the development, or the availability of sales facilities may seem to be deterrents to your physical control of the environment in which you are trying to negotiate sales. This is frequently the case in the pre-sale phase of a new neighborhood or in the clean-up stage after the majority of sales have been achieved.

When you cannot control the physical environment, you can compensate for it with a positive psychological environment, one that you personally generate. Be flexible in your approach and adjust to the criteria of the moment. Your willingness to use what you have at hand and to make necessary modifications in your presentation can help you overcome the negative elements which are not yet resolved.

There are some situations you *can* influence and control, however. If you see conditions in your sales environment that seem detrimental to your effectiveness in making presentations, attempt to have them corrected. Undoubtedly, the management team is just as interested as you are in seeing that everything possible is done to assure the maintenance of a positive sales environment. Living with something that is adversely affecting sales without reporting it to management is not a professional approach. Your company wants to sell all of the homes it builds and to have satisfied residents living in the new communities it creates. As part of the team, your observations and recommendations usually will be appreciated—if they are presented in an objective manner.

Personal Discipline

The attainment of any worthwhile goal requires effort and personal discipline. The time and energy you devote to self-improvement will pay dividends in all aspects of your life. This certainly applies to your earning capacity as a new home sales specialist. If you take care of the little things each day, the big things tend to take care of themselves. For example, if you keep your prospect records up-to-date, you will be less likely to miss opportunities that otherwise might be overlooked. When you are well prepared you tend to be lucky. Or, as someone else has said, *"The harder I work, the luckier I become!"*

Discipline yourself to set aside time each day to organize your activities. This is often best accomplished early in the morning or late in the evening before retiring. *Concentrate on your priorities.* Devote most of your time to the high-yield items that can generate more sales or help you to improve your professional selling skills. If you have low-yield things to take care of, try to avoid doing them during prime time, the time when you should be working with clients, following up on your prospects, and cultivating more business.

A well-organized approach to life gives you increased energy and frees your mind from time-consuming activities that are relatively unproductive. Then you can devote more time to the things that lead to greater achievement and satisfying results. The confused, disorganized individual is seldom as successful as one who is disciplined and systematically pursuing the details of daily activity schedules. Evaluate your own record keeping programs and your efficiency in managing your time. This book gives you various ideas and concepts on how best to organize and plan your time for increased productivity, which automatically leads to increased earnings.

Knowledge

Understand Your Profession and Your Products. The more you know about your profession, your products, and your programs, the more effective you will be. Knowledge is power, and is reflected directly in your personal earnings record. When you are able to provide the right answers to the questions and objectives you hear, you increase your capacity to achieve greater sales volume. The quality of your presentations has a strong influence on your customers' interests and decisions.

Your own self-confidence is reinforced by the knowledge you acquire and the skill with which you use that knowledge. *The more you know, the more you grow!* There is a deep sense of satisfaction in knowing you are improving each day. Like the sport of baseball, every time you get up to bat you have an opportunity to improve your batting average. You will learn as much from the practical experiences you have on the job as you will from other sources.

The information in this book has been designed to supplement what you learn in face-to-face selling situations. It is wise to index the areas on which you need to concentrate most and to work on those items first. No one learns everything at once. *Education, like most of the fine things in life, comes on the installment plan—a little at a time.*

Each day should provide you with new opportunities to add to your knowledge and personal selling skills. Review each day the things that worked for you yesterday and those that need additional attention. Selling is like any other skill—it is learned; people are not born with it. Education, practice, and consistent application of skills are the only ways to get better at any profession.

Understand the Decision-Making Process. The purchase of a new home is a major decision that certainly justifies rational conclusions. However, for most people it is also an emotional experience with side effects that are often uncomfortable and frustrating until they are resolved. When someone decides to seriously investigate the opportunities of buying a new residence, together with its attendant responsibilities of ownership, the process of reaching a decision usually involves conflicting forces. The desire to *proceed* is weighed against the desire to *retreat!*

Because it represents one of the largest investments most people ever make, the homebuying decision is seldom taken lightly by anyone. This is especially true for those individuals purchasing a primary home, as opposed to those investing in real estate with discretionary investment dollars. Consciously or subconsciously, people weigh major decisions in their lives. It is as though we had a scale in our brain that can be tipped one way or another depending upon how many "pluses" or "minuses" are there at any given point in time (See Figure 1.1).

Until people believe there are more positive than negative reasons for acting, they are inclined to do nothing. The homebuying decision is more complex than the minor judgments people face in the conduct of their daily affairs. In addition to evaluating the size of the financial

Figure 1.1. A mental scale.

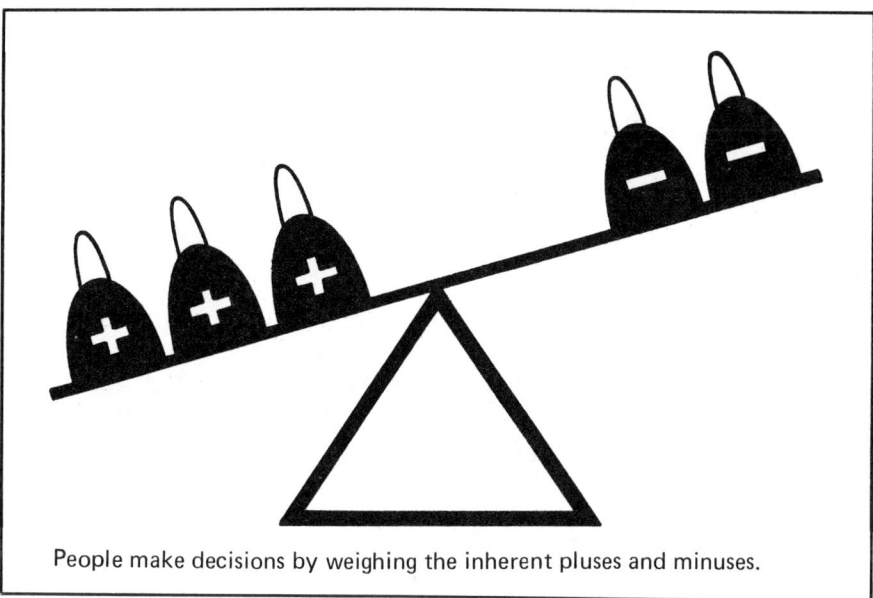

People make decisions by weighing the inherent pluses and minuses.

commitment, there are personal considerations, including lifestyles, community amenities, health facilities, transportation, and employment. People have subtle concerns for their security, comfort, privacy, and social compatibility with those whose lives will become a part of the housing environment they ultimately select.

When prospects arrive at your sales center, they bring with them their emotions and previous thoughts:

> *"Can we afford to buy, especially at these prices?"*
> *"Will we be happy living here?"*
> *"Is this the right time for us to buy a home?"*
> *"Can we trust the building company to do what it promises?"*
> *"Will we be able to resell the home for a profit if we decide to sell in the future?"*
> *"Can we sell our present home for enough to buy a new one?"*

These and many similar questions are weighed by your customers whether or not they openly share them with you. Often, the unspoken questions present the biggest hurdle to potential sales. That is why it is so critical to your objectives to make people feel at home and relaxed when they first arrive at the sales office.

The attitudes that are vibrated throughout the sales environment should generate positive responses. Your first role is to create a climate of trust and confidence while presenting the basic facts about your homes and community. The emotional experience is just as vital to your sales objectives as the information you convey. If your attitudes and actions do not stimulate your potential buyers in positive ways, then you may fail in your larger goal of motivating them to buy a new home today.

A Tempo of Success

A successful new home community has many complementary elements working together to create the climate for success. When everything is in harmony, you can feel the vibrance of the tempo that is communicated to the public. Your own positive mental attitude and personal enthusiasm are important ingredients in that total picture. It is your responsibility as a member of the team to be conscious of the larger objectives and to be a positive force for others as well as yourself. If there are negative influences in the scene when a prospect arrives, such adverse conditions lessen the customer's interest.

It is vital to protect and reinforce the relationships that are motivating factors in the sales arena. There is a synergistic effect when several people are working cooperatively within new home sales offices. A contagious spirit transmits itself to buyers, salespeople, and visitors when everything is going right. Your attitudes and actions, coupled with those of your associates, should be the catalyst for positive reactions from the prospects you so carefully try to attract from the marketplace.

Never forget that everything revolves around the sales effort. No one gets paid unless something is sold! Everyone in the company is directly or indirectly involved in the results of the marketing functions. Be proud of your association with your company. It is a mutual experience, and it should produce a sense of mutual responsibilities.

As you proceed through the rest of this book, bear in mind that the beginning of any sale is marked by the initial attainment of someone's interest in your homes in positive ways. People do not automatically want to buy; *they want their basic motivations satisfied in relationship to their abilities and needs.* As a new home sales professional, you can help your prospects achieve their goals while you are achieving yours.

MAKING THE MOST OF THE OPPORTUNITIES

Goal Setting

To really succeed in your profession requires a business plan. Such a plan encompasses much more than your day-to-day work of selling real estate; it includes a program for self-development, for education, for financial objectives, and for short- and long-range goals that relate to everything you want in life. Answering the three questions shown in Figure 1.2 are a good way to start setting your own goals.

Figure 1.2. Setting your own goals.

---
1. What are your motivations as they apply to your career of selling new homes?

2. List your abilities and personal strengths in selling new homes.

3. What are your basic needs?

Personal goals and a business plan are part of a willingness to accept today that which you must do to get where you want to be tomorrow. You can accept many things if you have dreams and visions for the future. Without them, you might be unwilling to accept some of the problems and sacrifices. Planning is like praying. A little each day is good for the soul.

Goal planning is most effective if you do it in writing. Writing down your goals helps you to keep them clear and specific. Figures 1.3 and 1.4 are examples of goal-planning records for use on a yearly basis. Figure 1.3 also contains a place to record achievements. If you have met an objective, pat yourself on the back. If you have fallen short, it is time to make a greater effort or to reassess your goals to decide whether they are indeed realistic.

Focus on Immediate Objectives. On a football field, for a player on the 50-yard line, the distant goal is important, but not nearly as important as carrying the ball for the next ten yards. The next down, the next ten-yard gain become immediate objectives, while the goal line remains in the distance. So it is with selling real estate. The builder

Figure 1.3. A yearly record of goals.

Name_____												Date_____	

My goal for this year is_____
Total income I need for this year $_____

Total commission I need, to achieve goal $_____

Number of prospects I must see, to get sales   _____groups

Number of sales I need, to achieve goal   _____sales

Number of prospects I must have, to make sales   _____prospects

Number of people I must ask to buy   _____people

	Jan.	Feb.	March	April	May	June	July	August	Sept.	Oct.	Nov.	Dec.	
Dollars broken down in monthly chart													Actual
													Goal
Contracts taken													Actual
													Goal
Prospects sold													Actual
													Goal
Sales closed													Actual
													Goal
													Actual
													Goal
													Actual
													Goal

Comments: _____
_____
_____

© Copyright T. Richey & Co.

Figure 1.4. A goal planning memorandum.

```
MEMO
    TO:    Sales Associate
  FROM:    Director of Marketing
  DATE:
    RE:    SALES ASSOCIATE'S GOAL PLANNING MEMORANDUM
```

PREVIOUSLY ESTABLISHED GOALS FOR PRECEDING TWELVE MONTHS:	
Number of net sales	Average monthly income
Projected annual income	Total dollars remaining in unclosed transactions
Total number of houses sold	Total number of cancellations
Total closings year-to-date	Total earnings paid to date
Special notations:	

GOALS FOR THE NEXT TWELVE MONTHS:	
Planned monthly income	To achieve income objectives, total number of homes to be sold
Average commission per transaction	Projected annual earnings
Projected cancellation rate	Cancelled transactions projected
Total net sales	

TO ACHIEVE THESE GOALS AND OBJECTIVES, I WILL NEED TO DO THE FOLLOWING:
1. _____   5. _____
2. _____   6. _____
3. _____   7. _____
4. _____

SPECIAL
NOTES: _____

DATE GOALS REVIEWED WITH DIRECTOR OF MARKETING _____

may be concerned about the next phase of the project and the hundred homesites or condominiums planned for the community. The lender may be concerned about the loan-renewal date that is six months away. The salesperson must be totally concerned about making and closing sales today.

What must you do to assure attainment of your objectives? In football, you play one down at a time. Golf you play one stroke at a time. The same is true of selling. If you worry only about the big goals and lose sight of the smaller objectives, you probably will fail to attain the desired score.

Concentrate on today; keep it in perspective and do not concern or frustrate yourself about tomorrow. You probably will accomplish far more than the person who lives only for distant dreams or is consumed with the problems but doesn't see what can be achieved immediately.

Time Management

It is easy to let time slip away in meaningless activities while wishing something better would happen. Time management makes you appreciate the value of your time. Through developing a plan for the day, the week, and the month, you weigh every activity in terms of its relative importance in helping attain your defined objectives.

Manage time instead of letting time manage you. Placing time in perspective and attaching priorities to activities will enable you to realize your ultimate goals.

High-Yield Versus Low Yield Activities. If you were to rate the hours and minutes of the day according to how much each of them contributed to your business and personal objectives, you might be surprised to discover how many of your activities are relatively low-yield. Too often, people get trapped into the performance of nitty-gritty detail work that has little or no relation to their total objectives.

There are 1,440 minutes in a day, of which a fair percentage should be devoted to yourself, your family, and your needed rest and sleep. If you assume that a ten-hour day is the average for a productive salesperson, that is the equivalent of only 600 minutes. How many of these are devoted to really high-yield activities?

High-yield activities include voice-to-voice, face-to-face contacts with prospects who can say yes, working on transactions you already have in the mill so that you can close them, developing new sources of business, creating centers of influence, and keeping yourself informed to be sure that you are ready when an opportunity presents itself.

Low-yield items are filing materials, filling out forms, talking to your associates about subjects that are unproductive, going out for coffee, spending time in conversations that lead nowhere, and merely waiting for something to happen.

There is no better way to increase your dollar yield than to increase the number of minutes you spend on high-yield activities. Whenever you are tempted to switch from a high-yield to a low-yield task, remember that you are reducing the value of that moment.

Multiply Yourself through Others. You do not have to do everything yourself to be successful; in fact, the contrary is true. Whenever you can get other people to assist you, you have increased your own value. In new home sales, these people include mortgage lenders, builders, suppliers, other salespeople, and secretaries, among others. They particularly include "bird dogs" who bring you new leads. The extra time you gain from the assistance of others can be used for higher-yield activities.

To obtain the cooperation of others, you must understand the value of their time. Organize yourself so that working together increases the value of that time for both of you. Lack of appreciation for other people's time means you do not understand the value of your own.

Develop Timesaving Systems to Prevent Problems. Time is managed best through a regular system for doing so. For instance, do not try to carry around in your head all the things that come up in a day. Write them down instead of attempting to make your head a warehouse for things you want to remember. One good system for doing this is to note the items for future follow-up on 3x5 cards or in a notebook. To lack a method of quickly jotting down things as they arise is to clog your brain and risk forgetting or possibly losing sales opportunities.

Making a checklist of the various tasks you perform is another good way to reduce the possibility of error. Some of the topics that deserve checklists are:

- Processing sales
- Qualifying prospects
- Following through with inventory
- Building referrals
- Handling objections

- Closing sales
- Financing (methods and sources)
- Servicing customers after a sale

Tickler files for remembering future dates are also part of a good timesaving system. A tickler file is a chronological index, either in the form of your calendar or something more elaborate. It can be kept on 3x5 cards. Such information as dates of move-ins and anniversaries you want to remember would be recorded here.

Every timesaving device you can develop increases your potential. Not to develop some kind of system means that you do not appreciate the importance of time, or the value of systems that will force you to grow and increase your own productivity. Such systems will make your job easier, help you to avoid problems, and create more opportunities for the future.

Today, Tomorrow and Someday. One real estate broker organized his time by dividing a notebook into three sections entitled *Today, Tomorrow,* and *Someday.* All the items he put behind Today were things he wanted to accomplish right away. Those behind Tomorrow could be delayed until the next day or the day after. The Someday section included things he would like to do that he would include in his plans if there were enough time.

This kind of thought process has great merit, provided, of course, that you do not postpone those things that you really should do today. The greatest labor-saving device in the world for most people is "tomorrow." Procrastinating may make the present easier, but the postponed responsibilities remain. Knowing the difference between what you should schedule for immediate action and what can be delayed can make a tremendous difference in the results you obtain from the hours you invest in your work.

The file marked Someday is really a brainstorming file. It lists the things that it would be nice to work on when there is time. Such a file is a place to incubate thoughts that might not be ready for immediate translation into action. If you have such a file, review it at least once a month, if not more often, and identify items that should be brought forward for immediate attention. In the meantime, concentrate on what is happening today. Place into the Today category the things that will make possible your continued survival and growth and give you a platform for the future.

Set Daily Priorities. When you take the time to list what you want to accomplish each day, in order to set priorities, you will accomplish more than when you do not. The best way to do this is to determine what you want to get done each day, perhaps at your desk in the hours before your work day begins or at home with a second cup of coffee. When the phones are ringing and the buyer you sold to yesterday is pounding on your desk over some unexpected delay, you can lose control unless you have a road map to come back to. You can take detours, but don't let the whole day become a detour. Figure 1.5 is an example of a form for use in daily planning. And don't forget your accomplishments: Figure 1.6 shows a form you can use for recording your achievements.

The hours that do not yield the most, because you are not face-to-face with buyers, can be used for more than filing papers. Use the time to prepare yourself for the next prospect or to follow up prospects who could return to work with you. Your own sense of priorities will increase the yield. If your schedule is packed with things that have to be accomplished, you will more than likely move faster and create a greater tempo of involvement than if you have no sense of urgency at all.

Stick with Your Goals. Few people in this world ever drop dead from overwork, but many curl up and die from lack of satisfaction. Achievement requires goals, and goals are meaningful only if they are brought down to today and the objectives at hand. For example, if you had a particularly difficult day when two of the sales you wrote yesterday were canceled, you learned that the builder was raising the prices by $3,000 per unit, and the mortgage market had just gone right through the roof, it would be easy to feel exhausted due to this emotional stress. You would then be unprepared for any new buyer to come along or for any other important event that might occur. Even the next day, or perhaps the following week, could be lost. Salespeople have taken as long as a month to adjust to truths they were unprepared to accept. These salespeople would have been better off to keep their eyes on their goals, and not to have let setbacks overwhelm them, even though following a goal can be difficult.

If you lose sight of cause-and-effect relationships and cannot control those things that are in your power to control, you are going to suffer the consequences. If you are unwilling to change, be flexible, and remain in harmony with the changes that occur, you will be the odd man out sitting on the sidelines and watching others do what you should have done. There is a price for success; it does not come easily. If you have a meaningful purpose and are prepared to pay the price, you undoubtedly can find success in the exciting profession of new home sales.

Figure 1.5. A daily planning guide.

Date_____	Day or Week_____
Primary Goals and Objectives Today:_____	

Time	Appointments	Phone Calls
7:30	☐ _____	☐ _____
8:00	☐ _____	☐ _____
8:30	☐ _____	☐ _____
9:00	☐ _____	☐ _____
9:30	☐ _____	☐ _____
10:00	☐ _____	☐ _____
10:30	☐ _____	☐ _____
11:00	☐ _____	☐ _____
11:30	☐ _____	☐ _____
12:00	☐ _____	☐ _____
12:30	☐ _____	☐ _____
1:00	☐ _____	
1:30	☐ _____	Priorities for the Day
2:00	☐ _____	
2:30	☐ _____	☐ _____
3:00	☐ _____	☐ _____
3:30	☐ _____	☐ _____
4:00	☐ _____	☐ _____
4:30	☐ _____	☐ _____
5:00	☐ _____	☐ _____
5:30	☐ _____	☐ _____
6:00	☐ _____	☐ _____
6:30	☐ _____	☐ _____
7:00	☐ _____	☐ _____
7:30	☐ _____	☐ _____
8:00	☐ _____	☐ _____
8:30	☐ _____	☐ _____
9:00	☐ _____	☐ _____

Other Notes:

Figure 1.6. Personal achievements report.

Name
Name of Supervisor _____ For Week Beginning _____
Building Project _____ Staffing Days _____

Minimum objectives for this week	Attempts for appointments		Contracts	Appointments	Presentations		Sales	New leads
	Phone	In person			Face to face	Close		
Monday								
Tuesday								
Wednesday								
Thursday								
Friday								
Saturday								
Total								

Notes: _____

What else could you sell that is as meaningful as real estate? Little else offers the same degree of involvement, excitement, and long-run influence on the lives of others as does the place and the community in which they live.

Someone once said that people do not fail because they do not know, but because they do not get excited enough about what they know. When you care about what you do and become excited about it, you can translate that enthusiasm into positive activity. The enthusiasm itself becomes a force that cannot be stopped, especially when it is born of sincere desire, personal belief, and persistance stemming from willingness to pay the price of the goal being sought.

CONCLUSION

To prepare for the chapters ahead, think about four words: *care, believe, dream,* and *dare.* They may help bring into perspective the topics covered in this book.

Care

If you care about what you do, the functions you perform, and the purposes you serve, then you will be willing to learn and become better prepared each day for your job in the real estate field. This, in turn, enables you to help your buyers and builders reach their objectives. Care is a matter of attention to other people and recognition that you cannot achieve your goals without satisfying the needs of others.

Believe

Believe first of all in yourself. Unless you do, you will accomplish little of what you set out to do. Next, believe in what you are doing. You are helping people to own property and to mold their environments for themselves, their children, and their successors. Real estate salespeople have more of a responsibility than most to help mankind use this earth to advantage. If you believe in what you are doing, you will spend more time and take more care with your assignments, and your accomplishments will therefore be more meaningful.

Dream

A dream is a vision of the future. Little would ever happen without dreams and imagination. When you have a dream, you can use your imagination every day to combine the things you know, believe in, and have experienced into bold new perspectives.

Dare

Dare yourself to do things that others might not tackle. There is no such thing as accomplishment unless it is preceded by a vision of that accomplishment. There is equally no accomplishment unless you act. The person who moves forward is strong and willing to risk failure. People will eagerly associate with someone who can offer them strength. People are attracted to strength, because it gives them a sense of security and a gentle guidance. It feels good to be around people who are more certain of themselves than we are, because it makes us a little stronger.

If you develop your talents so that you can give of yourself to others, you will enjoy not only the financial rewards of your profession but a feeling of self-confidence and self-esteem that can come only from such experience. Keep your goals in sight and the obstacles in perspective. Use your time wisely. Above all, do not try to copy anyone else, do not try to be like anyone else—be yourself. If you cannot be yourself, you are going to lose by trying to be someone else!

Selling new homes and new home communities is one of the most complex and at the same time one of the most exciting professions in the world. If you can accept the roles you play and the challenges you receive, you may well discover that, unlike many who go through life without any great sense of achievement, you will be able to look back on your life in later years and say:

> *You know what; I was pretty good. I helped a lot of people to own homes. I have molded a lot of lives. I influenced one of the most important things in the world—the way people live.*

2: Using Well-Planned Presentations

Professionals in the sales field know that sales messages achieve far better results when they are organized than when they are unplanned and unrehearsed. Each opportunity to help someone own a home deserves one's best sales approach. Every prospect is a valuable prospect!

Planning a sales presentation gives you more confidence when you are in an actual selling situation. By gaining product knowledge and improving your selling skills, you achieve mental security, which will lead to more efficient performance. Your closing ratios will be directly related to the quality of the messages communicated to your prospective buyers.

A successful presentation usually involves the following:

- A positive physical and visual environment;
- A positive psychological climate; and
- A flexible presentation plan that is logically organized.

How well you present yourself and your sales message ultimately determines your degree of success in the real estate profession. The ability to command attention and produce positive customer reactions is as vital as product knowledge and on-site merchandising programs. Unless you can dramatize the benefits of home ownership so that buyers feel personally involved with the concepts of the housing environment, both you and your prospects will lose.

In light of the many adverse influences that stand in the way of a prospect who is trying to reach a final decision on something as major as buying a home, it is only reasonable for a professional to take every precaution to overcome those hurdles. Your critical assignment is to control your customers and to overcome the obstacles. You do not control the events that occur before your prospects arrive or after they leave your sales center. You have no control over the competitive housing projects they will see or the way they will react to the various factors involved in making a homebuying decision. Therefore, you must exercise control in other areas.

When customers first arrive at your office, you must use every moment to your advantage, since you have no idea how much time you will have with them. It is what you do when you are with the customers that really counts. Your presentation and their reactions to it will determine whether you will be given the opportunity to help them fulfill their housing requirements or whether someone else will have that privilege. Worse yet, the customers may return to their present residence and not buy at all. When you are on stage, do everything you can to effectively involve your prospects in the ultimate benefits of owning the environments you represent. To be effective, you have to carefully consider how you will organize and deliver your basic presentation.

To that end, this chapter describes the importance of selling skills, the specific objectives that the presentation should aim to achieve, ways to build your presentation, management of sales exhibits, and the credibility of your presentation.

THE IMPORTANCE OF SELLING SKILLS

Like success in any profession, success in real estate sales requires knowledge, skills, and a willingness to practice certain basic principles. Remember, most of the fine things that make life easier today once had to be sold with great persistence and effort. Few products or services ever sold themselves.

Take, for example, the telephone. When he first invented the telephone, Alexander Graham Bell had no easy time convincing investors to put money into the scheme of providing communication systems between homes and offices. It required intensive effort to get people to experiment with the idea of a telephone.

Today's more sophisticated communication systems also require selling. Computers are one example. They didn't just appear and receive instant acceptance. They were a threat to many people as a replacement of human skills. Even today, the computer still has to be sold to those who do not understand how it can improve the quality of their lives and increase productive performance.

The automobile, too, had to be sold. Most people thought that it would never replace the horse. Likewise, the airplane was considered merely an entertaining, but risky, enterprise. Even today, taking a trip on a plane is, to some people, a traumatic event. Literally thousands of people have never flown because they are afraid of flying. It would be easy to cite many other, similar examples.

Merely having a worthwhile product is no guarantee that other people will understand or accept it. Selling housing opportunities is often easier than selling new forms of communication or travel. Certainly, real estate sales is no more difficult than selling an idea, such as life insurance, stocks and bonds, or other products that have little immediate perceived tangible value to the average person.

Be proud of your opportunities to present your merchandise to prospective homebuyers. Be prepared to do your best to convey the positive messages that will excite customers into a course of action that leads to fulfilling their desires and to completing your assignments successfully.

THE OBJECTIVES OF AN ORGANIZED SALES PRESENTATION

A variety of objectives should be accomplished in a well-organized sales message. Do not just try to do one thing, but do multiple things at the same time. Seven major objectives should be accomplished during the sales presentation:

1. Gain favorable attention.

2. Build maximum perceived values for the housing community.

3. Anticipate and answer questions or objections.

4. Create genuine interest in what is for sale.

5. Stimulate a desire to own a specific home.

6. Create a sense of urgency to act now.

7. Obtain a commitment to buy today.

The ultimate result of these seven steps is usually a successfully closed transaction, providing that the buyer has been qualified before the presentation was completed and that the ability to own has been clearly established. This chapter examines each of these steps in greater detail to show how they fit into the total picture.

Gain Favorable Attention

Before you can accomplish anything with others, you must have their attention. Attention is not easy to gain or hold. People with whom you are dealing have a number of things going on in their lives at any given time. Your messages and objectives are not necessarily the most significant factor influencing their thought processes.

Attention is the direct result of enlisting the senses of the person with whom you wish to communicate and channeling them toward areas of mutual interest. People pay attention only to what interests them. Thus, to get their attention, you must talk about the matters that interest them. You hold their attention by making the listening experience an exciting adventure, or at least one that is not boring.

The avenues to the brain are sight, sound, touch, taste, and smell. Real estate salespeople seldom involve the last three in the selling process. Certainly, you would not want to work in conditions that adversely influence sensory areas of taste and smell. There is often perceived to be a sixth sense, which is the nonverbal form of communication known as extra sensory perception (ESP). This is presently a relatively unexplored field, so it will not be seriously explored here. The point to bear in mind is that a person's actions and attitudes have an effect upon others. That is why enthusiasm and confidence are an essential part of the sales presentation, as emphasized in Chapter 1.

In most new environments, the salesperson must gain the prospective customer's attention quickly. Prospects arrive on their own and are prepared to leave on their own. They really have little intent to spend time with a salesperson, unless they find something of interest to them. Basically, they want information. They ask questions such as:

"Do you have a brochure?"
"What are your interest rates?"
"What are your prices?"
"How many are you going to build here?"

Salespeople must give them information, but should provide it to them on a *controlled* plan that allows the salespeople to achieve their objectives, while fulfilling the prospects' requests for facts. The information salespeople have is a resource they ought to use carefully. Firing facts at an unknown target achieves little. In fact, you can say things that will be taken out of perspective or may be totally off-target for an individual's requirements. Your comments can cause people to leave rather than stay. When considering the subject of communication

(Chapter 11), this book goes into greater detail on the important aspect of commanding and holding the favorable attention of others. Suffice it to say that without a method of gaining attention, none of the other things you want to accomplish in your sales presentation are likely to happen.

Build Maximum Perceived Values for the Housing Communities

Leading people to a decision requires messages that reinforce the values you offer. How do homebuyers know that the price you are asking is worth the values they see? Does the home meet their needs? Does it have values that are invisible? When they purchase the home, are homebuyers going to receive high-quality construction and builder service afterwards? Answers to these questions are part of the decision-influencing process and a factor in establishing values.

Beginning on page 44, this chapter discusses ways to build perceived values. The discussion focuses on a number of important areas, all of which should have sub-messages that are programmed to allow the prospect to feel that your particular home, location, method of financing, or whatever else you are discussing is a valid reason for them to consider the purchase.

Anticipate and Answer Questions or Objections

Seldom does anyone make a decision without some questions or personal concerns. Whether the concerns are spoken or not, most people entering a decision-making process for something as important as a home are carrying with them questions they need to have answered. Most often, they will verbalize the questions.

Part of the sales presentation is designed to answer questions before they are raised, so you do not have to shoot them down later. This particularly applies to objections you know you will have to overcome if you don't face a problem early in the presentation. Some conditions may be unfavorable to the sale; unless you put these into proper perspective at the beginning, clouds of doubt may develop and prevent the prospect from proceeding further. Chapter 5 deals with handling objections. That chapter goes into greater detail on this sales skill, but it should be understood that it is part of the presentation plan.

Create Genuine Interest in What Is for Sale

Before you can lead prospects to a sale, they have to have some interest in what you have to offer. That interest must be genuine.

In other words, it must reach the prospects' emotional and mental awareness, where it can ultimately stimulate a desire to act. A mental "move-in" occurs before the actual signing of the purchase agreement. This means that the prospects have begun to picture the benefits of ownership, and their interest level is now translated into something specific. A given homesite, a location, an opportunity to move by a certain date, a floor plan that intrigues the family, and a variety of other things, when interrelated, begin to excite the desire to act.

Creating genuine interest means involving the customer. You cannot close anyone without a measure of involvement on his or her part. Customers have to get involved! If they stand on the sidelines of the presentation, merely listening to you, they will have little stimulus to react to. People get excited when they are actively involved with the events that are transpiring, such as picturing how the home will be furnished, or visually enjoying the benefits of scenes they will have in their backyard or out of their future front window. This stimulation of interest leads logically to the next step of the presentation plan.

Stimulate a Desire to Own a Specific Home

Once you have won a customer's interest, pyramid that interest into a particular opportunity to own a given home or homesite that is available right now. All of your presentations *must focus on what you have to sell now.* Some salespeople are prone to show only the properties they like rather than the ones that need to be sold. They become emotionally involved with their own likes and dislikes and ignore the reality that there is a buyer for every home. What must be sold is that which is in the inventory today. A well-organized plan concentrates on creating a desire to own a certain model, speculative home, or a home that is to be built that is going to be available within the time frame prospects have in mind. Here, the specifics take over from the general interest that is described in the last step. You are thereby getting down to something prospects can decide upon!

Create a Sense of Urgency to Act Now

The area of urgency is a subtle part of the sales process. Chapter 6 includes an extensive review of the specific methods of creating urgency. In this chapter, the main point is that urgency should be part of the presentation. Urgency is conveyed in a variety of ways. One way to convey urgency is to provide evidence that homes are selling rapidly and that if clients don't act now, the home they want may be gone. That is why success tends to breed success. People get caught up in the house-buying fever when they see other people buying or when they realize that to delay could be expensive, costing them not only the house they want, but a higher price or loss of special financing that is available now.

Urgency is conveyed also by the salesperson's attitude. If the salesperson can successfully transmit a belief that this is the best time to buy a home, he or she is part of the psychological process that provides the background for clients' thinking and, hopefully, to their action. Ultimate urgency leads to a decision to do something today!

One fundamental factor that exists in all urgency is the underlying *fear of loss.* When people are afraid they are going to lose something they really want, they begin to feel a sense of urgency. If you can show the prospects benefits they do not presently possess and an easy method of acquiring them, a fear of loss will create a sense of urgency to act.

Obtain a Commitment to Buy Today

The final step in the process of building the presentation should automatically lead to a positive commitment if the buyer is qualified. A commitment to purchase is the summation of all the things that have preceded it.

Some instructors in sales tend to indicate there is a magic moment or a special time at which to close. That is unlikely. Closing is a by-product of all the things that have led to a positive conviction and a desire to own. You can often close early, but you then have to reinforce the decision that has been made. Sometimes you can close late, because you have the prospects so hooked and interested they will stay with you beyond that point of normal closing time. It is far better to close too early than not to close at all.

Obtaining a commitment to buy is founded on having provided information your prospects require, having seen evidence of their interest, having answered their questions, and having created a sense of urgency. Then, when you ask the questions that lead to the closing moments, you are in total control. The close seldom occurs before all other steps have been achieved. Trying to close before constructing a solid bridge from the point of initial greeting to the signing of the purchase agreement is to risk the whole transaction. Many a sale falls apart because the sale was not built on a solid foundation. When purchasers who have not been taken over the complete bridge of agreement go home and talk to third-party advisors or experience "after-buying blues" or "buyers' remorse," they often cancel. Cancelled transactions (except for unqualified mortgage situations) usually result from insufficient information or too little conviction to hold the sale together after the moment of inspiration in which it was conceived. Chapter 7 discusses actions that can prevent lost sales.

To review, these are the seven steps of the organized sales presentation:

1. Gain favorable attention.
2. Build values.
3. Answer questions.
4. Create interest.
5. Stimulate the desire to own.
6. Create a sense of urgency to act.
7. Obtain the commitment to buy.

HOW TO BUILD A PRESENTATION

The process of assembling information needed to construct a well-planned presentation is an important part of a new home sales specialist's assignments. Checklists are a helpful method for developing each segment of the total sales message. The checklist is a security device designed to prevent you from overlooking things that are important to your knowledge and to your presentation sequence. Unless all of the points on the checklist are understood and clearly identified in your own mind, they will not be there for your transmission to others at the appropriate time. This section provides a checklist for each of the modules that comprise the basic presentation. Review them, and, as they apply to your assignment, use them to rehearse your own presentation on each topic.

Build Flexible Modules of Information

One of the more successful techniques in organizing planned presentations is to have every part of the sales message broken into modules, or segments, which are self-contained and can fit into almost any position in the plan whenever that information is required. Integrating these modules into a presentation assures that prospects will have maximum interest and that you will not sound like a robot. Avoid "canned" or artificial presentations. They sound insincere and lack the creativity that a professional needs to meet specific situations.

There is a big difference between *canned* and *well-planned* presentations. Some sales trainers have taught for years that a canned presentation is the best security device. Door-to-door selling often has required fast-pitch canned presentations, due to the limited time the salesperson has in which to present the message. In those selling situations, a word-by-word rehearsed pitch may be the only way to get all the points across each time to every prospect. In new home sales, however, which involves dealing with so many variables and selling a complex item, you must be in a position to adjust to the requirements of the people with whom you are communicating. The modular system of developing presentations gives greater freedom, because you can insert whatever you need at a given point in the plan, without destroying or losing sight of all the other things you still want to cover.

With a checklist of flexible modules, you can keep your outline of information up-to-date. This is a vital consideration in the rapidly changing housing environment. What is true today probably will not be true tomorrow. Prices change, available sites are altered, and options may vary from day to day. Sometimes the objections you have to overcome apply only to specific situations. Therefore, checklists that are reviewed daily and used regularly will give you an opportunity to insert what you need now. Being current is part of being well prepared!

A new home sales presentation contains seven segments, each of which requires a checklist. Please do not confuse these with the seven steps and objectives of the presentation, just reviewed. The presentation segments are the elements that are at the heart of the information you use and will fit into any point of your message where it is appropriate. The objective of these segments is to see that your knowledge is indexed appropriately and used as required when you are face to face with a prospect. The following paragraphs analyze each of the seven segments of information that compose the heart of a well-planned presentation.

Identify the Principal Benefits of the General Housing Environment. As you assemble information to market specific properties, it is logical to begin with the overview of your community and the surrounding environments that affect that community. This should essentially be taken in three phases:

1. The benefits of living in your city or community.

2. The benefits of living in the neighborhood, surrounding dis-

trict, or area adjacent to your particular project.

3. The benefits of living in your specific housing environment.

The **benefits of living in your city** are much broader than those that apply to a particular subdivision or community. There is a long list of benefits for just living in the region or general area of the nation in which you are located. Your city and community have certain amenities and lifestyles that encourage people to live there rather than somewhere else. What makes your community a desirable place to live?

The first thing to sell is location. The location starts with the big view and then narrows to what you are marketing as a specific parcel of real estate. This is particularly true when trying to convince a transferee or newcomer to your community who is weighing the various advantages your region or general location offers compared to others.

Why should prospects consider living in your particular community? What are the advantages of your city? What are the advantages of your region of the country? Develop a broad checklist of items of information that can help you organize your data regarding the general region in which your housing projects are offered. If you do not have the facts on these subjects, you should research them. Customers appreciate talking to someone who knows the community and is proud of it. The more knowledgeable you are about your area and its environs, the more successful you will be in achieving a positive relationship with your prospective buyers. Not only will you be able to answer their questions, but it will be easier to convince them that you know your subject and believe in your project.

Figure 2.1 illustrates a checklist of regional characteristics you should be familiar with.

Once you have identified the benefits of the entire region and city, target those specific benefits that are applicable to your **immediate housing area.** The neighborhood district can vary in size based on the nature of the community. It has its own values and benefits for those who live there rather than on the other side of town or somewhere else. By indexing these correctly, you are ready to bring your story down to the particulars of your own project and neighborhood.

Figures 2.2 and 2.3 are checklists of neighborhood services you should identify.

Having now outlined: (1) the benefits of the entire region, and (2) the benefits of the larger surrounding neighborhoods, you are ready to checklist the specific benefits of living within your **new home community.** That brings you to the site plan and its amenities.

Figure 2.1. General information on regional characteristics.

General category	Facts needed	Sources of information
Climate	Temperature ranges Averages and variations Rainfall averages Number of sunny days Snowfall (where applicable) Other facts as appropriate	Weather bureau Chamber of Commerce Tourist bureau U.S. Department of Agriculture Industrial department of local government
Churches and temples of worship	Number of denominations Total number of churches/temples Location of each religious headquarters Services and charities offered by religious groups	Local council of churches All faiths roster Telephone directory Chamber of Commerce
Cultural activities	General scope of cultural events Art festivals Number/type of art galleries Number of libraries Number of movie theaters Number of museums Music centers Opera Night clubs Other factors	Chamber of Commerce Social sections of local newspaper Tourist bureau Art societies
Demographics	Total population Population mix Growth rates Average family size Average incomes Projections of future growth Professions and employment patterns Number of owners vs. renters Other facts	Census bureau U.S. Department of Commerce Chamber of Commerce Research departments of local governments Banking institutions Tourist bureau Private research companies

Figure 2.1. (continued)

General category	Facts needed	Sources of information
Educational Facilities	Number of schools Preschools Elementary schools Junior high schools High schools Colleges (junior) Colleges (industrial) Universities Adult educational program Special educational services Noted achievement or academic society Private schools and academies Other factors	Local school boards Department of education Chamber of Commerce Local government agencies Teachers' associations Information from institutions

Financial institutions	Nature of the financial community
	Number of banks
	   State charters
	   Federal charters
	Savings and loan associations
	Building societies
	Figures on bank assets
	Growth rates
	Availability of mortgage funds
	Availability of financial services
	Other factors
		State departments of finance
		U.S. Department of Commerce
		Local Chamber of Commerce
		Literature furnished by financial institutions
		Local bankers' association
		City directory

Fire protection	General status of facilities in region Local fire department facilities Fire rating facts Location of each station Nature of equipment Paramedic services Other services	Local fire department Firefighters' association Insurance underwriters Chamber of Commerce

Figure 2.1. (continued)

General category	Facts needed	Sources of information
Government	Type of city government County government State government Noted services Resident participation Other facts	Government offices Chamber of Commerce League of Women Voters Local political parties Service organizations
History	Background to civilization of area Historical events Notable people Cultural heritage Significant dates and local customs	Chamber of Commerce Historical societies Universities and schools Tourist bureaus
Industry	Nature of industry in area Number and rating of industries Employment figures List of major employers Economic factors related to industry	Chamber of Commerce Local department of commerce Industrial development of local government Regional business directories Banking research Institutional literature Assessor's office
Land planning	Master land plan for region Land use pattern Projections for growth Services affecting development	Local planning commission Government research studies Chamber of Commerce Zoning ordinances Engineers and land planners
Medical facilities	General availability of medical services Number of hospitals Number of doctors Number of clinics Health services Other facts	Medical society Medical roster Health department Yellow Pages Chamber of Commerce

Figure 2.1. (continued)

General category	Facts needed	Sources of information
Ordinances	Government agencies involved Ordinances affecting pet owners Ordinances affecting recreational vehicles Covenants, conditions, and restrictions affecting use of property Fire hazard ordinances Car parking ordinances Other ordinances	Licensing departments or local government Building departments Recorded property restrictions Bar association Published government papers Chamber of Commerce Fire department Police department City hall

Police protection	Nature of security services in community
	Size of police force
	Location of stations
	Patrol services
	General rating
	    Crime statistics
	    Achievement
		Police department
		Sheriff's department
		Office of the mayor or commissioner
		FBI
		Civic groups

Real estate statistics	General knowledge of real estate values in the region Rates of appreciation by type and area of region Average prices by housing type Ownership vs. rental percentage Vacancy factors Mortgage rates and availability Real estate turnover rates Resale market activity Land values	Published reports by Board of Realtors® Home Builders' Association reports Title companies Savings and loan associations Tax assessor's records HUD reports Appraisers' reports, SRA and MAI Chamber of Commerce Private feasibility studies Utility programs

Figure 2.1. (continued)

General category	Facts needed	Sources of information
Recreational facilities	Quantity and types of recreation in several regions	Department of parks and recreation Chamber of Commerce

	Location of facilities
	  Golf course
	  Tennis courts
	  Parks
	  Trails
	  Lakes/oceans
	  Swimming pools
	  Athletic gyms
	  Children's play areas
	  Sports arenas
	Other facts
		Tourist bureau
		U.S. Department of the Interior
		Civic organizations
		Golf association
		Tennis association
		Sports clubs
		Personal investigation

Service clubs and social groups	Number of service clubs in area Lists of all groups with times and places of meetings Services and charities supported Noted achievements Other facts	Chamber of Commerce City directory Tourist bureau Junior Chamber of Commerce Personal investigation
Shopping facilities	Regional shopping centers Neighborhood shopping facilities Complete list of most needed facilities General rating of shopping in area	Chamber of Commerce City directory Business rosters Yellow Pages Better Business Bureau Banking institutions
Taxation (real estate)	Basic tax rates Services performed by taxing entity Ratings of counties, cities, etc. Other factors	Tax assessor's office Local taxing authority Real estate board Civic groups of various kinds

Figure 2.1. (continued)

General category	Facts needed	Sources of information
Transportation	Total transportation services of region Present and future roads and freeways Bus service	Department of Highways Local planning agencies Department of Commerce Schedules produced by each service
	Rapid transit Railroads Taxis/limos Airlines Other services	City directory
Utilities	Electrical utility Gas utility Garbage service Telephone Water utility Sewer facility Liquid fuels Coal (where applicable) Wood Other fuels	Individual utility company Utility commission Chamber of Commerce Local government offices Energy planning groups

Figure 2.2. List of neighborhood services.

Emergency services	Address and location data	Phone
Ambulance		
Fire		
Medics		
Poison control		
Police		
Regular services		
Animal care		
Attorneys		
Auto rental		
Auto repair		
Bakeries		
Banks		
Barbers		
Beauty salons		
Book stores		
Bus service		
Carpet dealers		
Caterers		
Child care centers		
Churches		
Cleaners		
Clinics		
Clubs		
Decking		
Dentists		
Department stores		
Draperies		
Fences		
Florists		
Furniture dealers		
Garbage disposals		

Figure 2.2. (continued)

Regular services	Address and location data	Phone
Gardeners		
Garden and lawn supplies		
Glass dealers		
Golf courses		
Gymnasiums		
Handball courts		
Hardware stores		
Health clubs		
Heating contractors		
House movers		
Insulation companies		
Insurance companies		
Interior decorators		
Jewelers		
Landscape architects		
Laundries		
Lighting fixtures		
Locksmiths		
Lumber companies		
Marinas		
Nurseries		
Paint dealers		
Patio contractors		
Pet shops		
Pharmacies		
Photo stores		
Physicians		
Plumbing contractors		
Raquetball courts		
Restaurants		
Roofing contractors		

Figure 2.2. (continued)

Regular services	Address and location data	Phone
Savings and loan associations		
Schools		
Sprinklers		
Swimming pools		
Table service		
Television service		
Tennis courts		
Title companies		
Utilities		
Veterinarians		
Wallpapers		

Figure 2.3. Checklist of neighborhood characteristics.

General category	Specific services	Locations and notations
Churches and temples of worship	Catholic Jewish Protestant Others:	
Cultural activities	Art galleries Libraries Movie theaters Museums Music centers Opera Others:	
Educational facilities	Preschool centers Kindergarten Grade school Junior high High school Colleges Universities	
Financial institutions	Banks Savings and loans	
Fire protection	Fire stations Number of engines Medic services	
Government	Nature of local authority Key politicians Services provided Court house	
History of area	Historical events Notable people Heritage factors	
Industry	Employment centers Identity of major companies Distances to industry Other factors:	
Land planning and usage	Basic land plan Future projections Zoning ordinances	

Figure 2.3. (continued)

General category	Specific services	Locations and notations
Medical facilities	Hospitals Doctors Dentists Clinics Others:	
Ordinances of interest	Bicycle licensing Dog licensing Parking ordinances Recreational vehicles Pet control Others:	
Police protection	Closest station Size of force Security patrols Special services	
Real estate statistics	Growth rates Average values Appreciation rates Ownership (percent) Rental (percent) Turnover rates Other factors:	
Recreational facilities	Golf courses Tennis courts Parks Trails Lakes—boating Swimming pools Athletic programs Children's play areas Others:	
Service clubs and social groups	List of service clubs Dates and times of meetings Social services Other groups:	
Shopping facilities	Major regional centers Neighborhood shopping Other facilities:	

Figure 2.3. (continued)

General category	Specific services	Locations and notations
Taxation (real estate)	Basic tax rate Services performed Comparisons Other factors:	
Transportation	Freeways and highways Bus service Taxis and limousines Mass transit Airlines Railroads	
Utilities	Electricity Gas Garbage service Telephone Water Sewer Other:	

Here is a list of factors to use in creating housing values:

1. The socioeconomic groups who live in your community.
2. The price ranges of the homes.
3. The lifestyles of the people who live there.
4. Occupations and recreational interests of the residents.
5. The children's and teenagers' activities and educational opportunities.
6. The community's amenities.
7. The protected environments being created.
8. All other related factors.

After discussing those factors, recite the specifics that are applicable to individual homesites or models. By doing this, you are selling not only a home and homesite, but also the community. All of the factors that affect the community and, more particularly, the homesite can influence the sale. Know your community's advantages. For example, the interior site plan is well-organized with accessibility to all of the amenities created. Street patterns provide residential privacy. The community offers protection for children and security for retired adults. Views are protected and preserved. All of these are tailored to specific homesites that are available now. Figure 2.4 shows a checklist of benefits of a specific community site plan.

Develop Background Information about Your Organization. Part of your sales message includes statements about the quality of construction and the integrity of the company. Be able to point with pride at the management's consistency in its concern for seeing that your new home communities are places where people can proudly own homes and feel they have bought the best from people who care. People who are buying a new home are not just buying the mortar, bricks, roofs, and flooring—the things they can see. They are also buying the manufacturer behind the construction of the community. That is especially true in the early stages of marketing, when the neighborhood is in the formative process and you have little to show except models and floor plans.

The public's confidence (or lack of it) in a developer-builder often plays a major role in the decision to buy or not to buy. Many builders have created challenges for themselves by inadequate performance.

Figure 2.4. Benefits of a specific community site plan.

Category	Items to review	Notes
Present site plan	General characteristics or plan Building areas and sites Street patterns Identity of neighborhoods Areas of development Phasing of construction Topography factors Amenities in present phases Other relationships	Master plan presented management Evaluate pattern Sub-communities within plan Follow management's authorized information Know what is included and all relevant factors
Future development plans	General concept (qualified) Timing consideration Anticipated amenities (if any) in future phases Other factors	As per management's representations Focus on present development to avoid lack of urgency Quote future amenities with caution
Profile of residents and purchasers	Number of residents Age mix Children (average number per household) Professions Resident interests Social activities of groups in community	Information from resident and buyer profile forms Data to be verified by management before quoting

Often they have reputations that lead to public concern about the risks of buying from them. Homebuilding is known for having a substantial number of failures. The public is reasonably well informed through word of mouth, newspapers, government agencies, and other sources. Be aware of the public's attitudes and the precautions people take in dealing with anyone building a new home or buying into a condominium or planned development. The industry has had its challenges in marketing projects that did not always fulfill the representations made to the public.

It is also important to sell the people who work for your company. Big corporations are not necessarily loved. The fact that General Motors and American Telephone and Telegraph are big corporations does not win any great approval from the public. They are more concerned with the individuals who translate an impersonal organization into reality: the local managers, the people who service them, and the dealers. In the case of new home sales, convey the message about the individuals who are managing your homes and communities. *People buy people, not just property.* They want to know that management is as concerned as they are with the locations in which they are going to live.

This is true for all housing projects, but it becomes a critical factor when you are dealing with condominiums and common interest communities. Management of the condominium community—after the sale has been completed and possession taken—can be as important to the buyer (if not more than) as the home bought. With poor management, the best condominium community is going to be a failure. An average common interest community with superb management can be a great success. Market, with credibility, the programs and the service you offer.

It is not suggested that you stand in front of customers and declare how great your company is. They did not come to hear that story. It is more important to have detailed information and some visual evidence of the success of your builder team, which you can integrate into this module. You need facts about the company that will reinforce why people should deal with you rather than with someone else. It cannot hurt you to sell the company you represent. It can hurt you to lack sufficient information to provide this reinforcement, because one of your competitors may have done a better job of personalizing and selling its builders and managers than you did and can therefore win over your potential homebuyer. A checklist for developing background information about the company you represent is provided in Figure 2.5.

Sell the Features and Benefits of Your Homes. Hundreds of elements go into the construction of a home and a community of homes. Each of these elements may, by itself, seem relatively insignificant, but collectively they represent the quality of construction and overall inherent values sold to the new homebuyers. What people buy is the total package, but the focus is often on the individual elements that are

Figure 2.5. Checklist for the builder-management team.

Category	Items to review	Notes
The company's history	Years in business Areas of operation Number of projects and homes built Pictures and examples of projects Philosophy of company Financial strength Financial backers as part of corporate team Other factors	Policy manual provides basic history Current data available from managers Representations should be handled carefully
Key personnel involved in this community	Project manager Superintendent(s) Land planners Engineers Marketing manager Sales manager Property manager Support team Others	See manager for current list Review which portions (if any) should be emphasized
Recognition and testimonials	Awards Testimonials Service policies Publicity stories Government recognition Other facts	Marketing department maintains these records

visually important to the message of why they should purchase one of your homes instead of buying from a competitor. Here, the issue is the competitive positioning of your homes versus other available housing and the differences that can be perceived in buying from you rather than someone else.

The only way to be effective in this area is to know how your company builds homes, the specifications and features that are used, and what makes them different from the competition's. Admittedly, all housing has common ingredients that are relatively similar: floors, roofs, and walls seem to be obvious features. However, the quality of construction when craftsmanship of various products is compared can differ considerably.

Be able to discuss the cabinets, paneling, mitered joints, the care and detail taken to see that the home is finished with a pride of workmanship in all areas where the customer might not expect a builder to be that conscientious. This involves the quality of materials, such as windows, tiles, roofing, and masonry. Most of the elements that go into the home are purchased from suppliers who indirectly become part of your sales team. The more you know about the features of your homes and what they offer to your customer, the better prepared you will be to present them effectively.

It is not enough to just sell features. A feature means little until it is *translated into a benefit.* A benefit is something one can personally experience because the feature is there. For example, if you are selling six inches of insulation in the walls or ceiling, you don't just talk about insulation. You emphasize the quality of insulation, its thickness, and then translate that into the benefits of cooler homes in the summer and warmer, more efficient homes in the winter. Thus, the benefits are saved money, reflected in energy bills, and the joy of living in a well-insulated home that is easier to maintain because dust and foreign particles do not collect as easily. This same approach can be taken for air conditioning or any other element of the home.

Your company can supply you with background information on each of the homes it constructs. It is your obligation to review and understand the information you are given. When you think you lack sufficient information, ask those who have it. The suppliers, subcontractors, and superintendents on the project can help you. So can your executive manager. If there is not a basic orientation system for gaining that information from the company for new models and new projects, conduct your own research program.

On a day-to-day basis, you may encounter situations that require personal investigation. A prospect may compare your homes to a competitor's and make an observation they have something you do not have. What does that mean in translating your features and your product in such a way as to give people perceived values sufficient to justify their decision to buy one of your homes? In this regard, there is no substitute for competitive evaluations. Looking at your competitors' projects and studying what they are offering is part of the research that every salesperson should do personally. In some cases, management assigns responsibilities to individuals to provide such competitive data. However, professionals do not lean upon others for what they should be doing for themselves. You have spare time when you are traveling around the area or you can start a little early in the day and stop by someone else's community to look at that project and make comparisons.

Every home has its pluses and minuses. Make a total comparison of other housing to that which you represent. Then look for the differences that you can accent in your features and benefits in comparison to the competition. What you lack, you will not talk about. What you do have, you certainly can demonstrate and include in your presentation. This is more than merely using your features and benefits by simply identifying them. It is important that benefits are transferred to the buyers' understanding of your elements of value. Your checklist of features and benefits for a typical home should include most of the items shown in Figure 2.6.

Establish the Features and Benefits of Each Model and Floor Plan. Establishing the features and benefits of each model and floor plan is the heart of building your planned presentation. It goes beyond the features and benefits of the homes in general to the specifics of an individual floor plan or housing opportunity that you offer today. It is normal to have three, four, five, or more different floor plans at any given time. Each floor plan has its own benefits and lifestyle advantages. You may have a limited inventory of speculative homes under construction that can be different from the models.

The process of developing the presentation must lead to selling specific homes. That is usually done before you concentrate on a site location for the plan. When you have a home to show your prospects that is already under construction, normally it is best to use models as a prelude to showing a home. Begin the decision-making process by focusing on a particular floor plan that might interest prospects. Then, with the features and benefits of that floor plan in mind, introduce one or more available sites. To build maximum perceived values, the floor plan usually comes first.

The art of being able to see the merits of a home is a vital aspect of your sales presentation and skills. A home is not just a box or a place you just walk into and say, "Here's the living room, kitchen, and

Figure 2.6. Features and benefits of your housing.

(Note: If more than one, list all of them and identify separately)		
Material or system	**Features**	**Benefits**
Basement and/or foundation structure		
Frame construction		
Floor construction		
Exterior wall materials		
Roof systems and materials		
Interior walls and finishes		
Windows		
Doors		
Hardware and locks		

Figure 2.6. (continued)

Material or system	Features	Benefits
Heating system		
Electrical system		
Plumbing system and materials		
Water heater		
Bathroom fixtures		
Kitchen appliances (oven and range)		
Kitchen appliances (disposal)		
Kitchen appliances (dishwasher)		
Kitchen cabinets		

Figure 2.6. (continued)

Material or system	Features	Benefits
Bedroom closets		
Insulation systems and materials		
Air conditioning		
Fireplaces		
Other items		

bedrooms." A home is an integrated series of experiences; rooms have relationships, all of which have potential advantages and disadvantages. In the demonstration process, concentrate on individual properties, as discussed more specifically in Chapter 4.

In developing your presentation, you first need a checklist of the features and benefits of each model you represent. That checklist includes items such as typical profiles of people who might buy specific homes: their lifestyles, interests, and motivations. The checklist also would include information about living patterns within the home; orientation of the rooms to traffic flow among kitchen, family room, and dining area, and to other parts of the home; and the potentials of furniture placement. All of the features of the home as they relate to sites should be listed. Front views and rear views, impact from morning sunlight and afternoon shade are also checklist items when considering other locations, as discussed in the next module. Figure 2.7 is a checklist of things to be considered regarding each model floor plan you have to present.

Develop a Checklist of Characteristics for Specific, Available Sites. Having established the features and benefits for each model and type of housing offered, you are ready to concentrate on particular sites that are available for sale now. Regardless of how many homes are being constructed, you have only a limited number you can sell today, this week, or this month. *To any one buyer, you can usually sell only one home.* Inventory itself can become confusing when there is too much from which to select. Every location has its distinct advantages and disadvantages.

Figure 2.7. Features and benefits of each floor plan or model.

Alternatives and options	Lighting fixtures
Analysis of specific floor plan as example	Parking/garage/carport (accessibility)
Bathrooms	Plumbing system
Cabinets	Roofs
Ease of maintenance	Room arrangements/functions
Electrical outlets	Room sizes
Expandable areas/future additions	Square footage
Flooring	Storage/closets
Furniture arrangements	Walls
Heating system	Windows

Develop your presentation so that it is specific on why one homesite or location is superior to another or how it will be perceived by one customer versus another. A great percentage of the value of a home is in the location, not just in the floor plan, style of architecture, or the features of the home. Location may influence the total value of the home by as much as 30 percent to 40 percent (or more). This is notably true for highrise condominiums. There are the differences of value where the view on the top floor has certain advantages, and the characteristics of the first-floor locations have other advantages. For example, people who want easy access without taking elevators would be more interested in the first floor.

The proximity of the amenities has a bearing on the value factors of location. The sites should be rated according to the appeal each has to basic motivations of the people to whom you have targeted your markets. Remember the acronym CRISP. It stands for Comfort, Romance, Identity, Security, and Privacy, which are viable guidelines to the evaluation of site benefits.

It is also wise to use the comparative technique of selecting two dissimilar sites for which the same model or home can be offered. There is often a price differential based on advantages and disadvantages. In putting together a checklist for a given site, the items shown in Figure 2.8 are recommended. The information could be summarized on a lot rating chart, such as the one shown in Figure 2.9.

Know and Be Able to Present the Current Alternatives to Home Ownership and Financing. You are selling not just homes, but also financing, monthly investments, and the cost of ownership long after the purchase is completed. Many a sale is made or lost on the basis of the prospect's perceptions of its economic feasibility. The types and interest costs of available financing become critical for many individuals. Some people have difficulty acquiring a desired home or making a change in housing because they view the transaction in terms of certain rigid types of financing instead of exploring alternatives available.

Part of your education and your process of helping people buy a home is to know how many ways there are to finance the homes you offer and what you can do for a specific client. More than basic financing is involved, although that is an important consideration. Also important is to understand the variables that customers might apply to their own situations to become eligible for financing. You need to know all the things customers might do to improve their capital position or tax position, alternatives of selling or financing other real estate holdings, and contingent factors that are involved. The checklist of creative financing ideas is part of your presentation to those for whom

70 New Home Sales

this is a possible obstacle. Checklists for this area are covered in detail in Chapter 12.

Apply the Benefits of Home Ownership to Specific Customers. When all is said and done, the final step in the process is finding the home that fits a particular prospect's motivations, abilities, and needs. It has been said that no one buys a whole home—*they buy bits and pieces, and the rest comes free.* What interests one customer may not interest another. One person's motivations are not necessarily the motivations of another.

Figure 2.8. Characteristics and Benefits of Specific Sites.

Use lot rating chart

Items to rate
 ☐ Size of homesite (single family)
 ☐ Buildability (single, family, custom)
 ☐ Unusual topography
 ☐ Views
 ☐ Sun orientation
 ☐ Trees
 ☐ Parking (for owners and guests)
 ☐ Privacy, seclusion, isolation
     ☐ Traffic
     ☐ Buffers, landscape screens
     ☐ Proximity of adjacent homes
     ☐ Noise factors
     ☐ Visual privacy
 ☐ Security
     ☐ Protection from traffic
     ☐ Neighboring homes
     ☐ Accessibility
     ☐ Ingress and egress
     ☐ Lighting systems
 ☐ Gardening and planting areas
 ☐ Curbside appeal
 ☐ Access to amenities
 ☐ Special highrise factors
     ☐ Elevators
     ☐ Parking

Figure 2.9. Lot rating chart.

Lot number	Size	Views	Build-ability	Privacy	Amenities	Security	Prestige	Trees	Total points

NOTE: 0 = Average or base site for each amenity. The scale is then 1 to 10 above or below a zero. A dollar value to the adjusted levels or percentage value to dollars should then be established for the 1 to 10 rating. For example, if each one point above or below represented one percent of the lot value and the lot was priced at $6,000, then every point would be worth $60. Points should be rated according to the importance of that particular item to the salability of the site. The total on the far right represents the balance between pluses and minuses above and below the base lot. The first lot selected for that group should be as near as possible to being the average lot with no pluses or minuses in reference to the eight rated elements.

In the process of qualifying people and getting their reactions to your properties, look for clues, or "hot buttons," to identify their dominant interests. As you develop an awareness of these interests, tailor your presentation to emphasize the things these potential buyers need to fulfill their motivations. These motivations are often personalized, so it is difficult to provide a complete list, but the checklist in Figure 2.10 shows major considerations in the home purchasing decision. Find methods of seeing that your presentation includes positive resolutions to dominant problems. The sample checklist in Figure 2.10 contains broad categories of the motivations people may have with respect to a given home, and breaks them down into specifics.

Figure 2.10. Benefits of home ownership based on motivations.

Key motivations	General rating of plan	General rating of site
Total value based on resale potential		
Health and personal security		
Recreation and leisure		
Family needs (particularly children)		
Individuality and creativity		
Comfort and convenience		
Privacy (retreat)		
Romance (environment)		
Prestige (self-image)		
Return on investment		
Other (specify)		
Note: Use 1-to-10 scale, as in Figure 2.9.		

ADDRESS YOURSELF TO YOUR BUYERS' MOTIVES

Although all customers have personal motivations that are exclusively their own, it is worthwhile to learn to recognize the patterns in buyer profiles. Having identified the dominant buying motivations of a particular group, you can target your sales presentations to those factors most important to buyers in that group.

There are six broad classifications of homebuyers to whom specific sales approaches can be directed.

1. Family-oriented buyers.
2. Money-oriented buyers.
3. Self-expression buyers.
4. Prestige-conscious buyers.
5. Health- and security-conscious buyers.
6. Leisure/recreation buyers.

Based on past experience, the motivations of each of these groups can be described as follows.

Family-Oriented Buyers

Probably the largest and most dominant classification of single-family homebuyers in terms of controlling motivations is that loosely classified as family-oriented. What distinguishes them from the other groups is that they put *their families, their children, and their togetherness as a family unit* above all other motivations in making a home-buying decision. Frequently, the children come first, and the parents are willing to sacrifice many of their own personal desires to provide the things they believe are vital to their children's welfare and interests. Schools, safety, neighborhood influences, and recreation for the children are among the most important environmental factors. Even such features as better family rooms will influence which homes this group selects.

Family-oriented buyers do weigh the money involved and other factors that are important to them, but they make their final decision in terms of their love and appreciation for the family, and the interests of the children generally come before those of the parents.

When buyers are family oriented, spend more time on the features that would apply to their togetherness and particularly to the welfare of the children. Spend less time talking about money and other factors that would motivate someone else, because the final decision is going to be based on the buyers' willingness to provide the lifestyle they want for the family as a unit.

Money-Oriented Buyers

Although money is a major consideration for all homebuyers, to one particular group it is more important then general family welfare or any other areas of interest or personal fulfillment. The fear of losing money is usually an underlying factor, along with the need to justify the homebuying decision in terms of dollars, numbers, and facts.

People in this category are motivated by how much they receive for their dollars, and how well their investment is protected. They are interested in the details of square footage, construction quality, interest rates, and similar checklist approaches to value. Frequently, these buyers carry clipboards of competitive information and use their calculators to check your products against their predetermined standards.

With this kind of buyer, aim your presentation at justifying all values, and use your facts about the construction of the product to greatest advantage. These things are far more important to money-oriented buyers than choosing exactly the right home that would suit the lifestyle and interests of their families.

Self-Expression Buyers

Another group of buyers can be generally classified as individualists or self-expressionists. These are often creative people—artists, educators, and others whose professions have given them a sense of independence. Their homebuying decision is not based as much on family needs or money as the desire to express their personalities in their housing choice. Highly individual architectural styles or the excitement of a nontraditional floor plan may appeal to them.

These people often do not want to be burdened by maintenance and ownership responsibilities. They may select condominiums, townhouses, or apartments instead of a single-family home with maintenance burdens that would perhaps curtail some of their other activities. They are different, and they know it. Don't classify them as part of the general public, for if you do, you will probably lose them. They tend to be romantics. They buy the trees or the view, and the house comes free!

Prestige-Conscious Buyers

Some homebuyers make their housing decisions almost entirely on the basis of being with the "in" group. To them, the right neighborhood with a prestige address is the dominant buying motive, and it overshadows family needs, money, and personal self-expression. They often sacrifice things that are important to others just to have the psychological satisfaction of keeping up with the Joneses. Social life and social identification are controlling influences in everything they do.

With this group of buyers, emphasize the locations and the people with whom they want to be associated. They are also interested in making sure their peers are aware of what they are buying. So location and exterior appearance are more important than the interior of the home. They buy the address, and the house comes free!

Health- and Security-Conscious Buyers

Another group of buyers have come to a stage of life where their personal health or security is the dominant motive in the selection of a home. These buyers are usually older couples, widows, divorcees, or anyone suffering from a health problem.

Retirement communities where health and sunshine are the major emphasis cater to this group. In urban locations, the maintenance-free lifestyle of condominiums, patio homes, and townhouses also attracts a fair segment of this market.

Women who live alone normally are vitally concerned with their security and frequently will sacrifice many personal housing desires to find a home in which they feel secure.

Leisure/Recreation Buyers

A new group of homebuyers that is attracted to housing with substantial leisure/recreational benefits has been emerging for the past decade or two. These buyers are more interested in the golf courses, tennis courts, swimming pools, riding trails, and marinas than in housing itself. They are often empty nesters seeking a new fun-filled life, or people who have become affluent enough to enjoy their leisure time. Many are second-home or retirement buyers. With shorter workweeks and more time for recreation, more homebuyers than ever before are making their decisions based on the recreation and leisure amenities rather than on the housing alone.

Everyone is interested in leisure activities to some degree. Thus, this motivation is often a strong secondary factor even when one of the other elements of personal concern tends to dominate the decision.

Set Up a Logical Sequence of Topics to Be Covered

Having identified the benefits of living in your city, your neighborhood, and your project; the merits of your builders' specific homes and homesites; and the major objections and questions you anticipate, you are ready to begin building your sales presentation.

Do this by setting up a logical sequence of topics to cover with prospects during the initial presentation. Include the tours of the sales facilities, models, and sites. It is impossible for someone else to outline the ideal order of presentation, because every situation has its own requirements. However, it is best to begin discussing the broader regional interests and advantages and to work down to specific sites. That presentation sequence is an effective way to involve and qualify prospects.

Your outline should include any specific displays to be shown and tours you would like to conduct during that time. If, for example, a display located in the sales office should be used in the first phase of discussion, index what points to cover in that phase. Next indicate at what point to move to another display or out into your actual environment. The more thorough your outline of the points you want to cover in different locations, the better your presentation will be when you are face-to-face with your prospective buyers.

GUIDELINES FOR MANAGEMENT OF SALES EXHIBITS

Of great importance in the management of sales exhibits is to include involvement tools for you to use. Remember that a salesperson needs these tools in order to qualify and control the traffic. First, be sure that you understand all the tools. Then consider how to place them in the exhibits so that they are used to advantage.

Consider whether each tool truly helps or confuses in leading the buyer to a conclusion. If a tool does not achieve its primary objective, it should be modified, replaced, or eliminated. Many sales facilities introduce too many visual aids at the wrong time and place. The customer ends up having to look at and study more than is wise before seeing the product and the community. Any display that does not effectively help the sales agent is usually unnecessary. Exhibits that answer too many questions tend to replace the function of a salesperson. The basic ingredients of an effective sales facility are described in the following paragraphs.

The Plot Map or Relief Map of the Area

This is the most important tool in many sales offices. Maximum attention should be given to its development, location, and use. The ideal location of a plot map is on a horizontal table placed strategically between the customer and the floor plans or the major exhibits. It should be located off the basic traffic pattern so that the sales agent can, on busy days, determine how much time to spend with a prospect at this major marketing exhibit. It should be placed where the salesperson can use it to ideal advantage.

The plot map (or relief map) is visual evidence of the total environment you are selling and is vital to the decision-making process when considering available sites, models, and amenities. The plot map should clearly represent the area so that a customer can easily visualize it while standing in the sales facility. The customer should easily understand, in terms of directions and views, the total environment you are trying to portray. That means that the plot map should be organized so that it is facing the same way—north, south, east, west—that the community is organized. It should be easy for customers to determine their present location in reference to the entire project. One of the most effective arrangements for the plot map is to place it at bar stool height. The sales agent can work in a casual fashion, standing at the table explaining facts about the community, while the prospect sits on one of the stools. A bar-stool-height plot table or an environmental topography map is a focal point of attention in the sales facility.

You could have two different kinds of displays of this nature. One is a relief map showing the entire community with all of the amenities and villages, plus future development areas. You can use this to orient the customer to the entire concept. The second map shows the specific area currently being developed in the first phase, with the homes shown in a larger format. This gives you a chance to begin by setting the stage for the overview of the area and then move the prospect to a secondary display that shows what is currently being offered for sale.

Environmental Exhibits

In the sales office, prime consideration must be given to the exhibits that portray the type of environment you are selling and its benefits. Prospects should see this type of exhibit first when entering the building, and it should actively stimulate interest in the community.

It should be oriented along a route that takes the prospects toward major exhibits or out to the models if they are located nearby. In contrast, place those things you do not want prospects to see first where they can be inspected on returning from the models or as the sales agent introduces them.

The goal is not to have a prospect study renderings and elevation pictures of housing before seeing the entire environment; locate these exhibits where they are visible on the return trip. Environmental exhibits often include large photographs of the area, new shopping centers, recreational views, planned parks, golf courses, and mood shots depicting the way-of-life feeling about the community. This sets the stage for the specific information that will be conveyed in face-to-face conversation with prospects.

Location Map

Also of vital importance to prospects is a general location map showing nearby cities and towns. It should identify shopping centers, churches, schools, and other facilities that concern the prospect. The community may need two location maps—one for the specific immediate vicinity and one for the larger metropolitan area. Again, it is usually best to place the location maps somewhere near the entry area on the route to the first major exhibit. That way, the salespeople can quickly point out the prospects' location if they are not totally familiar with the community's orientation to the surrounding environment.

Feature Board

Major feature boards list the benefits of the community and the benefits of the housing products offered. To avoid confusing the two issues, maintain the environmental board separately from the specific features board for individual products. These feature boards can have merit if they do not replace the salesperson's functions. They should not contain all of the summary points that a sales agent must use. They should contain the basic points to increase interest in the community and the product. It is often wise to do this with mood-setting pictures rather than with words. The sales associate can then cover in detail the concepts involved.

Floor Plan Displays and Renderings

Floor plan displays and renderings are vital parts of the sales exhibits and are used as closing tools by salespeople. They should be located where the customer sees them on return from visiting models or so that the sales agents can show them after preliminary qualifying. Floor plans and renderings do not do the job adequately to pre-sell most merchandise. They often tend to confuse a prospect with too much to absorb too soon.

The floor plan in particular is a great closing tool after prospects have seen a particular home or a site that they could enjoy owning. Prior to that, it is difficult for many people to read the layout or understand what they see. These plans should be placed outside the traffic pattern where most of the initial qualifying and involvement will occur. They should be placed strategically so that they are visible to those already qualified and involved with the community when the salesperson is ready to get down to specifics in a controlled decision-making sequence.

Color Selection Exhibits

Once buyers have become interested in a particular product, they are going to want to choose properties and materials related to their particular home. It is desirable to have such exhibit areas completely isolated from the general sales facility. They might even be placed at the product's location rather than at the central sales office. In any case, they should not be openly visible until the prospects have begun to make a housing decision. If a customer gets involved in the selection of colors before selecting a home, you may lose control. Such exhibits are best placed in separate rooms, alcoves, or buildings removed from the heavy traffic of the major sales office. If they are discussed prematurely, they can create confusion and cause lost sales. In many cases, the best way to handle this function is to use the services of a decorator consultant.

Material Selection Exhibits

The recommendations about color selection also apply to material selection exhibits. That is, selection of tiles, cabinets, and other elements that go into a home is a tool to be used after you have involved the customer with larger concepts. In some subdivisions, customer decorating rooms are set up where buyers, by appointment, can sit and make their choices with the assistance of a color consultant.

Selling the Neighbors and the Residents of the Community

In many communities, it is desirable to emphasize the names of people who have already purchased. Thus, you lend credibility to the success of the project, and you impress prospects with the kind of people who already have made housing decisions. A neighborhood board or a list of buyers who already have made the decision can be helpful to sales.

In some communities, it is advisable to register the buyer's origin as well as property purchased. At some point in your presentation, this may be a valuable sales tool. It is particularly helpful in retirement communities and areas where most of the buyers are new and like to know the cities of origin of other residents in the community.

The list of buyers is often a part of the secondary plot map. The names oi the buyers are posted on each building site or on a separate list attached to it. Bear in mind that you should not use a purchaser's name without permission. Some people do not want their addresses or identities revealed to the general public. Privacy laws are designed to protect individual rights.

Nevertheless, additional exhibits are frequently in order because they help people locate others they already know. This gives the salesperson an opportunity to reinforce the buyer's identity and determine who will be making the final decision about buying a house. It does tend to build confidence and is a helpful tool to salespeople. Once you are well on your way with a history of success, this might be worthwhile to consider.

At other times, the marketing department decides not to provide the names of the present buyers for one or more reasons. That decision should be respected. It is often based on other considerations of greater importance than the marketing advantage of seeing the buyers' names or having testimonials. A community activity board is almost always justified. In addition, in owner association communities, the pictures and brief biographies of the board of directors, committees, etc., are excellent reinforcement for salespeople's presentations.

Other Exhibits

Many other types of exhibits can be permanently placed in the sales center. The ones identified here represent the most important. Any tool or exhibit should be weighed in terms of its impact on a customer and its ability to influence a favorable decision.

The philosophy behind the use of any handout materials or movable tools placed in the customer's hands during qualifying, involvement, and closing also should be carefully evaluated. The tendency in most subdivisions is to give the prospects too much material when they first enter the sales office. This deprives the salespeople of the very opportunities they need to get involved with the prospect in answering questions and using the exhibits to their advantage. Keep tools out of the customers' hands until they are of some value to your sales objectives. Basically, it is a mistake to give the customers too much to read when they first arrive. By controlling the information customers receive, you can direct the presentation to greater advantage.

Guide to the Model Homes. Many marketing experts in housing prefer to use an introductory handout less expensive than a brochure, which they sometimes call a Guide to the Models. The guide is a means of introducing the prospect to the models to be seen, their locations, prices, and a few basic facts without giving too much detailed information, which would tend to confuse the customer or reduce the salesperson's involvement. Further, the guide often contains a brief history of the builder and the community, which reinforces selling points about environmental factors and the integrity of those responsible for the community. The complete brochure is then used as an additional giveaway when the prospects return from inspecting the models or showhomes.

Subdivision Brochures. When used correctly, subdivision brochures are valuable tools. The most effective ones are those which can be assembled by the sales associates with individual sheets for the models and other items of interest. The salespeople are then in a position to introduce each of the models at an appropriate time and add to their controlling opportunities. All deluxe brochures should be introduced when the salesperson can effectively use them to involve the prospect in a qualifying conversation. Preferably, brochures should be located adjacent to the plot map, so the sales agent can use the map table and its lot selection potential to help get the customer interested in a specific site and model. Better yet, if brochures are hidden from customers' view, the salesperson has an excuse for keeping customers a little longer before giving them a brochure.

Price Breakdown Sheets. A good way to get a customer involved in a specific model or unit is to provide a price breakdown sheet filled out by the sales associate, which includes information only the customer is able to furnish. While the customer is waiting for this to be filled out, the salesperson starts a conversation, using suitable questioning techniques. In this way, the salesperson is in a position to lead the customer to a potential close. Usually one price breakdown sheet is given to the customer, and the salesperson keeps a copy with the name and address of the prospect clearly recorded for follow-up. Often, the agent will use an informal scratch pad rather than a preorganized sheet.

Floor Plans and Renderings. Handout copies of floor plans, the renderings, and occasionally acetate-covered copies of the same exhibits are effective tools to use to involve the customers. Again, they are usually best used when the prospect has been introduced to the product. They are often part of the brochure itself, but can be used separately if desired.

Plot Maps of the Area. Small plot maps showing the lots and environmental features of the subdivision are excellent involvement tools. They allow the customers to orient themselves as to where their homesites might be and, further, to establish a picture of the total community. Salespeople on busy subdivisions often use them to provide directions to interested prospects, so that they can check out the neighborhoods on their own.

Brochures about the Builder. Since the integrity and planning of the builder are important to the buyer, brochures about the people who have put the product together are often a valuable means to reinforce interest and secure a potential purchase. Again, these are frequently made a part of the major brochure.

THE CREDIBILITY OF THE PRESENTATION

Everything you say should be totally believable and factual. If you exaggerate the facts about your housing, or about the environment, you risk losing the prospect's confidence. You also risk future encounters with unhappy homebuyers who were told one thing, but who later found out something completely different.

Remember that the majority of today's homebuyers are well educated. They are more inclined to check on the integrity and reputation of the builders and their agents than was previously true. The soft-sell is still the most effective approach; you increase your chances of establishing a solid relationship with your buyers, one that is based on credibility and built on a foundation of confidence and trust. Homebuyers who live in the same community invariably compare notes after they move in, and special deals, false promises, and exaggerated claims have a way of catching up with those who promote them.

3: Qualifying and Counseling Prospects

Qualifying prospects is directly related to closing sales. The best closers almost always are the best qualifiers. Why? Because qualifying helps salespeople understand their prospects' motivations, abilities, and needs. You can reach people more effectively and guide them through a favorable decision-making process if you know enough about them to help them weigh the home purchase opportunity.

The techniques involved in qualifying and closing are essentially the same. They involve knowing the right questions to ask and using those questions during the presentation in a way that achieves positive answers and results.

At the beginning of your relationship with prospects, work on developing a "discovery process." You do not know what the prospects are thinking, where they have been, or where they are going. Therefore, you need to open the doors of communication to learn enough about them so that your decisions as to how to assist them will be practical and likely to result in a decision to buy.

Time is obviously a controlling factor. On-site new home sales personnel have less time to achieve their goals than do general brokerage sales agents. They also have less control over their prospects. Customers arriving in their own cars are free to leave at their own discretion. You do not control the events that precede their arrival nor those that occur after they leave. You may have little control over what they will see, even in terms of your own housing, unless you handle the presentation well. If model homes are available for customers to investigate, the customers often want to be on their own.

BEGINNING THE QUALIFYING PROCESS

When prospects first enter the sales office or model home area, you have only a few moments to quickly qualify and prepare them to see your merchandise. No matter how much time you have with any single prospect, it is essential to move along as rapidly as is practical, in order to leave time to work with other prospects that same day and to direct your time and energy to concentrate on prospects who are most likely to buy now. Learning how to quickly qualify while continuing to involve customers with the benefits of the housing environment is just as important as knowing how and when to close. If you do not master this early phase of the selling procedure, you probably will never reach the final one.

The best qualifiers can ask prospects one question that reveals multiple answers and opens up a number of areas to explore, while other salespeople have to ask more questions to obtain the same information. These better qualifiers are also better closers. Equally important, the most effective working relationships are with the prospects whom the salesperson has been able to qualify and establish rapport with prior to beginning the showing process.

The subject of this chapter is the art of qualifying and controlling prospects. Since the available time in which to work with prospects is limited, it is vital to know how to gain the right information as quickly as possible. This is especially true for a busy Sunday or a high-traffic day. When there are numerous prospects with whom to work, you cannot handle all of them at the same time.

Quick qualifying involves a careful mixture of salient comments about your community and your housing opportunities with well-phrased questions that are inoffensive and designed to encourage open response.

To fulfill your objectives with any prospect, it is essential to integrate your key questions and opening presentation points in a way that allows the customers to feel that they are getting information while they are giving information. *Customers do not want to be pressured at any time!* The art of selling is one of making them feel relaxed and at home while you are probing their degree of interest, their ability to buy, and their dominant motivations. It is important to remember that what *you* know does not matter until you know what *they* know. Use facts about your homes cautiously; do not fire them indiscriminately. One way of doing so is to turn almost every statement or comment you make into a question. That is a means of giving as little as necessary to get as much back as possible.

Matching Techniques to Circumstances

The appropriate approaches for high-traffic days and low-traffic days differ. On busy days, salespeople may have to use *knock-out questions* to set the stage for how much time to spend with one prospect rather than another. A knock-out question is one that is designed to quickly determine whether visitors are qualified buyers or are just looking at housing they cannot afford to buy or who are not really in the homebuying mood yet. When several people are standing in line, it is much better to be with *prospects* than with *suspects*.

Conversely, a low-traffic day when there is no one else with whom to talk (and it is even somewhat lonely to be there) is a good opportunity for sharpening skills on a suspect. Even if you fail to sell anything, at least you are practicing! Therefore, you might want to be less quick to qualify when you have the time to get to know people—and sometimes discover that they really are qualified but would not reveal their position at the beginning. There is always a risk in asking incisive questions early in the conversation. The risk is worth taking when traffic and numbers of prospects are at a volume that demands separation of the best qualified from those who are least likely to buy. It is not in your best interest to do this when you have a limited number of people with whom to work and plenty of time to achieve your objectives.

Knock-Out Questions

"Are you out house hunting today?" or *"It's a great day to be house hunting, isn't it?"*

"How soon had you anticipated making a move into a new home?" or *"How soon had you planned to be relocated in a new home?"*

"How long have you been looking for a new home?" or *"What size home have you been considering?"*

These are a few examples of polite questions designed to surface genuine interest. Most often you can obtain a "yes" or "no" response or some comment that leads you to tentatively conclude whether or not visitors are really in the market for a home today. Such incisive queries produce varied results. Even interested prospects may answer evasively when they are confronted with a direct approach. It is best to use the direct approach only when volume of traffic and the lack of sales personnel permit no other feasible alternatives.

Humor

Use of humor is another way to open up a conversation and get people to talk about themselves. For example, you see a lady with a baby in her arms, and you say:

> *"I'll take the baby for a down payment!"*

This will probably get a laugh and maybe even a revealing comment:

> *"We're really not in the market for a home; we just came to see your decorating."*
>
> *"We recently bought a home, and they told us you had some marvelous furnishings over here."*

If you get such a response, you can direct her to see the furniture while you work with a more valid prospect.

Never forget that you are in a public relations role as well as a sales role when you work for your building company. Everyone should be made to feel that the experience of visiting your project and seeing your homes is an enjoyable one. Be pleasant and hospitable to everyone you meet, and they may have a desire to send others to you as well as talk favorably about your community to others they know.

Practice your techniques for beginning the qualifying process by thinking of replies to the questions and statements shown in Figures 3.1 and 3.2.

QUALIFYING CATEGORIES

Do you know what you want to learn from each prospect? What must you know and how can you quickly learn it? Although there are many things you might want to discover ultimately, it is impossible to ask everything at once. Nor do you want to risk offending your customers by putting them through intensive interrogation before they have a chance to see your merchandise. Therefore, evaluate the areas of qualification you need to explore initially and the kinds of questions that will help you secure the right answers.

The categories of information you need from your prospects fall into the following six areas:

1. Experience.
2. Urgency.
3. Ability.

Figure 3.1. Handling prospects' questions.

> Practice your responses to questions asked by prospects during the initial qualifying interview by preparing answers to the following sample questions.

"How large are your homes?"

"How many square feet are in your homes?"

"How much do you require as a down payment on most of your houses?"

"What interest rate are you offering?"

"How many models do you have?"

"What class of people live here?"

"What extras do you give with the house?"

"How much are your taxes here?"

"How big are your lots?"

"What price are your homes?"

4. Status.
5. Requirements.
6. Motivations.

This chapter analyzes each of these qualifying categories and considers the various kinds of questions you might use to uncover prospects' true positions. The particular questions chosen for each qualifying objective may not be the best ones for you or for the project you represent. Selling approaches work best when adapted to your own individual needs and natural talents. Carefully analyze these concepts, and then adapt them to your selling style, using your own interpretations.

Qualifying a Prospect's Experience

The easiest areas to investigate first with any prospect are those that relate to past experiences and to present positions. Questioning here is designed to reveal such factors as:

88 New Home Sales

Figure 3.2. Responding to prospects' statements.

How would you respond to the following statements given at the beginning of your greeting and qualifying process?

"We won't be able to move until our lease expires."

"There are six of us in the family, and we're concerned about getting the most space we can for our money."

"Your competitor down the street says we should look at your homes first to get an idea of the value he has to offer."

"We're not sure we want to live on this side of town, but we wanted to see what you have anyway."

"One of our friends told us we should look at your houses."

"We may be transferred to your city, and we wanted to see what kind of housing was available."

"We sold our home and we have to move in 30 days."

"I understand your schools are not as good as those in some of the other districts."

- Where do they live?
- What do they know about our products or community?
- Where do they work?
- What have they seen?

In other words, what do they know, where have they been, and where are they now?

It is natural to begin questioning in these broad areas, since these subjects are relatively easy for prospects to discuss and do not create adverse psychological pressure in the early stages of qualifying.

Often the best opening question to reveal experience is this one:

"Is this your first visit to Greenfield Acres?"
   (insert the name of your own project); or
"Is this your first visit to a John Doe community?"
   (insert name of your own builder)

This selective approach quickly permits you to choose a course to follow based on their answers. If the answer is "yes," pursue one direction, and if the answer is "no," follow another, such as:

> *"It's nice to have you back again. Which of our model homes interested you and your family the most?"*

To help you improve your own approach, examine the following questions used by professionals to uncover these areas of experience. Compare them to the ones you are using and evaluate how you might improve your own approach.

> *"Is this your first visit to (your project)?"*
> *"Where are you living now?"*
>> *"How long have you lived there?"*
>> *"Do you also own other property?"*
>> *"Do you own your own home, or are you renting?"*
>> *"How is the resale market in your area?"*
> *"How did you happen to hear about (name of your project)?"*
> *"What new homes have you seen so far since you have been looking for a home?"*
> *"Have you seen anything you like?"*
> *"What has appealed to you?"*
> *"How long have you been looking for a new home?"*

From responses to these questions, you can determine your best approach in directing the prospects to your current housing opportunities. Degree of experience in knowing and understanding the real estate market is a primary factor in customers' ability to accept values and prices. If prospects are new to the area or have not seen many homes yet, they may not appreciate what your company has to offer. Educate an individual who does not know the market more than one who has been looking for an extended period of time.

Qualifying a Prospect's Urgency

Early in the qualifying conversation with any prospect, probe for clues as to the degree of urgency. How urgent is the need to make a decision, and how much time do prospects have to complete the move? *Urgency* and *timing* are critical areas of qualification. In many cases, the timing factors involved are also a part of the total motivation and will be critical in helping you target a specific property that meets a prospect's possession requirements.

Urgency and timing should surface quickly in qualifying sessions, so that you can make the decisions on what to show and how much time to devote to any single prospect. Here are some ways to uncover this vital area:

> *"How soon had you planned to be in your home?"* or
> *"How soon would you like to make a move?"*
> *"How soon had you thought of making a move if you found the right home?"*
> *"Are you planning a move in the near future?"*
> *"How soon will you need your new home?"*

> *"How much time will you have to see homes today?"* (very important for out-of-towners)
> *"How long will you be in town?"*
> *"Where are you staying?"*
> *"What have you planned to see while you are here?"*

> *"How long have you been seriously looking for your new home?"*

> *"When were you planning to give possession of your present home (or apartment)?"*
> if renting:
> *"How soon will your present lease expire?"*
> *"Will it be necessary for your lease to expire before you make the move to a new residence?"*
> if the home is sold:
> *"How soon will your sale close?"*
> *"How soon will you be receiving the funds from the sale of your home?"*

Qualifying a Prospect's Ability

Certainly one of the most critical qualifying factors is prospects' financial ability to purchase the property you represent. When the selection of merchandise covers a wide range of possibilities, this is even more significant. You will not want to introduce properties that do not meet prospects' potential capacity to buy.

Determining financial ability basically involves relating prospects' answers to several areas of questioning, so as to complete the qualifying puzzle. By fitting these pieces together, you can match the clues and get the total picture.

Probing for financial qualifications can be a delicate and sensitive area for many prospects, especially in the early stages of conversation and before a specific home has aroused their interest. *Approach this subject gently, but do not be afraid of it.* The areas of questioning on ability should involve the following:

- Profession or employment;
- Ownership of real estate or other assets;
- Open questioning;
- Examples and comparisons;
- Defining mortgage requirements;
- Exploring hidden assets;
- Reviewing people who might be of assistance to the buyers.

Normally, prospects will disclose the first two pieces of information easily, often as a by-product of questions regarding experience and urgency. The others become more incisive and must be investigated with great care so as to avoid putting the prospect under mental pressure too soon. Your sense of timing and the way in which you ask the questions are crucial to your objectives.

The following paragraphs examine each area of questioning in greater detail.

Profession or Employment. A good way to begin obtaining information is to ask a prospect about his or her profession or employment. This can be done with questions such as the following:

"May I ask your profession?"
"With which company are you associated?"
"Where will you be employed when you transfer to our city?"
"Are both of you working at this time?"
"How long have you been associated with A.B.C. Company?"

Ownership of Real Estate or Other Assets. Another approach is to ask questions about what real estate or other assets prospects own. Such questions could include:

"How much do you feel you will realize from the sale of your present home?"
"Will it be necessary to sell your present home to buy a new one?"
"Have you made other real estate investments?"
"How long have you lived in your present home?"
"Have you recently had your home appraised?"

Open Questioning. Another area of questioning on financial ability is open questioning, which requires relatively involved responses.

> *"How much of your savings have you planned to invest in a new home?"*
> *"What price range have you been considering?"*
> *"How much do you feel will comfortably fit within your housing budget?"*
> *"How much have you set aside for the initial investment in a new home?"*
> *"What type of financing have you considered?"*
> *"What did you have in mind?"*

Examples and Comparisons. Examples and comparisons are a helpful tool in qualifying. Some illustrations of this technique follow:

> *"Our homes range from $70,000 to $95,000 in price. What price range have you been considering?"*
> *"This model you are now looking at is priced at $125,000; that includes all of the finishing details except for the furniture. How does this compare to what you have in mind?"*
> *"A minimum investment in these homes would be approximately $50,000. How does that fit into your plans?"*
> *"How do our homes compare in price and value to others you have seen?"*

Establishing Mortgage Requirements. When working with prospects who may be marginal in their ability to qualify, it is usually necessary to explore the specifics of mortgage qualifications relatively early. This is particularly true for lower income groups and those who are seeking minimum terms because they have limited reserves and income. Questions might include the following:

> *"Since you are interested in using FHA financing terms, you will need to qualify for the maximum available loan with a minimum of $26,000 in annual earnings. How does that figure compare to your present income?"*
> *"Are you familiar wth the qualifications that will be needed to establish your credit for a mortgage? If not, permit me to briefly review them with you. . . ."* (and then review them)
> *"What types of financing have you considered so far?"*

At this point, with marginal qualifiers, it may be best to sit down and summarize mortgage requirements with a checklist of key factors, so that both you and your prospects understand what is involved. You would not normally use this technique with higher-priced homes, at least at the outset of your qualifying, or for individuals whose responses to previous questions clearly indicate they are financially capable of meeting your lender's requirements.

This approach to qualifying is normally pursued with one specific home in mind. You are thus playing the role of educating a prospect who has evidenced interest in one particular plan. It is usually best to do this kind of qualifying with previously prepared examples or case histories. It is easier to help someone understand facts and figures when they are in writing. As we will explore in the chapter on closing buyers, this qualifying step is frequently the prelude to making the sale. The summary sheet or scratch pad becomes a closing tool, as well as the basis for qualifying criteria.

Exploring Hidden Assets. People frequently have assets that they fail to consider when trying to qualify for the purchase of a new residence. When buyers need additional resources to strengthen their financial positions, it is necessary to explore for the things prospects tend to overlook. Since this line of questioning can be delicate or —even worse—threatening to customers, carefully weigh when and where to pursue it. Normally, such questions are reserved for the sit-down session in the pre-closing period. Tackle then only when it is obvious that the customers cannot make the qualifying mark without adding something to the picture.

Some of the questions that explore hidden assets are the following:

> *"Will you be converting any of your other investments or assets to complete your purchase of a new home?"*
>
> *"Have you recently evaluated your assets to see if they might be a factor in preparing a financial statement for a mortgage lender?"*
>
> *"Do you have cash-valued life insurance that you might use as collateral for an insurance loan?"*
>
> *"Have you established relationships with any credit unions, banks, or private lenders who might be of assistance to you in financing a home?"*

These are only examples of the areas you might explore to find hidden resources. Another approach is to use a checklist of proven ideas for helping buyers, which you can introduce at the appropriate time. Chapter 12 reviews the matter of creative financing in greater detail.

Reviewing People Who Might Be of Assistance to the Buyers. Many a new home sale is consummated because people in the buyers' sphere of influence give financial assistance in one way or another. Co-signers, co-investors, gifts, and a wide variety of other potential resources can be pursued involving individuals who have some motivation to help the prospective homeowners. This is people leverage!

Here are a few examples of questions you might ask to discover if there are people who could be added to the financing picture to improve the buyer's position:

> *"Have you discussed your desire to purchase a home with anyone close to you who might be willing to help you if necessary?"*

> *"May I inquire about your parents' professions?"*
> (for young buyers)

> *"Would your parents be in a position to be of some financial support to you if it were needed to help you qualify for mortgage financing?"*

> *"Are you familiar with shared equity mortgages?"*

This last question can be followed by an explanation of how people can share equity in different ways. Case histories can be used to show the prospective buyers how this concept might be of value to them. This subject is examined in greater detail in Chapter 12.

Qualifying a Prospect's Status

The term *status*, with regard to qualifying prospects, refers those factors that will affect prospects' ability to make a decision *today*. What problems must first be resolved? What contingencies in their situation could prevent them from making a total buying decision at this time?

If qualifying has progressed smoothly on the categories of *experience, urgency,* and *ability,* you may uncover most of the contingencies involved and the decision-limiting elements in a prospect's current status. When in doubt, however, explore them in greater depth before trying to attain a closing opportunity on a specific property. When the customer gives you the clues to the conditions affecting a homebuying decision, seize that moment to investigate the details more fully.

Here are typical questions designed to reveal these potential sales hurdles:

> "What arrangements have you made for your move to our city?"
> "What steps have you taken to sell your old home?"
> "What is the status of your present lease?"
> "Will you need assistance in making arrangements to secure the initial investment for your new home?"
> "What other points would you like to explore at this time?"

If a husband or wife is looking at housing alone, it is wise to ask about the interests of the other party:

> "When would your husband (or wife) be available to see the home?"
> "Have you and your husband (or wife) reached agreement on the type of new home you both have in mind?"
> "When will your husband (or wife) be free to approve the home you select?"

Questions on status must be framed to meet the individual situations you will encounter in your daily sales activities. Care also must be taken to avoid prematurely raising an issue that becomes a problem only because you discussed it with a prospect. This is a matter of judgment and timing. However, it is usually better to anticipate contingencies or other potential issues before they can become real stumbling blocks. If you are investing considerable time with one prospect (such as would be true in resale brokerage or custom home selling) it is advisable to begin the inspection tour by asking a question such as:

> "Mr. and Mrs. Jones, if we found a home today that truly met your needs and desires, is there anything that would possibly prevent you from making a decision today?"

If they reply "yes, we must first do this or that," you will know the obstacles you face and can plan your course of action accordingly. If they reply, "no, there isn't anything," then you are in a stronger position to close that same day when you find the right home.

Qualifying a Prospect's Requirements

A primary target area for qualifying your prospects is the basic matter of personal requirements. This covers all the specifications of *size, floor plans, style, location, amenities,* and *price,* as well as many individual items.

If you have well-organized sales centers and a good choice of model units, the product itself provides the basis for qualifying customers. They react to what they see, and you merely have to determine what they like best in light of their financial ability to purchase housing. As customers return from an inspection trip through your models, you might inquire:

> *"Which of our model homes do you prefer?"*
> *"Which of our homes do you feel best suits your needs?"*
> *"Which one of our models would you like to come home to?"*
> *"How do you feel about the (name of) plan?"*
> *"Which of our model homes would you like to take home?"*

In each case, you are using the product to help you qualify the prospect's interests and requirements.

In the event there is a wide selection of possibilities, or if you can custom design products, it is necessary to qualify customers' requirements by in-depth questioning. Here are some of the questions that are most effective for such counseling sessions:

> *"What special features do you feel are important to you in a new home?"*
> *"What style of home appeals to you the most?"*
> *"Describe your present home for me. What do you like about it? What don't you like about it?"*
> *"How many people will be living in the home?"*
> *"Do you prefer a home that is formal or informal? How do you prefer to furnish a home?"*
> *"What have you seen so far that you like?"*
> *"Are you looking for more room, or less room, than you have now?"*
> *"What floor plan arrangements have you considered most desirable?"*

Normally, this line of questioning leads to the use of specific examples or floor plans that can be introduced for the customers' reactions. Chapter 5 reviews how to demonstrate homes and use them for opportunities to either close or qualify.

Qualifying to Uncover a Prospect's Real Motivations

The pros in new home sales soon learn that prospects' *specifications* are seldom, if ever, their *motivations*. When prospects start describing the homes they would like, it is usually in terms of size, style, price, and features. Their underlying motivations may not be evident. What are they really trying to achieve? What are the "hot buttons" that will trigger a positive reaction and a sale? Real motivations are emotional in nature and difficult for most people to adequately express. It takes sensitivity to discover the motivations and to know how to read or interpret them correctly.

Basic motivations include such things as a desire for:

- Privacy;
- Comfort;
- Romance and beauty;
- Personal identity;
- Security;

and many other things that may be of a very personal nature.

Here are questions that can help you uncover real *motivations*, as contrasted to *specifications:*

> *"What appealed to you most about (name of) model?"*
> *"What special interests do you and your family have that you would consider important in buying a new home?"*
> *"How do you like to live?"*
> *"How do you enjoy spending your leisure hours?"*
> *"Of the homes you have lived in during the past, which one gave you the greatest personal satisfaction? Can you describe it to me?"*
> *"Of the homes owned by your friends or associates, which one appeals to you most and why?"*

These questions are designed to draw the prospects out and help them talk about the subtle but important aspects of living that influence decisions about the homes they purchase. Ultimately, although you give many facts, and prospects give you many specifications, only one or two major motivations will be the key to the decisions made. *People tend to buy on emotion and justify with facts, rather than to reverse that process.*

Using Questions for Maximum Results

This section has suggested many questions that cover the six primary qualifying areas that should be explored with prospects. Obviously, no prospect is going to let you ask that many questions. You must select the best questions to meet your specific objectives and reserve the others for special situations. Like a physician, you have a total kit of knowledge from which you can draw out the things you need when conditions indicate they should be used.

If you have the six broad categories of qualifying in mind and you practice various ways to uncover them, you will find that some questions will do a better job than others. Try to start with questions that produce better answers and cover more qualifying areas. Certain questions act like "open sesames," whereas others are more restrictive.

In your basic qualifying approach, develop eight to 12 solid questions that are most productive for you. Ten of the best are shown in Figure 3.3. These questions have the power to open up the prospects and help them express their thoughts. They explore areas where you need information, so you can choose a course to follow.

Figure 3.3. Ten of the most effective qualifying questions.

Topic	Question
Knock-out	"Are you out house hunting today?"
Experience	"Is this your first visit to Greenfield Acres?" "How did you happen to hear about us?" "Where are you living now?"
Urgency	"How soon had you planned to be in your new home?"
Ability	"May I ask your profession?" "How much of your savings have you planned to invest in a new home?"
Status	"What arrangements must be made before you complete your move?"
Requirements	"Which of our model homes do you prefer?"
Motivations	"What appealed most to you about the *(name)* plan?"

In any given situation, be prepared to alter your direction when the prospect gives you clues or questions that should be promptly pursued. *Flexibility is essential!*

QUESTIONING TECHNIQUES

Ask Questions with Interest

There is an art to asking the right questions in ways that generate interest without being offensive. One key point to remember is that your voice inflection should always end on an *upswing* rather than a *downswing*. This will reflect personal interest rather than a cold, prying attitude.

The way in which you ask questions can make a tremendous difference in the reception you obtain. To illustrate that point, practice the following questions, first by dropping your voice to a lower pitch at the end of the sentence, and then by ending on the upswing, with interest and enthusiasm:

> *"Is this your first visit to our community?"*
> *"How long have you been looking for a home?"*
> *"How much had you planned to invest?"*
> *"Where do you live now?"*

Did you notice the difference in how the questions sounded?

Prospects are normally hesitant to tell you everything they know, for fear it will either hurt them or force them to become involved too soon. That is why it is important not to put them under any psychological pressure, especially when they first arrive at your sales office. By asking questions in ways that indicate genuine interest and respect, you help to reduce the pressure and eliminate their resistance to telling you what you want to know.

It is best to project your voice in soft, warm tones, so that what you say is pleasant to the ears. If you have not heard yourself lately, practice with a tape recorder and compare the results with the sounds you would prefer to project to your listeners.

Blend Questions into Your Presentation

As you ask each question, give the prospects reason to answer. You earn that right by giving them information they want to know.

Thus, your basic sales presentation should be interwoven with the qualifying questions.

It is normally wise to ask only part of the key questions prior to showing your models, and the rest of them later. If you have a wide selection of models in scattered locations, you will be in a better position to thoroughly qualify at the beginning of your interview. Each sales situation has its own criteria, and you should adopt your techniques to fit these demands.

Be a Good Communicator

All qualifying and related steps in the sales process depend upon your ability to communicate. Never take communication skills for granted.

Remember that it is more valuable to ask questions than it is to give information. There is more power in asking the right questions than there is in knowing the right answer. When you ask questions, you are in control. Others respond to you. Nonetheless, people do not respond when they sense that someone is prying into areas that they consider private. They are also hesitant to answer when no cooperative relationship has been established and when they feel pressure or any other possible threat to their personal security. Making prospects feel comfortable, relaxed, and at home is the first part of the greeting and qualifying process.

As you give information, do so with interest and expressiveness, allowing other people a chance to respond. Do not race at too fast a pace. Make sure your voice carries a warm tone, reflecting genuine interest and concern for others. Be a friendly person. Everyone likes positive, friendly people, while few enjoy people who are negative and cold.

Selling is the art of helping people express themselves, to help them do what they want to do. Only by releasing customers' unexpressed wants and needs is it possible to assist them in that all-important step forward—a homebuying decision.

As you proceed through the rest of the face-to-face discovery process, keep in mind the need to review and qualify even while handling objections, closing on urgency, and leading to the final step of asking for the order. You are never through qualifying, because you need confirmation at all points of the process.

The types of questions asked have their own specific values. At the beginning of your presentation, use open questions, which are designed to open people up. An open question is one that cannot be answered yes or no and never suggests an answer. You want people to respond. Most open questions begin with *who, what, where, when, why,* and *how.* Some examples are:

"What did you have in mind?"
"What have you seen so far?"
"How much of your savings have you thought of investing?"

These questions are structured to help people tell you whatever is on their minds without leading them to any specific conclusions.

Later in the sales process, as you lead to closing, your communication skills become more directive in trying to steer prospects to a decision-making event. Do not try to steer them when you are just getting to know them. At that point, it doesn't matter what they say, as long as they talk. The most difficult customers in the world to sell are the ones who fail to respond at all. They are frustrating individuals with whom to work. Part of the role of helping them open up is to make them feel that you are genuinely interested in *their motivations, abilities, and needs, and not just your own.*

If you are working from a posture of interest in your customers, it is likely they will feel confident in sharing some of what they know. There are, however, customers who never say anything. With them, play a waiting game and make a patient presentation, structuring questions that are inoffensive. At some point, you may have to become a little more incisive, in order to help them realize that, for you to be of service to them, they must share their real thoughts.

The way to demonstrate genuine interest in helping customers is to obtain information that enables you to know what to emphasize and what properties to select and show. Practice asking questions in ways that do not offend others. This will improve your qualifying skills. These skills grow in direct proportion to your awareness of how important to your objectives this aspect of communication really is.

SELF-EVALUATION

Review the questions suggested in this chapter for each of the six areas of qualification. How many of them can you improve? Draft your own questions to uncover these same critical factors. Use the questions in this chapter if you think they are the best for you, but do not accept them just because they are easy to use. Think them through and improve them as you see fit. In all cases, relate the questions to your own present assignment.

One way to practice the concepts introduced in this chapter is to work with another sales associate. Ask permission to audit your colleague's qualifying session with prospects. Question your colleague about different approaches he or she uses and review the concepts suggested in this lesson.

Another practice technique is to acquire a small tape recorder and place it where it will not be obvious to others while you are qualifying. Replay your own tapes to evaluate your effectiveness in achieving your qualifying objectives.

Think back over the last five sales you made, and ask yourself these questions:

How important was your ability to qualify each prospect in terms of realizing your ultimate closings?
Which sales came easiest, and why?
How much of a factor was timing in your qualifying and closing?
Did you create any unnecessary problems for yourself because you failed to ask the right questions early enough in your interview?
How would you rate your own qualifying ability based on these sales? How much improvement do you feel you need?

Think back on the last five prospects you thought were qualified but did not buy, and ask yourself these questions:

How well did you qualify them in terms of all six primary qualifying areas?
In any of these cases, were there critical points you did not discover until it was too late, as a result of which you could not close?
Evaluate each of these cases to the best of your ability and decide whether you lost the customers in the qualifying stage or in the closing stage.
Compare the last five sales that you successfully closed with the five you failed to close, and ask yourself how they differed in terms of qualifying. Were there any circumstances surrounding this phase of selling that differed from one group to the other?
Compare the closed sales to the lost prospects. How many homes or models were involved in each case, and how long did it take you to zero in on the right ones?

As a final self-evaluation, read the case histories in Figure 3.4. These are examples of selling situations that might arise. Answering the questions for each case is a way of practicing techniques for confronting possible problems. When you confront difficult situations in the real world, your problem-solving skills will be more developed.

Figure 3.4. Case histories.

1. A prospect arrives at your project in an apparent rush. When you greet him and his wife, and try your normal approach, he says, "Please give us a brochure and the prices of your homes. We just want to look at them quickly today as we don't have much time to spare." What questions, if any, would you ask, and why?

2. Three groups of prospects arrive at the same time on Sunday afternoon, and you are the only sales associate on duty. The first couple is young, casually dressed and under 25; the second is middle-aged, well dressed and apparently affluent; the third is an older couple apparently out for a sightseeing tour on Sunday. All six come through the door, almost together. How would you approach them? What questions would you ask? Which couple would you attempt to qualify and involve first? Why?

3. A man and wife arrive at your sales center with a handful of brochures and literature from other subdivisions and projects. Would you ignore this fact and proceed as you would with others, or use a different approach? What would it be, and why?

4. When you ask prospects how much they plan to invest in a new home and they reply, "That depends on how much we like the home," what would you say or do?

4: Demonstrating New Home Values

THE IMPORTANCE OF NEW HOME DEMONSTRATIONS

The intrinsic value of a home cannot necessarily be perceived or totally understood merely by a casual inspection. When you first walk through a property, you seldom see everything that the home has to offer, even if you have the trained eyes of a professional in the building and construction business. A home has many subtleties and literally hundreds of ingredients in its composition, each of which justifies evaluation by a discriminating buyer. As a specialist in new home sales, be totally prepared at all times to demonstrate the homes or condominiums you represent in a way that accents all their benefits to a potential prospect. Then use only the information that is important to the particular prospect with whom you are working.

A new home represents one of the largest single investments made by the average family. The homebuying decision is not something that people make without serious thought, and it is accompanied by emotional as well as rational reactions. As people become involved with property, they typically begin to debate many things, including:

- How will they live in the home?
- Will their furniture fit?
- Is it worth the price?

Customers become emotionally involved when they begin to want a home and start envisioning where they are going to place furniture, or what kinds of drapes they might design. *These are closing signals.* The intervening process is one of becoming familiar enough with the property to sense that there is a justification for owning it. This entails a mental review of the facts. The decision is whether there is sufficient evidence that giving up something—such as the home or apartment prospects are living in today—is justified by buying the new home.

Consumers' Need for Credible Information

People need facts and a credible explanation to justify the decisions they make. That is particularly true of a large investment, such as the financial commitment needed to purchase a new home. People do not buy automobiles, homes, or any other major purchase with the mere flip of a coin. Rather, they consider and weigh the many factors involved. Once they have started to become interested, they need credible facts to justify that interest. When someone asks them why they made a certain decision, people want to be able to give a rational answer. Customers who say, "Well, we looked at a number of homes, and this one has these features and benefits," or "We think it's an excellent value because . . .," are often repeating the very ideas you have given them in presentations to reinforce their decision. If they do not have enough facts to go along with the emotions that their experience has generated, they may hesitate or even cancel a decision they otherwise would have made.

Credibility and consumer confidence are major factors in today's marketing. It has always been important to be truthful and honest, but there have been periods in all sales professions (and particularly real estate) where customers were not necessarily considered bright enough to have all of the facts. Today, the market is characterized by knowledgeable people. It does not pay to operate on any premise other than an honest one. It is your credibility in what you say and how you say it that will give the customer the confidence to make a decision.

There is no perfect home or situation, so be proud of whatever you represent. The prices, locations, styles, quality of construction, and everything else you present are worthy of your best attention. Emphasize the values of your homes, so that your customers will have the proper frame of reference when they compare your models to other opportunities. If you make mistakes in what you say, it may cost you sales because you have not won the customers' confidence.

Without credibility, the best product in the world would be difficult to sell. It is the salesperson who represents the merchandise who must carry the weight of authority in the presentation. A number of these points were covered in Chapter 3.

A demonstration is a particular aspect of presentation, a more specific part of it. It is the process of showing one or more homes to a prospect in positive ways that build and create sufficient interest for a sale to be ultimately achieved in the majority of cases. This chapter examines the reasons why showing prospects new housing demands more skill and thought than is typical in a residential resale operation. Resale people frequently just show property, letting the buyer see what reality is and without justifying anything. More often than not, the property carries no warranties, and it is a used or pre-owned home that has been modified to the present owners' interests. The facts in such a situation must be presented carefully, to avoid potential misrepresentation. A new home is different. It is a manufacturer's product, and it has particular aspects of demonstration that are not applicable to most resale properties. Consider the following:

The Relative Costliness of New Homes

Builders and developers experience today's prices for materials, labor, land, and all of the related costs that go into producing a home. They experience these costs today, not tomorrow and not yesterday. The difference between inflation and appreciation is a valid consideration. The true cost of the house is what the builder pays for the materials, supplies, etc. The appreciation is the increased demand for that location and the additional, created values.

As will be emphasized further in Chapter 6, inflation and appreciation are different elements of value. Inflation is the *cost of reproduction,* and appreciation is *accelerated land values* resulting from the force of supply and demand factors.

Builders and developers, as manufacturers, are living with the reality of today's costs and must reflect those costs in the prices asked for the property. Older homes experience the effects of aging, or depreciation. These factors must be considered when weighing an older home against a new one. An older property does not have all the warranties and the newness of materials and conditions that a new home offers in its early years. Conversely, a pre-owned home has other things going for it, such as complete landscaping, rugs, drapes, and other items that are usually included. Also, the aging process might be masked by the fact that the home has been lived in and is furnished.

Never overlook the fact that builders are entitled to a reasonable profit on their investment. For most builders, that is a very small percentage of the total gross sales price of the home. Between 5 percent and 10 percent of sales price is a common target amount. Unless this profit is protected, the building enterprise will fail. It is the salesperson's role to see that the prices asked for the homes he or she sells are justified to buyers. The demonstration process, along with the thorough presentation of other related facts, reinforces those values.

Sellers of older homes usually have more equity with which to negotiate their position. Their motivations also differ from those of a builder. A resale property owner has only one house to sell. There have been a number of years for equity to build. The owner can sell for less or negotiate positions because he or she is primarily concerned with moving to another home. A builder is thinking of staying in business and making a profit, in order to realize out of the total project a reasonable return on his or her own efforts and the efforts of others. New homes and resale homes often are in competition with each other. A demonstration process is designed to show why a new home is worth the price and why its advantages outweigh any considerations of an older home with negotiated values.

Appraised values in real estate frequently place new homes at a disadvantage. The appraisal system is based on data that come from a variety of sources.

- *Cost of reproduction;*
- *Market data or comparables;*
- *Income (return on investment use).*

There is often a three- to six-month time lag in the market data reflecting current costs of reproduction between that experienced by builders and that which is actually shown in the resale market through multiple-listing systems, comparables, and historical information. Thus, when a new home is priced and offered today, it may well cost more than a resale home of the same size simply because the resale property does not yet truly reflect the impact of cost reproduction for current values. The salesperson must offset that fact by stressing what goes into a new home and emphasizing its inherent advantages over older properties that were not designed to meet today's standards. Older properties usually do not have the protected environments or many of the warranties that go with new housing communities.

Future-Oriented Benefits

Resale properties are normally in established neighborhoods where surrounding homes and conditions are complete. They are there for everyone to see. Although these are not always positive conditions, they are visible and easily understood. A new home is presented in an entirely different environment—one that seldom is complete at the time of sale—and adverse influences may arise from the stages of construction in which it must be shown.

When representing new homes and their developing neighborhoods, you seldom, if ever, have ideal conditions in which to show your housing values. That is the reason for working so hard to offer effective visual documentation of what will happen when the subdivision is completed. You paint dreams through the graphics in the brochures and literature that reinforce the future values being created. A common way of doing so is to use models that you display to give people an idea of the environments that they will enjoy when their homes are completed and the neighborhoods around them have come together, with finished housing fully occupied and landscaped.

Dramatize dreams, showing what the future will be, because the present reality is less than what you are trying to convey as being the ultimate that prospective buyers will experience when the homes and environments are completely established. *In new housing, you are selling tomorrow's values, not today's values.* Since the values today are usually inadequate to justify the finished product, you must dramatize and romance to maximum advantage the homes you are marketing.

New homes have warranties and disclosures that need to be emphasized clearly in the process of selling. This is especially important in selling from floor plans without models and without completed inventory to show the prospect. Here, the dream is created through all the visual tools and documentation furnished plus your own presentation of what a home will be like when finished. At that stage, you need the best graphics and the most effective salespeople to paint the dream. Later, when you have homes that can adequately demonstrate values, it becomes a little easier. This is particularly true if you have models with exciting decor and conditions that are designed to display their features to advantage. Bear in mind the concept of the dream versus the reality when comparing your sales process to that of a resale agent, who usually "discovers" the home with the buyer. They go through the house saying, "Here's the living room, kitchen, family room, and the price is. . . ." Resale agents do not have to demonstrate a home the way a new home agent does, and often they are unwise to do so. *Conversely, demonstrate your values, or you may lose to a resale property or to a competitor whose salespeople do a better job.*

Cost Compared to Perceived Value

Also recognize that merely because the price of a home, a homesite, or the options that go with a home is set at what the item costs (plus a reasonable profit margin), it does not necessarily mean that the public will automatically perceive values equal to costs. *Cost alone does not equal value.* For example, you might elect in the planning process to include more expensive lumber or better grade fixtures in a home than the competition is offering in comparable housing. If the cost-price relationship forces you to charge more, and the potential customers do not see the added value or perceive that it is worth the price, they will resist purchasing at that price. The fact that a home cost more to build is unimportant to the homebuyer.

Working with the Differences. Every builder makes mistakes sometimes. If money is spent where it is not necessarily appreciated, adjustments are occasionally required in order to bring the property into line with what the customer perceives. Most of the time, the values can be justified if the demonstration and presentation are adequate. That is why values must be translated and communicated in ways that assure the customer's interest and acceptance. You cannot afford to assume that prospects understand why a given home in the community or a specific site location is worth the price established for it.

The rehearsal process is part of the demonstration preparation. By going through the property and talking it out with yourself, you can determine the property's values and rehearse how to demonstrate a home in a way that fulfills your sales objectives. In other words, demonstrate homes to create values in the minds of your customers —those are the only values that really count. If the potential buyers do not believe a home is worth the asking price, they will not buy it for that price.

Locational Differences in Perceived Values. A subdivision or plat map has a number of sites, whether in a single-family community or in a high rise condominium development. Each location has unique advantages and disadvantages. Here, the cost of a specific site is less important than the total value of the project and the differences among locations. It is best to rate your sites and create a realistic pricing structure that takes into consideration the variables of site preferences as the public will perceive them. To do this efficiently, use a lot rating form.

To appreciate the truth of this concept, merely look at the pattern and pricing of resales in a new community once the builder-developer has departed the scene. Two or three years after a community has been sold out, study the resale values of that community. Almost always, there are differences that the market discovered even if these were missed in the original sales presentation. For example, a corner site with a big tree might produce an extra thousand or two thousand dollars from someone who wants such a location. Or, the location that has the greatest degree of privacy or the best view might command several thousand dollars more, simply because it has those amenities. Conversely, some sites may not experience much appreciation because they lack some of the same benefits at the beginning. It thus should be evident why it is so critical to your objectives to demonstrate your housing opportunities thoroughly to all potential prospects.

PLANNING A DEMONSTRATION

Profile Prospects and Target Specific Motivations

The first step in planning a demonstration for new homes is to profile the typical anticipated buyers for the specific home or site offered for sale. Research may have already provided the necessary criteria and marketing demographics. Perhaps your company maintains adequate records, and profiles are compiled in advance when a new community is placed on the market. If so, these should be reviewed and tested against your own actual marketing experiences. Each salesperson should evaluate the profiles developed by others and check them against his or her own identification data.

The best sources of profile information are those that draw upon the demographics of the people who have purchased similar housing. Your own resident owners are the best resource. Therefore, it is wise to survey buyers at the time of purchase and then after they have taken possession of their new homes. Some of the basic information needed can be extracted from mortgage application records, but it is better to prepare a more comprehensive survey or summary that digests many factors not revealed in financial profiles.

Among the things you should know about your profiled prospects are the following:

- Age of head of household;
- Ages of others in the family;
- Marital status;
- Professions of earners in the home;
- Household annual income;
- Lifestyle interests;
- Recreation/leisure time activities;
- Social activities and interests;

Personal interviews after occupancy should focus on the reasons customers like a particular housing design or floor plan. These provide the clues to the motivations of other potential buyers.

Figure 4.1 is a typical profile sheet used with new home buyers at the time of sale.

Objectives of the Demonstration

Essentially, demonstrating a new home should accomplish five major objectives:

1. Accent the benefits of each plan and location as related to the interests of that buyer.

2. Anticipate and overcome potential objections.

3. Translate features of construction into benefits to the clients.

4. Create perceived values sufficient to justify the offering prices.

5. Sell the inventory and plans you have available to sell today.

Determining What Should Be Demonstrated in Each Home

Evaluate the room arrangements and traffic patterns within each home in terms of what deserves the most attention in one plan versus another. For example, a home that has a beautiful country kitchen and a small living room might be accented by concentrating on living pleasures of the family kitchen with its multiple usages and its orientation to the other living centers of the home. That would be better than to try to make a small living room a real plus. Every home has its accent points, and there is no perfect home. Therefore, avoid concentrating on negatives. It is much more important to work on positives.

Interpret each home in terms of your prospects' basic motivations. Such elements as comfort, romance, identity, security, and privacy need interpretation. Think in terms of the living zones and multiple uses of the home. A well-designed home has taken into consideration how people live in it. Be able to tell people that the sleeping wing of the home is isolated from the activity center; that the entry area of the home provides transition between the formal and informal parts of the home, while serving as an open area that adds to the home's entertainment value when the owners have guests. The concept is to bring your presentation to the specifics of how people live. Emphasize the things that motivate them to be interested in a home, not just the fact that it has three bedrooms, two baths, and a family room. It is not just a house, but an entire experience in living.

Figure 4.1. New home buyer profile sheet.

```
                                        DATE _____

 1. NAME _____
 2. PRESENT MAILING ADDRESS _____
    TELEPHONE: (home) _____ (work) _____ (H=Husband, W=Wife)
 3. MARRIED ____ SINGLE ____ DIVORCED ____ WIDOWED ____ (MALE ____ FEMALE ____)
 4. HEAD OF HOUSEHOLD AGE _____
 5. SECOND APPLICANT AGE _____
 6. HEAD OF HOUSEHOLD ANNUAL INCOME _____
 7. SECOND APPLICANT ANNUAL INCOME _____
 8. HEAD OF HOUSEHOLD OCCUPATION _____
 9. SECOND APPLICANT OCCUPATION _____
10. AGES OF DEPENDENT CHILDREN ____ ____ ____ ____ ____ ____ ____
11. IF OWNED PRIOR TO PURCHASE, APPROXIMATE VALUE OF HOME ____ OR CONDOMINIUM ____
    (CHECK ONE)
        ____ $20,000 or less    ____ $20,001-$30,000    ____ $30,001-$40,000
        ____ $40,001-$50,000    ____ $50,001-$60,000    ____ Over $60,000
12. IF RENTED PRIOR TO PURCHASE, APPROXIMATE RENT PER MONTH (CHECK ONE)
        ____ $100 or less   ____ $101-$150   ____ $151-$200   ____ $201-$250
        ____ $251-$300      ____ $301-$350   ____ $351-$400   ____ Over $400
13. HOW DID YOU FIND OUT ABOUT OUR DEVELOPMENT?
        ____ Radio or TV    ____ Newspaper   ____ Signs      ____ Referral
        ____ Drive-by       ____ Other agent ____ Mail       ____ Other (specify)
14. HOMESITE PURCHASED _____    BUILDER _____
    PROJECT _____    DATE OF CONTRACT _____
    PRICE _____    PLAN _____

                                          SALESPERSON _____
```

The real professional anticipates furniture placement alternatives. You may be fortunate to have decorated models, but often you will be forced to work with speculative inventory or homes that are unfurnished. Even if you have models, your builder cannot furnish every home for sale. That would be prohibitive. Knowledge of furniture placement and the alternatives for locating the key elements of furniture can be of great value in the demonstration process. You can plant ideas with your customers while they are envisioning living in the home:

> *"How do you feel about this home, Mrs. Adams? Where would you suggest that the divan and the chairs be placed?"*

Or you might say

> *"Mr. and Mrs. Smith bought this same model, and they decorated it in an interesting manner. I'd be glad to show you their home if you'd like to see how they did it."*

The skill of knowing how to relate the furnishings of a home, the decor, and the living pleasures to something other than just the room dimensions gives you the sophistication of being a real pro who can help people picture what it might be like to occupy the residence.

This does not mean you should tell people what to do. Remember, people are different, and they have widely varied interests and lifestyles. First try to anticipate what interests your prospects have, and then talk about the kinds of furniture they have or anticipate buying. Variations in room furniture arrangements can make a great deal of difference in how a home is shown and whether you can overcome some of the objections that might be there if what customers see does not fully meet their expectations.

Use Decorating Guidelines from Outside Experts

Perhaps your company employs decorating services and also recommends color decorator consultants. If you have one on staff, work with that person for guidance and direction. Sometimes it is wise to involve the consultant at that important point when a customer is beginning to be interested enough to anticipate furniture placement and yet you cannot stimulate the sale without going through the mental move-in experience. Homebuyers have their own preferences in taste, and this demands an awareness that people are different. The decor featured in models may not necessarily suit the majority of the customers you sell. Sometimes you decorate a model merely to create interest, knowing that the majority of the customers would not want it that way. When you have a model that evokes reactions like:

> *"Well, I'd never furnish it that way,"*

your demonstration process should point out,

> *"We furnish homes in a variety of ways to give people ideas, knowing that they are going to want to create their own environment with their own tastes and furnishings. Fortunately, everyone is unique. We have people that can give you ideas on decorating. I would be glad to introduce them or to share some thoughts on how the variations might apply to this home."*

Use a sample checklist of key elements often worthy of demonstration within a home. Figure 4.2 is an example of such a checklist.

Draw upon the Advice of Experts

When a home and a community are created, many people are involved in their development: architects and designers, the building department, land planners and engineers, suppliers and subcontractors. Each has a potential contribution to make to your sales presentation. The architect or designer may be unable to spend personal time with you, but questions and ideas you would like to explore certainly can be channeled to him or her. Your local manager or builder can be in a position to tap those resources for greater input than is possible without seeking such advice. The builder knows why something was built a certain way, whether due to costs, engineering requirements, or building restrictions, or is tied to the administration of housing projects.

When customers ask you about a home, you want to be in a positive role of telling them why things were done in a particular way. To lack the answer is to be less credible—and to achieve less of the confidence that you need for the sales process.

The suppliers and subcontractors also are good resources for specific demonstration information. Each of the subcontractors knows his or her own trade and services better than anyone else. That is why salespeople should review the specifications and material lists that can be provided by the subcontractors. The salespeople can extract the portion of information that is applicable to a given situation or to specific buyers.

Outside consultants and marketers are sometimes employed by building companies to give advice (including research and review)

Figure 4.2. Checklist of features that can be demonstrated in a new home.

General features
☐ Designs/floor plans
☐ Architecture
☐ Energy conservation construction elements
☐ Foundations
☐ Roofs
☐ Siding/masonry
☐ Exterior finish

Entry area
☐ Entry flooring (when applicable)
☐ Definition of space
☐ Guest closet/coat closet
☐ Lighting fixtures

Living room
☐ Location advantages
☐ Dimensions (when appropriate)
☐ Furniture placement alternatives
☐ Paneling/wall treatments
☐ Sound engineering systems
☐ Functional use for entertaining
☐ Windows and window treatments
☐ Heating and air conditioning system
☐ Special effects (such as vaulted ceilings, step-down areas, conversation pits, fireplaces)
☐ Indoor-outdoor relationships
☐ Decorating alternatives
☐ Other items

Dining room or dining areas
☐ Functional relationship to kitchen and entertaining areas
☐ Dimensions (when appropriate)
☐ Dining room table placement and alternatives
☐ Buffet serving area
☐ Lighting fixtures (when applicable)
☐ Wall treatments
☐ Indoor-outdoor relationships
☐ Windows/patio doors (when appropriate)
☐ Other items

Kitchen
☐ Locational advantages (accessibility for grocery delivery)
☐ Dimensions (when appropriate)
☐ Cabinet space and extra storage areas

Figure 4.2. (continued)

Kitchen (continued)
☐ Countertop space/finish
☐ Appliances
 ☐ Range
 ☐ Oven
 ☐ Dishwasher
 ☐ Garbage disposal
 ☐ Refrigerator
 ☐ Other appliances
☐ Lighting fixtures (when appropriate)
☐ Electrical outlets
☐ Serving functions
☐ Food preparation functions
☐ Indoor-outdoor relationships
☐ Visual screening from formal areas
☐ Conversational opportunity with family in other areas of home
☐ Wall treatment(s) (application to care and maintenance)
☐ Floor covering(s)
☐ Windows, pass-throughs, doors (where applicable)
 Other items

Family room or area
☐ Location advantages
☐ Dimensions (when appropriate)
☐ Furniture orientation
☐ Functional uses of room
☐ Fireplace (when applicable)
☐ Wall finishes
☐ Flooring or floor covering
☐ Patio doors (ingress, egress)
☐ Lighting fixtures (where appropriate)
☐ Sound controls (particularly entertaining and children's activities related to rest of the home)
☐ Special effects (beams, vaults, lofts, step-downs, conversation pits)

Bathrooms
☐ Locations (accessibility, privacy)
☐ Bathroom fixtures
☐ Lighting fixtures
☐ Cabinetry/storage areas
☐ Counter surfaces
☐ Wall treatments
☐ Safety devices
☐ Plumbing fixtures

Figure 4.2. (continued)

Bathrooms (continued)
☐ Mirrors
☐ Decorating alternatives
☐ Other items

Master bedroom suite (other bedrooms as necessary)
☐ Location (privacy, accessibility to service)
☐ Dimensions (when appropriate)
☐ Bed placement alternatives
☐ Dressers
☐ Wall treatment(s)
☐ Flooring or floor covering
☐ Lighting fixtures (when appropriate)
☐ Indoor-outdoor relationships
☐ Mirrors
☐ Closets (demonstrate space when a positive)
☐ Accessibility to bath and dressing areas
☐ Windows
☐ Doors, patios, decks (as appropriate)
☐ Other items

Service area(s)
☐ Locational advantages
☐ Washer-dryer (space)
☐ Plumbing outlets
☐ Floor treatment (safety, care, maintenance)
☐ Sound conditioning factors
☐ Water heater
☐ Furnace
☐ Air conditioning
☐ Cabinets and storage
☐ Other items

Other areas of demonstration as applicable
☐ Basements (lower levels)
☐ Garages, carports
☐ Outdoor storage facilities
☐ Decks, patios, balconies, porches
☐ Attic storage (access)
☐ Expandable areas of the home
☐ Special-purpose or multi-purpose rooms

before and during the development of a community. Such people may be an additional source of information.

Mostly, however, you must do your own researching of facts. Review all the literature and information that is provided. That literature is there for two reasons: One, to help the customers when they need to take something home with them, and two, to help you in the process of a demonstration by giving you key points to emphasize. If you do not have a reasonable explanation, ask.

There are two kinds of knowledge: that which you have and that which you know where to find. If you do not know something, ask someone who does; it will not hurt. Usually somebody can help you. An inquiring mind that searches out new avenues usually enjoys the greatest rewards.

COMPETITIVE RESEARCH

To learn how to demonstrate a home and what you should accent in your communities, it is wise to inspect and know your competition. Only if you understand what the other company is offering will you know how to give your homes the attention they need to be perceived as being a better value. Ignorance is neither bliss nor a profitable approach to new home sales.

First, identify your immediate competition in the primary market. What are your customers looking at and making comparisons with? To whom are you losing prospects and sales? Answers to these questions give you clues as to which merchandise you need to research and know more about. Then study your competition in terms of your prospects and anticipate the comparisons they will be making.

USING A VALUE INDEX SYSTEM

As noted in Chapter 3, every home, condominium, or community has unique values. The homes you sell will have a value index system related to the things your builder thinks are important for that price range or style of housing. Other builders in the same market will furnish their own merchandise with what they think will create sufficient differences for them to achieve their sales objectives. The outcome of this thinking is what registers in the buyers' perceptions.

One method to help your buyers appreciate the differences, in favor of your homes, is to build a value index chart for your own use.

This is particularly helpful in determining what features to emphasize in the presentation and demonstration.

THE WALK-THROUGH AND REHEARSAL

In preparing a demonstration, there is really no substitute for personal rehearsals and private practice sessions. As you walk through a home, you are experiencing what a customer would feel when seeing the property. Always view the property from the eyes of the potential buyers. Observe the people to whom you actually make a presentation to see the things that cause them to react.

Rehearsal is even more effective if several people are involved, such as two or three salespeople walking the same floor plan and talking it out. One can play the role of the buyer and the other the role of a salesperson and then switch roles to see how thoroughly the presentation has been created. Objections that are commonly heard can also be introduced at the same time. Role playing with others adds to the learning experience. Don't be afraid to participate in a free-for-all exchange of ideas.

When you plan your approach, plan it to accent all the benefits that might offset negatives or at least balance the scale in favor of your housing versus that which the buyer has inspected from competition.

THE DO'S AND DON'T'S OF SHOWING A NEW HOME

The professionals have learned many things about the showing and demonstration procedures. Following are two lists, one of which summarizes what the professionals have learned to do, the other of which summarizes what they have learned *not* to do.

DO

- Plan your presentation by practicing walk-throughs and rehearsals.
- View the home through the eyes of a potential purchaser.
- Give each room the feeling of maximum space by positioning yourself so as not to detract from its values.
- Anticipate all questions and objections you might hear, and rehearse your responses.
- Practice demonstrating special items such as appliances, removable windows, screens, and countertops.

- Anticipate lighting and visual experiences, and see that all lights, drapes, etc., are used to advantage.

DON'T

- Stand in front of windows or other sources of light when showing a home.
- Talk too much when touring prospects; make your points hard-hitting and brief.
- Crowd the space in small rooms or hallways. It's best not to enter such areas. Let prospects inspect alone.
- Rush the showing. Let your buyer mentally picture benefits of ownership without discussing them.
- Justify the home against the buyers' reactions. Let them talk it out with you.

ACHIEVING THE PURPOSE OF THE DEMONSTRATION

The demonstration of a new home is designed to get buyers totally involved in the concepts of the home, so that they begin to mentally picture ownership. If a demonstration does not achieve that objective, then it has failed its purpose. When model homes are available, use the demonstration process in the model, where everything is completed so the customers can carry a vision of the model with them to the inventory homes you plan to show. When they arrive at the unfinished property, they at least have a total mental picture of what it will be like to fulfill the dream of living there.

Sell the model home first if it is like the property you are going to demonstrate or show, because it will work better for you as an example of what it can be when finished. Conversely, if you do not have models that are just like your inventory, it is sometimes wise to show the inventory first and then use the model as a backup for demonstrating furniture placement, decor arrangements, and quality of construction. That variable must be based on your reaction to the homes you have and the sites that are available. Most of the time, your model should be selected and demonstrated first. Then when you get to the unfinished property, you will have the advantage of mental pictures working for you.

The sequence of events from the original presentation of general concepts to a specific home thoroughly demonstrated should lead to positive action. Help people to picture the benefits of ownership by planting ideas, reinforcing interest with facts, and giving them opportunities to use their imaginations in positive ways. Do not just show property to prospective buyers; help them to experience its values with you. Remember, the sale is not made until the customer mentally moves in.

5: Converting Objections Into Closing Opportunities

Knowing how to respond to a prospect's inquiries, objections, expressed fears, and problems can make a tremendous difference in how successfully you close potential buyers. The real pros in real estate sales have learned how to achieve and maintain control over their customers while negotiating the hurdles created by the questions and objections customers raise. To become more effective in these situations, pay attention to what you are saying and to prospects' reactions. Through increased sensitivity, you should be able to detect the real significance of the comments buyers raise.

THE NATURE OF THE HOMEBUYING DECISION

To fully appreciate buyers' questions and objections, be aware that the decision-making process for buying a home is far more complex than for most other consumer product transactions. Buying (or selling) a home represents a big change in people's lives. The decisions made may affect their lifestyles and alter their personal motivations.

Homebuyers are trying to determine what factors will dominate their daily environments and affect their financial positions. They are concerned about the neighborhood in which they will raise their family and the impact this new environment will have on their children's education and attitudes. They face a major consideration in terms of the financial commitment they must make. The entire relocation experience brings out age-old fears of having to pull up roots. Thus, it is perfectly understandable that any sincere prospect will approach the purchase of a home with a genuine concern for making the right choice.

Homebuyers may not openly express the following questions that are deeply worrisome to them:

> *"Is this really the right thing to do at this time?"*
> *"What would happen if there were an economic downturn and we were unable to earn as much as we do now?"*
> *"Are we sure this is a good value? Perhaps we should look at more homes before we decide."*
> *"What are we going to do about the house we own now, which must be sold before we can buy another one?"*

Buyers may not directly express such inner doubts and fears to you. Often, they are masked by other comments that seem totally unrelated to these underlying questions. Examples of such comments are:

> *"It is certainly a lot further from the office than we wanted to be."*
> *"This bedroom is much smaller than the one we had in mind."*
> *"The price is really more than we wanted to pay for a home."*
> *"I think we should have Uncle Louie look at the place before we make a decision."*
> *"Let's go home and think it over. We'll be back later."*

These and hundreds of other objections are common defenses of hesitant homebuyers. Often, they are not genuine expressions of the prospects' inner doubts. Prospects may be afraid to voice their true feelings for fear they will become too involved or forced to face issues with which they are uncomfortable at the time.

AVOID JUMPING TO CONCLUSIONS

It is so easy to open your mouth and say something that you later regret. Most salespeople have lost sales because of saying the wrong thing at the wrong time. All humans are capable of making mistakes. Avoid reaching early conclusions as to the real motivations behind prospects' questions and objections. What your customers say and what they mean are often different; that is why you cannot afford to respond impulsively. To do so is to risk creating additional problems for yourself, some of which may be impossible to overcome.

TYPES OF OBJECTIONS

When you first hear a comment that sounds like an objection, remember that it may not be one at all. There are at least four possibilities. The comment may be:

1. A mere comment with no real significance.
2. A request for additional information.
3. A buying signal that indicates mounting interest.
4. A real problem that must be resolved at the right time.

When you encounter an objection, you can seldom be sure which of these possibilities is actually involved.

The Mere Comment

In the process of trying to think through the complexities of a housing decision, homebuyers often feel the need to talk out their formative thoughts. This is one of the ways people negotiate the emotional hurdles standing in the way of making a decision. One of the primary roles of a professional sales agent is to act as a sounding board for prospective homebuyers. Those who are good at the job will help customers express their thoughts without interference. Thus, when a prospect makes a comment that sounds like an objection, avoid making it one by checking your own reactions.

For example, suppose you are showing a home to a couple, and the wife comments, "This bedroom is terribly small." Now, that does not mean she does not like the house or that the couple will not purchase it. The comment could be a sincere and immediate reaction, but it is possibly only a minor point. The woman could have been thinking about the furniture she owns and contemplating how it would fit in the room. Or, she could be comparing the room to another home they have recently inspected. In any case, when this objection is first introduced, you do not know what she means. Thus, treat it *gently*—if at all.

The Request for Information

A prospect may make a negative comment before the facts that would counter the objection have been presented. Sometimes it is wise to cover the matter briefly there and then; at other times it is best to wait until the timing is right.

Timing is everything! If an issue is raised prematurely, you may decide to wait until the total presentation has been made to be certain the information you impart will be meaningful. For example, assume you are showing a home to a couple, when the man asks:

> "How much are the taxes and the monthly payments on principal and interest on this place?"

You have not yet had an opportunity to show the entire property, so it is probably wisest to avoid a direct answer by giving a credible reason for postponing it:

> "Mr. Smith, I will have all of those figures for you when we have completed our inspection of the home. There are a number of variables I do not want to misquote. When we have seen the entire property, I will put all the figures in writing on a Home Estimate Form."

This protects you from prematurely quoting facts and figures that could be misunderstood. It also protects you from directing the buyer's attention away from the benefits of ownership before he or she is ready.

The Buying Signal

Look back over your past sales transactions. Probably few, if any, were consummated without at least one or more serious question or objection being introduced. In fact, the prospect who never raises a single question or objection is seldom, if ever, a qualified buyer.

When, for example, you ask a prospect how he liked your models, or which home he preferred, and he answers,

> "Fine, I liked them all!"

you instinctively know you do not have a real prospect. Then, after trying to bring the discussion down to one specific home, you ask,

> "What did you like most about that particular home?"

and the response is,

> "Everything!"

At that point, you begin to worry. A qualified or interested buyer would invariably qualify the answer in a way that indicates serious thought about the house:

> "Well, we like the home but we are worried about . . ."

Those who "like everything" without questions, objections, or mental reservations are seldom genuine prospects. They are suspects, who rarely buy.

Sincerely interested prospects will almost always have things to talk about. They will express the ideas in ways that sound as though the prospects are objecting to the merits of the product. They do so because they are more than passively interested in the home.

So-called objections or negative questions can, in fact, be buying signals. As emotional pressure builds to the point where it becomes obvious the prospects are headed toward a buying decision, the buyers' natural instinct is to bring up obstacles that will slow down the onrushing conclusion. It is natural to want to delay until there is more time to think the whole thing through.

Homebuying is always a big step, and it usually precipitates inner conflicts and doubts about the wisdom of making such a major move. Remember this when you hear an objection, and think first about the possibility that it may be a clue to start closing.

The voice itself may give away the fact that the so-called objection is really a buying signal. For example, if a wife says, with longing in her voice, "Oh, honey, this is more than we planned to invest in a home," you can hear the interest and enthusiasm that belie the objection. Such situations should be treated differently from those that involve a real issue that must be resolved.

The Real Objection

Once in a while, objections are evidence of real problems that must be resolved before a sale can ever be consummated. Even the tone of voice in which objections are expressed normally indicates the seriousness of the matter, although not always. Buyers can hide their reactions in ways that make it extremely difficult to detect the nature and depth of their concern. This is particularly true if you have not yet had time to win the confidence of your prospects so that they feel free to communicate their thoughts openly.

The ability to communicate with customers is vital to success in understanding and solving their problems. It is not a question of how valid you think the problem is; the only issue is how vital it is in their minds. Everything is relative; what may be insignificant to one prospect may be critical to another.

WHEN TO BE HARD OF HEARING

Some salespeople learn to treat negative subjects as though they did not hear them raised. They wait until the appropriate time to answer the questions—if they must be answered at all. Whether or not this technique is wise for you is a matter of judging your own style. Do nothing to lessen your credibility.

Spending time discussing a comment that sounds like an objection can sometimes make it become one, for you risk the possibility of increasing its importance in the buyer's mind. This does not mean that you should always avoid early discussions of potential objections, because there are times when they must be faced to avoid losing the buyer's confidence. Whenever you can avoid talking about negative subjects early in the game, however, you should do so.

One way to handle negative comments when they arise is to try to skirt them politely without indicating any lack of interest on your part. For example, you might say:

> *"I'm sure you will understand how that can be handled when we come to the details of financing the home. How does this basic floor plan appeal to you?"*
>
> *"We will come to that point in a few minutes. In the meantime, let's review the merits of the home in terms of your own needs."*
>
> *"I will cover that with you before you leave. Now, how would you like to look at that homesite we were discussing?"*

Tactfully postponing topics that can produce negative overtones is a practical technique for maintaining control of the sales conversation so that it remains on a positive course. You owe it to the prospective homebuyer to protect him or her from the desire to know everything at once. If the customer cannot digest the information, you have done him or her a disservice by talking about it. You really cannot handle negatives successfully until there are positives to offset them.

AVOID DEFENSIVENESS

It is easy to become defensive, often without even realizing it. At times, pressure builds up to the point where the slightest thing can trigger an explosion. For example, a salesperson who has had no sales in a month is under tremendous psychological pressure to achieve certain pre-established goals. That person is probably tense and may automatically become defensive.

Such tension can arise when you work with a difficult property for a long time, and you hear the same objections over and over again. For example, you may be selling small lots, and every prospect seems to say:

"My, these lots are certainly small!"

You are certain you have lost sales because of this, and each person who repeats the comment only magnifies its importance in your mind. You are tempted to say something like:

"Oh, no, they're not! Let me prove it to you!"

Overreacting or becoming defensive automatically creates psychological barriers between you and your prospects. The buyer senses the fear and anxiety of a salesperson who is pressing too hard or who reacts defensively. You must work from strength, not from weakness, if you are to win. Attaining your objective requires you to remain in control of your personal feelings. Keep cool and radiate reassuring confidence, and you will be able to handle even the most complicated situations.

STAY ON THE PROSPECT'S SIDE

Keep the channels of communication open. Let prospects know you respect their feelings and are genuinely interested in their reactions. If you stay on a prospect's side, you keep yourself from becoming defensive.

The magic words to remember are:

"I understand how you feel."
"I appreciate your feelings."
"I know why you feel as you do."

These words of understanding are like oil on troubled waters. They soften the impact of differing positions, and they lessen resistance to a reasonable exchange of ideas on the subject.

To be really effective, speak the words in ways that demonstrate your own sincerity in trying to put yourself in the prospect's shoes. Mentally and emotionally view the situation from the customer's vantage point. Otherwise, you will limit your ability to remain in psychological control, and so be unable to help the customer over the emotional hurdles he or she has to negotiate to reach a final decision.

THE SEVEN STEPS TO HANDLING OBJECTIONS

There are seven essential steps to remember in order to handle objections efficiently and successfully:

1. Sidestep an objection when it first arises if the time is not right for discussion.

2. If it must be handled, always question the objection before you give any answer.

3. Hear prospects out. Let them explain fully the reasons for their objections.

4. Question the statement and verify that it is the real objection.

5. Answer the objection by converting it into a positive point, due to other advantages, or diluting it to insignificance by concentrating on the other benefits of the product.

6. Confirm the answer with the buyer.

7. Close that point and continue with your sale.

The following paragraphs go over each of these steps in greater detail.

Sidestep an Objection When It First Arises

Earlier, this chapter discussed the various reasons why it is usually wise to avoid discussing any question or objection before demonstrating all of the benefits of your housing. Even when you have all of the psychological advantages working for you, tackle the question only if you sense that it is standing in the way of a sale. Many times, you will discover that early objections are never raised again, as the prospects become more and more involved with the total benefits. Some salespeople adopt the attitude that nothing is an objection unless it comes up twice or comes up at closing.

Question the Objection Before Answering It

Before answering an objection, force a more complete explanation. One reason this is so practical is that it gives prospects a chance to resolve their problems before you have to do anything about them. By tossing the question back, you give the prospects a chance to play with it and to either find their own solution, clarify their thinking, or reveal the real objection, which may be something else entirely.

You know the danger of assuming what customers mean when they say something. Don't risk saying the wrong thing. For example, if a buyer says; "It's too far to drive," you should promptly toss back (if the objection must be answered); "To where?" or "What did you have in mind?" or some similar query that will force a more complete explanation.

You do not know what the prospect is thinking or how important that comment really is. He may be thinking about driving to work each day, or may be worried about how his wife is going to get the children to school or go to the shopping center because she doesn't drive. Anything you say could introduce another problem the prospect hadn't even thought of until you brought it up.

The kinds of questions you ask can make all the difference in the responses you receive and the general course of the conversation. The most effective questions are open questions, which cannot be answered yes or no and do not suggest answers for the customer. Some of the best standard replies to objections are these:

"What did you have in mind?"
"That's interesting. How did you happen to think of that right now?"
"What have you thought about doing in that regard?"
"How important is that to your total objectives?"
"Which alternative do you think will work best for you?"
"When you weigh that factor with all of the many benefits we have discussed, how do you feel we might resolve that one point?"
"Why do you feel that is a problem?"

As with most open questions, they begin with one of the seven key openers: who, what, where, when, why, which, how.

Hear the Prospect Out

After you have asked a question, give the prospect time to answer it fully and to think it out with you. Do not interrupt unless absolutely necessary. One such occasion might be when you must keep the conversation from going in the wrong direction. This is a critical time in helping prospects solve their own problems. If you short-circuit the communication process by introducing your own thoughts before buyers can express theirs, you may miss your only opportunity to help them either to reach their own solution or to reveal clues as to their real hidden objections.

As prospects speak, listen not only to what they say and how they say it, but also for the things they omit. Sometimes the fact that certain things were left unsaid is more important to your discovery process than the points that were covered.

Question the Response

Even after customers have given you a further explanation of their objections, it is often wise to question their responses once again in a manner that will permit them to either amplify or resolve the objections. The most effective technique for this is to repeat to the speaker a summary of what he or she has said with an implied question that requires some sort of confirmation. An example is:

> "Mr. Jones, you think the home is more than you and your family can really afford right now, because the monthly investment will be about $300 more than you are currently paying for the older house. Is that right?"

Given this second opportunity to discuss a concern, the buyer might open up to you more readily than before and begin to share the real doubts that lie beneath the surface. He or she might then say:

> "Well, that's not the real problem. You see, we are worried about the state of the local economy and we wonder if it is wise to take on that much additional expense at this time."

With the real objection on the table, you are in a far better position to solve it than if it were buried. In this case, if you had documented statistics and projections that proved your community was going to continue to grow and prosper, you might well overcome this potential barrier to a sale.

Answer the Objection

If the customer does not find a solution—or conclude independently that there really is no problem—you will need to answer the objection in one of two basic ways:

1. Convert it into a positive.

2. Or, lessen its importance by emphasizing the other benefits of the transaction.

Almost every objection is related to some offsetting benefits. Know these benefits for every key subject and learn to convert objections to advantages by rehearsing all of the favorable features related to each one.

Consider the previous example of the objection about the small lot. The buyer thought the lot was too small, based upon what he or she had anticipated or was used to. You could then emphasize the following benefits of a smaller lot:

1. Less land to maintain—to water, mow, and plant; thus, less work for the owner.

2. Lower cost of water bills and related expenses for caring for a large site. Thus, the buyer is able to save money for other purposes.

3. Less wasted space that tends to collect trash and unsightly items. (This is particularly true where side yards have been reduced or eliminated.)

4. Lower taxes because tax values are based on the total size of the lot and the related value.

5. Convenience of being able to travel and do other things and not be tied to a large piece of property that demands constant attention.

6. Examples of how others have landscaped small yards to create more privacy and beauty in less space.

This exercise should be performed for every objection you hear more than once. In your presentation, always remember that people are more interested in benefits than in features. The question your buyer is asking is, "What does it do for me?"

When emphasizing the plus side of anything, be sure to interpret all of the features in terms of specific advantages to the prospect. For example, you might begin your points with such benefit phrases as:

"*You will save money because . . .*"
"*You will enjoy the extra hours you save because . . .*"
"*Your home will be protected from the hot rays of the sun and will be more comfortable to live in because . . .*"

The other proven approach to answering an objection is to list all of the benefits of the property, and thus dilute the importance of the negative factor. Sometimes you cannot directly convert a negative into a positive. It may be obvious to everyone that the objection is valid. In light of all the other benefits the buyer will receive, however, it may be a reasonable compromise to make.

As previously stated, every homebuying decision requires some compromises because there is no such thing as a perfect home. In most cases, the issue of the small bedroom cannot be resolved by focusing attention on the bedroom. Rather, you have to point out such things as the efficiency of the floor plan or the magnificent view from the living room, or the value of the home in terms of the limited money the prospects have to spend on housing. Your reply might include the following points:

> "I realize this bedroom is not quite as large as you would have preferred, but notice how the living space of the home has been maximized by carefully investing the construction dollars in the family room, the kitchen, and the living area, where you will enjoy most of your waking hours. The costs of constructing a home limit how much space we can offer. However, we have discovered that most people prefer to have the extra footage in the living center of the home rather than the sleeping wing. After all, that's where you will spend most of your waking time and where you can enjoy that magnificent view of the mountains."

This approach can be used for almost any objection where the prospect can perceive offsetting advantages in the total picture.

Confirm the Answer with the Buyer

Once you have made your point in response to an objection, confirm the answer with the buyer. Give the other party a chance to accept and acknowledge the reasoning. If you have failed to resolve the objection, you will want to know it. If you have succeeded, you need to obtain agreement so that the subject will not come up again to haunt you. You might now ask affirmative questions like these:

> "That is reasonable, isn't it, Mr. Smith?"
> "That solves the problem, doesn't it?"
> "Don't you agree that is the logical way to look at it, Mrs. Jones?"
> "How does that fit into your thinking?"

> "Weighing all the benefits of ownership, doesn't that seem to be a reasonable compromise?"

Close That Point and Continue with the Sale

When you have received the prospect's agreement on the solution to any objection, you should immediately close the door on the matter and proceed with your normal sales process. This is often a great time to go directly into the close—if all the other groundwork has been properly laid.

> "Now that we have cleared up that point, let's review how you can arrange to enjoy this beautiful home before the summer months are gone."

Sometimes an objection can be made to serve as the final step to making a decision. This is known as closing on a final objection, and it will be covered in detail in Chapter 8.

ANTICIPATE MAJOR OBJECTIONS

To let questions arise without anticipation or thorough preparation is to lose many opportunities. When you are given any new selling assignment, take the time to list all the advantages and disadvantages of each home involved. Then list the questions and objections you think will be fired at you. Using the guidelines in this chapter, prepare alternative answers for each one and, with the assistance of others, review the best methods of handling them. Group workshops are frequently the most effective means of developing answers to the daily problems each individual sales agent faces.

There are some objections you should cover before your prospect raises them. These are the kinds of things that can work against you unless you first put them in perspective and prepare the customers to accept them in a positive rather than a negative light. Any question or objection that you hear from the majority of your clients falls into this category. It is a case of offense being the best defense. Abraham Lincoln once said that if you want to defeat your opponent in a debate, just anticipate his arguments and then include them as points in your presentation. This technique has the advantage of taking you off the defensive when you are forced to respond to difficult questions.

Suppose you hear from almost every prospect who inspects a specific inventory home that the rear yard is too steep and difficult to landscape. As a result, you have not sold this particular home. As your prospects walk into it, their eyes are immediately drawn to the rear yard, and they become negative before they even have a chance to fully experience the benefits of the home itself.

To let that negative hit you every time, without doing anything to counteract it, would be ridiculous. At least tell the prospect in advance what he or she will see. On the way to the property, say something like:

> *"Ms. Johnson, this home I'm going to show you has one very unusual feature. The rear yard is screened by a rather high, sloping bank because the homesite was cut out of the hillside to provide a good view of the valley below from the large living room. It is different, and it has some real possibilities for creative landscaping. I'm sure you'll appreciate that point when you see it."*

Thus it will not come as a surprise when the prospect enters the home. For many people, it may still be a negative, but the odds are it will be less serious with this approach.

THIRD-PARTY STORIES

Another way to handle the hard-to-sell rear yard would be to find a good example of how someone else treated a similar property and use it as an example of how such sites can be landscaped effectively. In fact, the third-party story is one of the better ways of fielding difficult questions or objections. It is easier for people to be more objective about others than about themselves. Be sure, however, to stay on the prospect's side as you relate the other party's experiences:

> *"I know how you feel, Mr. and Mrs. Green. Mr. and Mrs. Smith felt the same way you do, and after they moved into the home and lived with it for a while they found. . . ."*

The formula for introducing these valuable true stories is:

Feel   Felt   Found

You know how they feel. Someone else felt the same way. And they found a solution. Remember this easy word sequence whenever you need to reach for a good third-party story.

In addition, make a list of all the examples you will need and the names of real people and events you can effectively use to illustrate your sales points. There are always plenty of case histories you can find with a little research. If you have too few examples of your own, ask others in the company for their recommendations, or take examples from previous subdivisions. Again, preparation is your best defense.

THE PRINCIPLE OF REDUCTION

When dealing with issues that involve money, distance, or size, one of the best techniques for handling them effectively is the *principle of reduction.* The concept is based on limiting the discussion to the differences between what the buyer is prepared to accept (or understands) and the total amount involved. The objective is to reduce the figures or facts into smaller, more easily acceptable segments. Rather than discuss or debate the entire subject, first establish a base of reference to which your buyer can relate, and then deal only with the differences beyond that base.

For example, suppose the prospect is objecting to the 15 percent interest rate on the mortgage. She says:

"That's too high. I don't plan to pay that much for financing."

Your response (using the principle of reduction) might be:

"I understand how you feel, Ms. Jones. How much do you feel is reasonable for financing your new home today?"

If she replies,

"Well, other builders are offering 12½ percent interest—and that is the most I should expect anywhere!"

You could say,

"You are probably right about some builders offering lower interest rates. Many of them have been forced to do so because their housing values have not been acceptable to the public. Fortunately, our homes and this community have been perceived by our homebuyers as a real housing value, so we have not had to discount our prices or financing. However, when you analyze it more carefully, isn't the 2½ percent we are talking about really

> *a small factor when compared to the total benefits of the home and the protected environment?*
>
> *And here in the United States you have the advantage of deducting the interest and real estate taxes from your annual income tax; which, in effect, makes the 2½ percent even less. Perhaps, if you are in the 30 percent tax bracket, we are talking about only 1.75 percent of true difference. That is only 1.46 per month per thousand.*
>
> *Compare our homes and this new community to others in terms of their future appreciated values and I think you will agree that the few additional interest dollars are insignificant compared to the thousands of dollars of anticipated equity growth."*

This is the way you bring large numbers down to bite-size pieces that you can more easily handle.

The same principle works when you are discussing the distance from your community or housing to employment centers, shopping, etc. Suppose your prospect says to you:

> *"It's too far to drive!"*

You might respond:

> *"May I inquire what you had in mind? Is it the distance to your office that you are considering?"*
>
> *"Yes, it is."*
>
> *"How far is it from where you live now to where you work?"*
>
> *"About ten miles."*
>
> *"How long does that usually take you to drive?"*
>
> *"About 15 minutes."*
>
> *"How much further would you say this is—about an additional five miles or perhaps another ten minutes each way?"*
>
> *"I guess so . . ."*
>
> *"Wouldn't it be worth an extra ten minutes to come home to this environment, considering how much more home you can afford to own here than in close-in locations?"*

To this reduction approach you might then reinforce your message with a good third-party illustration.

> *"I know how you feel about the extra driving time. Mr. Harrison, who lives over there, felt the same way you do when he first investigated our community of The Meadows. But since he has purchased, he has found that the small driving time difference is more than offset by the fact that he comes home to a happier family who truly enjoy the improved lifestyles we offer here. In fact, he was telling me the other day that he finds some advantage to the fact that he has a little more 'attitude adjustment time' on the way home from work, which he uses to debrief himself and to get ready for the recreational activities he enjoys with his family here at The Meadows!"*

This is an example of reducing the potentially big issue to a small one. The big issue is driving 25 minutes a day each way. The small one is only a ten-minute consideration, which is then offset by the many advantages of the new housing environment.

Another application of the reduction principle is handling objections about size, square footage, or design concepts. For example, suppose you are selling a patio home designed along the zero-lot-line land use plan. Your customers complain that the 1400-square-foot home is smaller than they wanted and the lot is only 50' x 100'—which is also small in their opinion. Your approach, using the reduction principle, might be as follows:

> *"At first appearance, our patio home might seem to be smaller than you anticipated. You were thinking of perhaps 1800 to 2000 square feet—right?*
>
> *"The 1400 feet in this plan look like 600 feet less than some other homes you have considered. When you study the design carefully, however, you will discover that because of the efficient use of the total space, it is like having 5000 square feet of living space for which you have to heat, air condition, and maintain only 1400. You see, because the entire lot is incorporated into the floor plan, you have indoor-outdoor relationships that maximize the value of the home. You have a private patio off your living room, another one off the kitchen, another off the master suite, and a fourth extending the family room.*
>
> *"It is not really the amount of footage in a home that counts—it is how usable the total space really is!"*

Wherever numbers or statistics are an issue in your sales approach, try to reduce the total figures to some amount that is easier to understand and explain. This applies to the following items, and many more:

- Housing prices
- Down payments
- Interest rates
- Monthly payments
- Real estate taxes
- Homeowners' association fees
- Room sizes
- Lot sizes
- Distances to or from a specific location
- Settlement costs
- Utility costs

When reducing these items to the smallest common denominator, use the following guidelines:

- Reduce dollars to value differences
- Reduce size to use differences
- Reduce distance to time differences.

DOCUMENTATION

The one sure way to reinforce your arguments when facing the obstacles of serious questions or real objections is to have available documented evidence of the facts you use. When you rely exclusively on your verbal presentations, you are only partially effective. People tend to believe and remember more of what they see than what they hear.

Some subjects are best handled by visual documentation, such as graphs, charts, pictures, and newspaper stories. If someone else has published an article about how great your product is, it is always more believable than you can be. If others have compiled statistics to prove the merits of a certain financial arrangement, they will be far more effective in convincing a buyer than you. You should have as much visual evidence as possible to help a prospect accept the truth about any critical point in your presentation that requires reinforcement. The sources of such material are numerous; with a little investigation, you will probably find most of them within easy access of your present sales operation.

PREPARE A WORKING PLAN FOR DEALING WITH OBJECTIONS

Here is a list of basic categories of subjects in which questions and objections are likely to arise. Review each item and list the objections and/or questions you might hear about each. Imagine how you would handle them. Then develop a number of different responses and weigh the merits of each.

Construction

Appearance
Quality
Material selection
Maintenance
Options and extras
Service and warranties

Design

Architecture
Floor plan
Functional use
Room sizes
Decorating
Land plan
Orientation to other buildings

Location

General characteristics
Access to shopping
Distance from other areas
Access to the community
Neighborhood influence
Schools
Topography
Land plan
Lot sizes and orientation

Timing considerations

Occupancy dates
Need to sell old home
Season of year
School transfers
Too much inventory—no urgency
Need for third-party approval
Wait for new models or lots
Wait for better economy
Interest rates must come down first
Want site in undeveloped section

Financial considerations

Price
Financing terms
Closing costs
Future costs anticipated
Maintenance
Homeowners' association fees
Resale potential

With each category of questions or objections, prepare a working plan to handle them when they arise. For example, under the topic of construction, you must develop a chart like this:

Item	Points to emphasize	Strategy
Construction	Reputation of builder	Awards Testimonials Publicity History Success Third-party
Materials used	Evaluation of competition	Inspection Evaluation sheets Checklist of benefits
Systems and products used	Demonstrated quality	On-site demonstration Builder's warranty Underwriters' ratings Manufacturer's warranties Manufacturer's literature Research
Price	Maintenance savings	History of owners Builder's service policy Manufacturer's experience Testimonials

COMMONLY HEARD OBJECTIONS

Here is a list of commonly heard objections. Practice your responses, and review with others how they would handle them. Try some role playing with these questions or similar ones that apply to your products and community.

1. We want to think it over.
2. I want my lawyer to approve this first.
3. We don't have enough money for the down payment.
4. Your taxes (or interest rates) are much higher here.

5. We want to see more homes before we make a decision.

6. We have to sell our old house before we can buy.

7. Uncle Louie is a builder, and we need him to give us his opinion.

8. Your prices are very high.

9. I don't like that kind of siding material.

10. The bedrooms are too small.

11. There is not enough cabinet space in the kitchen.

12. The lot is so very small.

13. It is further out than we expected to be.

14. The values in this area are mixed and we are worried about reselling in the future.

15. We can't put our grand piano in the living room.

16. Our king-size bed won't fit in that bedroom.

17. Your school district is not as good as (other school).

18. We need more room for our cars.

19. It will take too long to have the house built, and we must move now.

20. There is no room for our dining table.

21. It will be hard to resell the property if we have to move in the next three years.

22. We have been told this building material is difficult and expensive to maintain.

23. For about the same price, the other builder gives us (name of a product or amenity).

24. The association fees include the maintenance of the pool and other things we will not use.

25. How do we know that we will be comfortable with the other people you sell to in this community?

26. They sure don't build houses like they used to!

27. I will wait until interest rates come down.

SUMMARY

The ability to effectively handle objections and serious questions can make a big difference in sales volume. Being prepared to meet these potential obstacles can turn stumbling blocks into stepping stones.

The way to get better at anything is to keep practicing until you have mastered it. In the new home sales profession, that means using every selling situation as an opportunity to improve your communication skills—and that includes converting objections into closing opportunities.

6: Creating Urgency to Induce Action

An essential element of the sales process is *the motivating force of urgency*. If no factors were creating a sense of urgency, the average customer would postpone housing decisions until forced to act. Some people delay forever. That is like the story of the real estate salesperson stating to a buyer, "You seem to have a hard time making up your mind." The buyer's response was "Well, yes and no."

Hesitant buyers frequently make statements such as:

"We want to think it over."
"We'd like to sleep on it."
"We want to look at more homes before we decide."
"We must check with our advisors before we buy."

These and many similar phrases indicate uncertainty—and a desire to avoid making a big decision that the buyer thinks can be delayed.

The reaction is completely normal for most homebuyers, particularly when the decision represents a major commitment. As most people approach the decision point, they begin to exhibit resistance. It is far easier to do nothing than to take affirmative action. Shock waves build a barrier to positive action, and deflection or retreat seems the most comfortable way to avoid psychological pressure.

One of the salesperson's most important roles is to create and maintain the tempo of urgency that acts as a positive psychological force to help prospects over emotional barriers when closing opportunities occur. The salesperson is there to assist prospects in making a decision they should and want to make. That does not mean high pressure. It means genuinely conveying to the prospects the facts they need on which to base a decision and generating a sense of urgency to act now.

EVERYTHING IN THE SALES ARENA SHOULD CONVEY THE MESSAGE OF URGENCY

The old maxim is true: Nothing succeeds like success. People gravitate toward successful events. They find themselves caught up in the momentum of successful activities because they like the excitement. In addition, most people are followers, not leaders or adventurers. They like to be reassured that other people are doing the same thing. A saying that captures this is:

There are 3 percent who think, 12 percent who think they think, and 85 percent waiting for a slogan.

Therefore, all of the visual and psychological conditions with which you work should be positive elements that will bolster the buyers' confidence and stimulate their desire to take action. Figure 6.1 is a checklist to review to see if conditions are all favorable to the urgency climate.

Sources of Urgency

Urgency is based on two emotions:

1. Desire to own.
2. Fear of loss.

All urgency is founded on these two basic emotional drives. Once a person wants something that is unique and desirable, the fear of losing it is frequently the motivating reason to act now and buy it. Most people have experienced this human response more than once, whether the object is a marriage partner, a fine home, or a special item. In sales psychology, this factor can and should be honestly precipitated.

Give customers credible reasons why they should not postpone making a decision, once their interest has generated a desire to own one of your homes. Customers need the stimulus to act and the justification for their actions once they have consummated a decision. There are valid methods to generate a sincere sense of urgency, once it is evident that a prospect likes and can afford one of the homes you are showing. The following paragraphs describe the seven most important elements in producing these results:

Uniqueness. One of the inherent qualities of real estate is its uniqueness. Every home, condominium, or homesite is truly one of a

Figure 6.1. Checklist of factors that can influence buyers' sense of urgency to act.

Exterior appearance of the homes and community

Positive evidence of construction activity ☐
Sold signs on property and evidence of occupied homes ☐
Clean exterior of the homes that are for sale ☐
A limited number of For Sale signs—not so many that they would evidence too much unsold inventory ☐
Vacant lots cleaned and all growth controlled ☐
Models (if any) landscaped and maintained neatly ☐
All signage fresh appearing, not faded or looking as though it had been there for an extended period of time ☐

Interior condition of speculative homes and models

General cleanliness and fresh appearance evident ☐
Model furniture in good condition and rooms light, properly ventilated, and cheerful ☐
Plants and flowers where appropriate ☐
Drawers, closets, windows, etc., all easy to open and not cluttered or dirty in any way ☐
Display material (if any) in neat and clean condition ☐

Sales office conditions

Clean and orderly office ☐
Evidence of success displayed visually in a number of ways ☐
Prospects feel at home and comfortable ☐
Coffee, tea, soft drinks, etc. ready to use to help people relax with you ☐
Site map up-to-date; Sold signs prominently featured, here or in another location ☐
Graphics neat and ready for use ☐
Current photographs, especially of items depicting success ☐
Fresh plants and flowers as appropriate ☐
Sales desks business-like and uncluttered ☐
Literature in good condition and organized for use ☐
Pictures of resident activities ☐
Newspaper articles, publicity, and testimonial displays ☐

Personal psychology

Positive mental attitude ☐
Friendly and relaxed ☐
Confidence exhibited by actions and attitudes ☐
Prepared to help people make positive decisions ☐
Cooperative, with concern for impact on the total sales environment ☐

kind. A substantial portion of the value of any piece of real property is in its location—the specific site with all its positive features, as well as possible negative influences. Typically, 20 percent or more of the total price of a home is represented by its exclusive land values or site location. There are always differences among sites, and often numerous perceived unique characteristics that set one location apart from the next one. Normally, in any community, a wide selection of sites is available at any given time, and each should be appreciated for its own distinction.

The capacity to translate those individual features into perceived benefits for a specific homebuyer is the prelude to closing on one-of-a-kind urgency. Once a particular home or site has been sold, it is usually off the market for a long time. *The fear of loss* is real for people who want a home and then begin to realize they may not own it if they do not act soon. It may then be lost to them forever. To accent the benefits of the location or home, you need to know everything possible about it. The checklists provided in Chapters 2 and 4 give clues as to how you can achieve that objective. Prepare yourself to sell what you have to sell.

While on this subject, it is appropriate to again emphasize the importance of controlling inventory. Whenever prospects have too much from which to choose, it is easy for them to become confused, and also to sense little urgency for taking any action now. Even if you have many properties to offer, you have only one of a kind for each customer, and you can (normally) sell that customer only one property. Your role is to select from the inventory the appropriate locations for the styles and types of homes involved and to concentrate on one or two properties for a given customer.

Focus on the limited available inventory, and work with tools that assist you in that regard. For example, point out the site map for each neighborhood where the Sold signs clearly indicate what is left, the limited amount that is open for delivery within a reasonable time frame, and the differences of site locations. Here, the lot rating chart is helpful. As you understand the differences of location, you can focus on the points that will reinforce in the buyers' mind the exclusiveness of that property versus others you have for sale.

Cost and Price Increases. In new housing, even more so than in resale housing, price increases that reflect escalating costs of construction and development are used as justification for not delaying the decision to purchase. Land, materials, labor, services, financing, and marketing costs continue to rise in all areas of the nation, especially in high-demand markets.

Price increases normally are structured to give early buyers in a new building area a distinct advantage. As a community or neighborhood achieves greater sales activity and success, prices are raised to reflect accelerated values as well as the increased cost of reproduction. A pricing strategy should be designed to assist sales momentum. By scheduling future price adjustments in advance, developers can give salespeople the advantage of creating urgency, which will stimulate more closed transactions. In a new community, there should be distinct marketing phases during which predetermined pricing objectives are used to generate sales activity. That strategy is further developed later in this chapter.

As other chapters of this book have implied, there is a difference between inflation and appreciation. The combined effect represents the higher future prices people pay for property. To fully communicate the impact of rising prices, you should be able to explain to your customers that there is a difference between inflation and appreciation. Appreciation applies essentially to land values, and is based on increased demand for specific locations and areas: *more people want a certain property and location.* Inflation is directly related to the national economy and the cost of doing business, which escalates prices of everything we buy. Inflation typically adds 5 percent to 20 percent per year to the cost of building a new home.

No one reasonably expects inflation to be totally eliminated in the foreseeable future. The question is merely how much it will be controlled. Thus, housing costs probably will continue to go up even in low-demand areas of the nation. It simply costs more to do business each year. In contrast, real appreciation occurs only when more qualified people want the same property or the same general location and are willing to pay for the privilege of living in a particular region, community, or home. The combination of inflation and real appreciation of land values results in higher prices for new homes every year. Builders and developers normally create added values as their communities mature.

The best building teams believe in creating added values by the way they design and complete their housing projects. When you sell a new home, you are selling more than just a house; you are selling a new environment backed by people whose success depends upon meeting their responsibilities. If you are working in well-planned communities that have inherent values in their design, you have a real advantage in the protection of future values.

Values are also enhanced by controlling inventory. When you release a limited number of housing units at each phase of development, you avoid oversupply as well as provide the company an opportunity to increase prices as sales occur. This positive method stimulates buyers to act today rather than experience higher prices tomorrow.

It does some other things too. First, it increases the value of homes already purchased. There is no one happier than buyers who have already made money (sometimes even before they move in). If the property is worth more shortly after they purchase it, they become solid buyers and great supporters of your sales objectives. They can be your best referral source, helping you bring others to the community. They are less likely to cancel when they learn they have already made a profit before the homes are delivered.

The second benefit of controlling inventory to enhance values is that it stimulates action on the part of customers who delay. They know that the longer they wait, the more it is going to cost them.

The Availability and Cost of Financing. Financing a home is often just as important as the price of the property, if not more so. The financing terms available can and do influence most homebuyers. In the last few years, the housing industry has experienced tremendous fluctuations in financing. Interest rates, the availability of mortgage money, and the qualifications to obtain credit approval have varied from month to month, making predictions difficult for homebuilders and homebuyers. Consequently, salespeople have learned to be more creative in their approaches to financing homes and condominiums.

The major point to remember is that any terms offered now for the purchase of a new home can be used as a valid reason to buy while such terms are still available. Whenever you can feature rates or terms that are better than the competitive market, you have an even stronger closing tool. Sometimes prospects will say they are going to wait until interest rates come down. At that point, it is important to show them the net effects of waiting for lower interest costs while the price and demand of available homes are rising steadily. No one can predict future conditions with certainty, but you *can* prepare yourself to give an informed opinion. As covered in Chapter 5, documentation and current data about market activities, prices, and interest rates experienced in other communities, and about the money market, help you to convince homebuyers that it may be more costly to wait than to buy now. Property normally can be refinanced, once you own it, but unless one freezes the price and locks in the opportunity to own today, that advantage is also lost.

There are distinct advantages even to paying higher interest when it is compared to the tax benefits and the appreciation growth of property. Consider, for example, a home with an $80,000 selling price and a 20 percent down payment ($16,000), a 29-year mortgage of $64,000, and $700 estimated annual property taxes. The buyer is in a 33 percent income tax bracket. Assume a 9 percent interest rate, a 6 percent inflation rate, and monthly payments of $576 including principal, interest, and property taxes. (Note that there is usually a direct relationship between inflationary factors and interest factors. When inflation is higher, so are interest rates.) With these assumptions, the following calculations can be made:

> The first monthly payment of interest
> and taxes $538

The savings would be:

> Income tax savings (interest and tax
> payment times 33 percent tax rate) $178
> Equity build-up in loan (the portion of
> the $576 monthly payment not going
> to interest or taxes)   38
> One month's property appreciation
> (6% x [$80,000/12])   400

> Total benefits to homeowner in first month $616

The first month's net benefits to the homeowner can be calculated by subtracting the $576 monthly payment from the $616 total benefits, resulting in $40. Note that this means the owner lived in the home rent-free and still made $40. (A salesperson making such a presentation should be sure that the customer understands he or she will not actually receive $438 of this income until he or she sells the home.)

No alternative return on investment for the $16,000 down payment was considered in these calculations. If a 9 percent return on that investment is taken into account, this would be $1,440 per year, or $120 per month. This would mean the owner lived in the home for a net cost of only $80 the first month (i.e., $120 foregone return on investment less the $40 benefits to owner).

Now assume a 16½ percent interest rate and a 12 percent inflation rate, with the same conditions otherwise. The first monthly payment of interest and property taxes would be $938. In this case, the savings would be:

Income tax savings (33 percent bracket)	$ 313
Equity build-up in loan	8
One month's property appreciation (12% x [$80,000/12])	800
Total benefits to owner in first month	$1,121
Monthly payment	(946)
Net benefits to owner	$ 175

Note that with a 9 percent yield on equity ($120), the buyer had a rent-free home and received net benefits of $55.

This illustration shows that owning real estate, even at higher interest rates with higher inflation, is still safer and has a better rate of return than many other things in which people invest.

Financing becomes one of the tools by which you show the leverage value of purchasing today with the tax credits received (according to an individual's own bracket) and appreciation gained. This is especially true in comparison to other things people might have done with the same funds. An important truth about real estate is that it is one of the few investments in which the investor has the capacity to borrow 70 percent to 90 percent of the value of the property, usually on long-term financing. Most other investments require substantial cash investments or short-term borrowing to handle the risk, without the assurances of normal appreciation gains, which can be projected with some degree of certainty in almost every demand market.

The availability of special financing has its own unique urgency advantages to help you motivate a prospect to buy now. Since the time period during which a specific financing program is offered is usually limited, that fact alone can be effectively used to precipitate action. The salesperson might say, for example:

> "Mr. Clark, I appreciate your desire to wait a little longer before reaching a decision. However, one consideration is the fact that we have special financing available today and I do not know how much longer we will have that advantage. If you act now, I am sure you can secure approval of this favorable package and complete the paperwork in time to close before there is a rate change."

When your builder has given you any financing advantage, it should be used as an additional incentive to buyers to act now. Since you do not control such matters, you can honestly say to your prospects:

"I do not know how much longer we can feature this financing plan. It is in your best interests to take advantage of this program while we have it."

Possession Dates and Scheduling Production Items. Possession dates almost always are part of the consideration in a housing decision. Most prospective buyers have a date in mind by which they would like to move or enjoy the benefits of home ownership. In resale housing, occupancy dates are usually sooner than in new homes, which must be finished or built on a production schedule. Of course, a completed speculative home may provide opportunities for immediate possession, but such homes, if available, are usually limited in number. Their availability can be a supply factor that creates urgency for someone needing prompt occupancy. Where secondary or vacation housing is involved, possession may be less critical, but it can be important in terms of enjoying the benefits of use or rental investment.

Know what approximate time frames are involved in the construction of a new home and, more specifically, the anticipated production schedule of each home released by your management. One of the qualifying areas in the initial counseling session with prospects should be the matter of possession and use. The homes or sites you select to show a particular customer should be dictated in part by the occupancy consideration. When people express a desire to delay purchase, you can emphasize the estimated time frame for completing construction of the home they like, and the importance of ordering the various items that must go into the production sequence.

There is an added factor when the builder places production emphasis on homes that are sold. In a market area where you have a controlled production sequence, the home customers want completed may not be given any attention until they have made the decision to purchase.

If you have a production schedule sheet at hand, you can use it to validate the urgency of deciding now. Even weather conditions can sometimes be important, although less so in Florida than in states farther north. Production dates are just one more element in the package of urgency factors which can help you to influence your prospects to decide today.

Optional Items. Related to production scheduling, but a separate element of urgency, is the matter of selecting the optional items that go with the purchase of a new home. The choices are sometimes limited, but there are normally at least one or two areas in which buyers are permitted to make a selection. In the case of customized homes, the choices are usually numerous. Whatever the options and alternatives provided by the company, they do represent opportunities to precipitate decision making. For example, at the critical point when your buyers are hesitant you might say:

> *"I realize that you want more time to think it over, Mr. and Mrs. Smith; however, we are at that point in construction when a number of decisions have to be made regarding the various elective items that go with the home. Colors, floor coverings, tiles, and wall coverings must be chosen now in order to have them in your home on time. You still have an opportunity to make your own decisions rather than those of our decorator if you act today. You also have the advantage of today's prices. Let me show you what items are available for your approval."*

The color selection room or exhibits can be helpful in closing the sale, based on using the minor point of choice with the overriding factor of urgency to make the decision. It is a subtle but valid consideration. Delivery and installation dates play equally important roles in this situation. Remember also that the availability and prices of options are subject to change. Buyers are at the mercy of subcontractors and suppliers who may be out of stock of a particular item, or the prices may increase without notice. As for installation, subcontractors who are busy may be unable to meet desired schedules unless notified sufficiently far in advance. These factors combine to add further reality to the urgency of making a housing decision while conditions are in the buyer's favor.

Introduction of Contingencies. Frequently, there are contingent conditions tied to a real estate transaction that can be used to facilitate the urgency factors. Any "subject to" or "contingent" consideration may produce the opportunity to help you trigger a sale if properly handled. The most common example is the sale of a new home based on the sale of another property owned by the buyers. Company policies on handling such contingent sales will vary from time to time and by project, because of market conditions as well as the sales status of specific building operations. Always check with your manager about current procedures before writing any contingent contract.

Even if your company does not allow contingent sales, you can still use step-up buyers as legitimate opportunities to make or create extra transactions. The equity in the other property can be the basis of the sale through noncontingent decisions. There are a variety of ways creative financing can play a part in solving the challenge of unlocking equities. For example, you might suggest that a hesitant buyer who has an equity in an older property release that equity in the other home through a well-established marketing plan working with a professional broker who has been recommended by the company.

Some other considerations for making the decision *now* can be:

- the season of the year;
- the activity of the resale market, which indicates that it is a good
- time to market the home;
- the added time customers will have to sell the older home while
- the new one is being constructed;
- the availability of financing for the older home;
- the cooperation of selected brokers who are willing to offer
- guarantees or equity release programs.

The specifics of handling trade-ins and guarantees are not dealt with in this book. Information on this specialized subject is available from the author and other sources.

Another contingency, if prospects are living in an apartment and are under a lease agreement, is to offer the landlord sufficient time to find a replacement tenant or to help the prospects find one while they are making the arrangements for the new home. The more notice given the landlord, the less likely there will be a problem in securing the release or forfeiture of deposits.

Sometimes special incentives are offered with limited time considerations. Examples of these are a free membership in a country club or a special consideration that goes with that particular homesite and not some of the others for sale. Any contingent condition, even including getting customers' children registered in schools on time, can be a helpful device in encouraging the buyer to make a decision now.

The Personal Benefits of New Home Ownership. The personal benefits of enjoying home ownership may, in the final analysis, be the most important motivator to get customers to act now rather than wait. The new environment, with all of the amenities and features your community and homes offer, is in itself a major reason why prospects should not postpone their decisions.

> *"If we select a home now, you and your family will be in the new home to enjoy the wonderful summer months here at Quail Lakes! Your children will have the parks, pools, and tot-lots in which to play, and you will be able to enjoy your new home and pleasant environment."*

This same concept can also be used for almost any season of the year:

> *"Be in your new home before Christmas and enjoy the holidays in your new environment."*
> *"Be in your new home before spring so that you can plant your own flowers—and enjoy them during the summer."*
> *"Move in before school starts so that you and your children are settled prior to the beginning of the school year."*

In sum, effective face-to-face closing strategies include emphasizing uniqueness, likelihood of a price increase, availability of financing, and contingencies related to buying now. You can use these strategies to accent prospects' fear of losing out.

Maintain a Tempo of Excitement and Urgency

Another way to create urgency is in the sales facility and in the community. Everything from the customer's sense of arrival at a community, to the proper maintenance and signing of the sites and models, to the attitudes, involvement tools, and tempo in the sales facility are important psychological factors.

Have you ever noticed that activity and excitement are contagious? When things are happening and a lot of activity is generated in a new home community, everybody seems to want to get in on the act! Department stores have learned the secret to this mass-buying psychology. They hold special sales to draw the crowds and then sell more expensive merchandise that would not have moved without the stimulus of the sale. They pile goods on the tables, and clerks pore over them to attract the interest of shoppers. As the customers move in, the clerks disappear and the merchandise starts selling. Customers get caught up in the spirit of the event. If everyone else is doing it, there must be a reason. "Perhaps," they think, "I too should buy before it is too late!"

There is a tempo of success in a well-operated new home sales facility. The sense of urgency is created by the number of people looking at the models, the activity in the sales office, the Sold signs on the homes, and, when appropriate, the names of the owners on the plot map, not to mention the feeling of excitement in the air. The time to buy is when others are buying!

Salespeople can help generate and maintain that feeling of activity by the little things they do in the total sales environment. Maintain a neat sales office, move plants around, and keep fresh flowers in the office and in the models. Remove excess signs, have directional signs repainted when needed, place Sold signs on all sold lots and (with permission) include the buyers' names on the Sold signs. You can create extra tempo, and thus urgency, by conducting and advertising a series of open houses with refreshments, art shows, or other special events. A busy sales pavilion helps build interest as the volume of prospects coming through your project increases.

TEAMWORK

There should be a feeling of teamwork among sales agents, even if they are competing for sales commissions in the same sales environment. When two or more sales representatives are in the same office, they can help each other to close more sales, without being artificial or using high-pressure tactics. Salespeople can ask each other questions that are designed to accelerate urgency features and the desire to confirm decisions.

For example, if your prospect shows interest in a particular property but hesitates to take the first step, you might ask the other sales agent:

"Bill, is it lot #135 that your Dr. Hayes has been considering? Do you expect her back tonight?"

In other situations, the alert sales agent can assist the one trying to write a sale, by using a little reinforcement:

"Are you writing up lot #135? Well, I guess my prospects are going to miss out on that one!"

We are not suggesting you create artificial situations; just use the facts you know to strengthen the buying attitude.

PHASING AND MARKETING STRATEGY

The tempo of a building project can be greatly accelerated by effectively planning the various phases of introduction to the marketplace. To realize the greatest impact from initial marketing efforts, it is best to establish a promotional strategy that is designed to build interest and general sales from sequentially programmed events and activities. The opening of a new project, model, or lot release program gives salespeople an opportunity to bring the new products to the attention of the buying public in ways that stimulate their own momentum.

As an example, suppose you and the marketing team were given the responsibility of planning the initial marketing strategy for a 100-lot, single-family subdivision that will include introduction of three speculative models or show homes. Your research shows that the potential absorption rate for these homes and sizes will require approximately one year to achieve. Your objective is to build maximum tempo and achieve the optimum number of sales by the efficient implementation of your marketing plan. The following steps might then be logically pursued to fulfill that goal:

Step 1: Limit the Initial Inventory in the First Phase

To avoid having too much inventory on the market at one time, the decision is made to offer only 25 sites out of the 100, constituting about 90 days of projected sales. The inventory should be balanced to represent the broad categories of properties available, with a high percentage of the better sites saved for the later phases.

Step 2: Target for Highly Qualified VIPs and Pioneers

Little or no advertising is to be done during this period. This is a very low-key marketing phase, during which the primary appeal is made to target groups who have been identified as likely prospects. Direct mail, home calls, personal presentations, and a limited amount of on-site marketing occur at a relatively subdued level.

Step 3: Begin Preview Marketing Campaign

After several days or weeks of the pioneer phase, the preview campaign is inaugurated. At this stage, there are an effective on-site sales facility (possibly with models about ready) and a low-key advertising program. Special parties and open house events are held for the following groups:

- Local residents;
- Previous purchasers;
- Prospects who did not buy in an earlier phase;
- Press and centers of influence;
- Cooperating brokers;
- Suppliers and subcontractors.

Step 4: Hold Grand Opening or Major Event

Once the prelude period has been completed, the big event can be held. The grand opening is a very special time in the marketing program. If the previous phases have been successful, a number of presales will have been made, so the impact of the opening is even more dramatic than would be possible without that sales success. When the general public is first made aware of the new housing, the site map will already have Sold stickers on it, which help to build a tempo of success.

Step 5: Follow Through with a Post-Opening Campaign

The post-opening phase includes consistent advertising or other promotional programs that capitalize on the success of the sales made in the previous weeks. If inventory was limited to a 90-day supply, the sales should now reach the majority of the target goal—permitting the release of the next group of sites. If some inventory is selling slowly, refer to the tips in Figure 6.2, to get it moving.

At the appropriate time, another step-by-step phasing plan is put into operation for the opening of the next section. This whole process allows the tempo to be maintained. Prices also should be increased some small amount to reinforce the previous buyers and create a sense of urgency to act for all new prospects.

SUMMARY

Do not let the decision to buy be postponed because of too many options and choices. Arrive at a decision with your prospects by narrowing down involvement to one or two properties and then developing a sense of urgency to buy now.

If your sales tools give your prospects too many alternatives and thus permit them to justify postponement of housing decisions, you will find it difficult to make sales. This problem often arises with the plot map or plot table display, which is usually the most important exhibit. When the buyer can see too many unsold lots or housing units, the urgency to make a decision is diminished. When it is obvious that there are plenty of sites for sale, there is also plenty of time to make a buying decision. One way to avoid this problem is to display only that portion of the total project that is for sale now. The remaining areas can be identified as future development without defining lots, prices, or styles. This helps you to circumvent having too much to see and avoids extensive discussions of the entire development plan. Your

Figure 6.2. Ways to move stalled inventory and speculative homes.

1. Look for ways to increase the value of the unsold property so that prospective buyers will perceive it as worth more. It is better to increase values than to decrease prices. Investment by the builder/developer in improving values can be made at a substantially lower cost than the purchaser would have to make to achieve similar results; therefore the perception of value will be greater.

2. Improve the ease of ownership of the properties that are not selling well. This may mean lower down payments, special financing terms, or even lease option and equity accumulation plans.

3. Re-evaluate the prices of the unsold inventory and balance them so as to place greater value differences that are sufficient to stimulate the sale of the properties that are proving the least acceptable to the market. If necessary, adjust the prices of that which is not selling in favor of that which is. One approach is to lower prices for one group of homes or lots while raising prices for others, so that the total income from the community remains about the same but the perception of differences increases.

4. Provide bonus incentives to salespeople for those properties most in need of being sold. This same incentive system can be used with outside brokers if you are working with cooperative real estate companies.

5. Furnish one or more of the spec homes as a method of presenting them to better advantage. A furnished model or home has been demonstrated to show better and thus to sell better.

6. Add special incentives for purchasing specific properties in specific time periods. The following examples are some of the things that have been done in the past:
   - Include a membership in the nearby golf and tennis club at no extra cost if purchase is made immediately.
   - Include special items with the home, such as a refrigerator or microwave oven, if the home is purchased now.
   - Use prepaid interest association fees, etc., as urgency closing tools.

7. Raise the prices of the new phase or new production while keeping the present unsold inventory at the older price. This is often justified on the basis that it was built or developed under the previous budget and therefore is available at advantageous prices as compared to the new inventory. You can publish the new inventory price and make the comparison so that the salespeople will have a tool to emphasize to the buyer in documented form.

8. Carpet and drape certain spec units so as to add to the visual appeal of the unsold inventory, and include the items in the price if they are not already

Figure 6.2. (continued)

> included. Mainly it is a matter of making the inventory look more salable or look occupied.
>
> 9. Do something special for one home at a time. For example, take one home and add a larger deck, a patio, or a fire pit and use that one home as an example on which you are experimenting. If prospects are interested in that home, sell it to them for the same price as the standard home, using the addition as an incentive if they buy now. Some of the other things you can add are finished rooms such as a recreation room, or landscaping on one side at a time. The key to this approach is that this one property on which you are offering the feature is unique and available only on a limited basis.
>
> 10. Open the sales to outside brokers if you have not already involved them in the past. The designated or preferred broker approach is often better than the multiple listing system. Select those brokers who work with your kind of clientele and target for their involvement on an increased commission level over which you have been paying your own people. Never penalize your own salespeople if you can avoid doing so.
>
> 11. Provide special allowances for the equities of older homes for contingent trade-up buyers. This may mean the willingness to take some "paper" or provide some guarantees on just those properties that need to be sold, where you might not be doing it for the entire project.
>
> 12. Run small classified ads on one home at a time as though they were individual resale properties. This is designed to get the phone to ring from those individuals who may be seeking bargains or looking for resale or for-sale-by-owner properties.
>
> 13. In the single-family housing market, include a landscaping allowance which can be applied to the initial investment. The value is twofold; it helps to sell the specific property on which it is offered, and it adds to the curbside appeal of the adjacent sites that may be unsold.
>
> 14. Train and educate your sales staff to work on one or two target properties at a time. Sharpen their presentation on those properties and make certain that the properties themselves are in physically good condition for showing.
>
> 15. *Reduce the inventory.* One of the more important aspects of increasing sales on properties, where inventory has begun to build up a surplus, is to reduce that inventory even if you have to withdraw some properties from the market. If you have more than 90 days of inventory on the market at any given time, you have created your own competition and decreased the urgency to buy now.

Figure 6.2. (continued)

> 16. Explore *bulk sales* or an investment approach to selling off a group of your homes with special prices and terms. This approach is valuable only if you can create an investment package that makes sense to an outside group.
>
> 17. Use *target marketing,* which aims specifically at prospective buyers who are profiled to fit the properties you are trying to sell. Under this approach, selling inventory focuses on those specific people who should know about the properties, makes them aware of the properties, and offers incentives to buy.

presentation should emphasize the availability of a limited number of sites rather than review all the alternatives that may be available in the future.

If the plot or topographical display permits you to easily identify all sold units, do so and keep it current every day. If you make sales during the middle of the week when traffic is relatively low, it may be wise to do the actual posting and update your plot map or environmental display boards on Sunday afternoon while potential buyers are watching. Buying fever can be heightened when prospects see that others have made the decision to buy.

Some offices display signs without identifying the purchasers; others display names of buyers too. There are usually good reasons for both approaches. One advantage of using actual names is that your Sold signs are more credible when they are identified with real people. Such a sign accomplishes at least two objectives:

1. It gives potential buyers an increased sense of urgency.

2. The actual buyers more strongly identify with their purchase as they show the site to others.

Use a pedestal registration book only in high-volume sales facilities. Prospects do not like to feel they are the only ones who have visited the project in the last few days or that they are the first ones to visit on a particular day. In low-volume subdivisions, use prospect cards to keep a record of visitors and avoid openly visible documentation that might decrease the sense of urgency.

Make sure every model home is clean and attractive. People do not get excited about shopworn and damaged products. Figure 6.3 lists tips on maintaining inventory. Make sure the plot map, renderings, and brochures are all up-to-date and in superb condition.

Figure 6.3. Make certain that inventory is in good condition.

> It is difficult enough to sell inventory property without having to work against adverse influences. You can help your cause by keeping your inventory in good condition. The following questions are designed to guide your efforts in doing so.
>
> 1. Does the community have a clean, fresh appearance, particularly around unsold properties?
>
> 2. Are the yards policed constantly to see that they are free of weeds, rocks, papers, etc.?
>
> 3. Are the streets clear of debris?
>
> 4. Are the houses clean inside and out, dust free?
>
> 5. Do doors and windows work easily on all the unsold merchandise?
>
> 6. Are there any broken windows that are in sight of the customer?
>
> 7. Is paint free from chips or peeling, and has the finish been completed, especially on the high-visibility areas such as front entries?
>
> 8. Are the houses free of obvious construction oversights such as loose floor tile, poorly fitting cabinet doors, and sloppily layed carpet pads? etc.
>
> 9. Are glass windows and doors reasonably clean?
>
> 10. Does the inventory's appearance imply that you are successful and what you have to offer is fresh?

It helps to have considerable construction activity under way. The sound of hammers pounding and saws rasping stimulates interest in the project and lends to your credibility as a community on the go. The builder controls this activity, but the salesperson can effectively use it in timing his or her sales efforts.

Regardless of whether you are working from plot tables, models, or homesites, remember the old saying, "The longest journey begins with a single step." Your role is to get the customer to take that first step. Any degree of mental or emotional involvement customers feel on first inspection of your products normally will lead to greater involvement in the future. If all you achieve is an appointment for the prospect to return, that is a partial buying decision and well worth your effort.

Most important, the people in the sales area should keep each other on their toes and maintain a positive and exciting tempo, which is contagious and will spread to the prospects as they circulate through the area. As a salesperson, create a feeling that the prospect is important. Think of ways to apply the principles in this chapter to your own situation. Questions to guide your thinking appear in Figure 6.4.

Do not let your actions proclaim:

> *"Come back any time, I'm always here,"*

but rather:

> *"I have a very full calendar, but I think I can arrange some time for you—say, tomorrow afternoon at 2."*

Do not say:

> *"We have many models to choose from—take your pick";*
> *"We anticipate building another 350 homes in the next year";*
> *"Lot #123 is an example of the kind of home I think you might be interested in—go check it out—let me know what you think,"*

unless you work in a community where you are fighting off prospects from your front door. If you do not express enthusiasm and a sense of urgency, your customers will not have these positive forces influencing their attitudes and actions.

Figure 6.4. Review techniques for creating urgency.

1. List some pending events that could help create urgency and encourage a prospect to make a decision to buy today.

2. List the kinds of impending events you could use on *your* products to create urgency.

3. Practice the urgency closes reviewed in this chapter. Index the ones that work best for you. Experiment with other ways to create urgency that help you close buyers.

4. Why is it important to maintain a tempo of excitement and activity in your sales area? How can you do it?

5. What can sales personnel do to help each other in creating buyer urgency and reinforcing interest in the community?

6. From an objective point of view, study every aspect of your sales environment and your sales tools to see if new customers will really experience a sense of urgency and an excitement that could lead to buying. Review this matter with others in your company to see what can be done to pick up the tempo.

7. Inspect your subdivision and ask yourself whether or not there is a feeling of urgency and excitement that leads to positive decisions to buy. Analyze what might be done to pick up the tempo of activity and stimulate the buyers to take action now.

8. You are staffing a subdivision that has 43 unsold completed homes based on only four floor plans. Thus, you have ten or more of each model. How do you create urgency for a buying decision today?

7: Generating Sales with Be-Backs

THE IMPORTANCE OF BE-BACK BUSINESS

Most new home sales are made to *be-backs,* those prospects who visit the properties more than once before they finally decide to purchase. Stone Institute studies of numerous new home sales operations throughout the U.S. have found that fewer than 25 percent of prospects make the total buying decision on the first day they inspect the properties they ultimately purchase. More than 75 percent of the sales are completed on a return trip. This is usually after the buyers have inspected several competitive products and explored other alternatives.

This does not mean that some projects do not achieve a high ratio of first-time buying decisions. If a property is a real *barn-burner* (an outstanding value) or there has been a prolonged housing shortage in certain economic ranges or locations, buyers might be standing in line to purchase your homes the day you open. For most, however, that is a rather rare event. Gone are the days when a salesperson could make a good living just by getting in the way between the buyers and the merchandise. Today, salespeople must depend upon their selling skills, as well as upon the value of the products they represent. Salespeople must successfully involve their customers with the homes. If a salesperson cannot close a prospect today, the salesperson must try to get him or her back tomorrow for another opportunity to bring about a favorable decision. For the majority of salespeople in the new housing market, if they lose the be-back business, they lose 75 percent or more of their potential sales volume.

Marketing experts in new home sales know that one of the surest ways to measure and predict sales trends for any new home community is to analyze the quantity and quality of the be-back business. *The first indication that a project may be in trouble is when few people return to take a second look at the models.* If you have good traffic for initial inspections but few of these prospects ever come back, you can be reasonably certain you have a major marketing problem. It may be prices, location, plans, environment, or possibly the sales personnel on duty.

The traffic report forms used by developers who are concerned with the total impact of their marketing programs usually cover these factors in detail. An example of such a form is shown in Figure 7.1. An effective traffic report measures not only the number of people who visit the models, but also the number of potential buying units and the number of be-backs each day. This kind of information can be extremely valuable to marketing directors if it is accurately recorded by the sales personnel who staff the subdivision.

Sales associates sometimes avoid disclosing how many customers visit their sales areas for fear it will adversely reflect on their sales abilities. Only if that vital information is made available to those who must make marketing decisions and plan sales strategies, however, can those people find the answers that will ensure effective use of the marketing budget.

On any project, and under almost any sales conditions, the professional in new home selling achieves a greater proportion of be-backs and closings. Involving prospects with you and your homes in a way that will encourage them to return and buy is an art. Its success depends on what you do the first time you meet new prospects. *If you do the right things, and then follow through, you can create additional sales that otherwise would be lost to competition.*

Qualifying skills are very much a part of the story. Knowing how to qualify customers is the first step to any sale. You cannot target well for specific properties that will match buyers' motivations, abilities, and needs unless you discover what factors influence their decisions. There is a direct relationship between ability to qualify and ability to close. There is also a relationship between qualifying skills and the degree of involvement obtained on the prospect's first visit to your models or new home community.

GETTING BE-BACKS BY GENERATING EMOTIONAL INVOLVEMENT

Emotional involvement is essential. The sooner prospects identify with one specific home in the community, the more likely they are to become sufficiently involved to ultimately decide to purchase that home.

Figure 7.1. Sample traffic report form.

The first time prospects are exposed to your housing environment, they should experience enough emotional involvement with a model or homesite to motivate them to return and, hopefully, to buy. The salesperson's role is to help them develop a sense of personal identity with one home they can picture owning and enjoying. They must begin to feel a part of what they see and experience. Part of this involvement should be with the various elements of the total environment, but that alone is insufficient. Prospects must also become involved in one property they can envision as their potential future home. There are many ways to generate involvement. Some are discussed in the following paragraphs.

Focus on One Property

It is extremely difficult for prospective homebuyers to remember a number of models or homes inspected in one day. If they visit several projects (as they often do), the impact of the number of properties seen will tend to confuse and dilute the relative values of any single home.

If customers leave your office without taking with them a *vivid impression of a specific home they liked,* they will have little reason to return for another inspection. As they drive away from your sales area, their interest may fade. Their attention can be diverted to competing events and alternative housing projects. Only when their picture of ownership and personal enjoyment is clearly focused on one property (never more than two), is there a dominant motive strong enough to draw them back again. Understanding this point is vital to closing success in this profession.

Always try to isolate prospects' interest and attention on one (or, at the most, two) properties that can be purchased now. Then, create as much urgency as possible, so that they will have an intense desire to take positive action today!

While it is necessary to sell the "big picture" first, if you spend too much time on the larger concepts, you may not have time to concentrate the buyers' attention on one property that fits their individual motivations, abilities, and needs. Too often, new home salespeople are tempted to lecture rather than involve their prospects. They extol the virtues of their builder's products and the advantages of their subdivisions without relating them to the customers' personal interests and motivations. At times, sales associates stand at plot tables or other sales exhibits, sermonizing on the merits of their homes and communities. While doing so, they waste time on subjects unrelated to the private motivations of their listeners. If you spend too much time in making the big presentation, you may never have an opportunity to guide your prospects to properties that fit their individual needs.

Timing is everything, and time is always limited. It is a fleeting, intangible element, impossible to recover once lost. Since you never really know how much time you will have with customers, nor what events may compete for their attention, try to make every moment count. You cannot afford to give your prospects a "museum tour" or conduct a sightseer's approach. The sales agent who repeats a canned presentation like a robot has no chance to involve anyone with a new home environment. The robotlike salesperson says:

> *"This is an early American home, this is the living room, this is the kitchen, this is the bedroom . . . (ad nauseum),"*

and the customer asks:

> *"Where is the door?"*

As soon as you have been able to determine prospects' general interests and qualifications, begin directing their attention to specific models or homesites that could satisfy their needs. The amount of time they spend in one or two homes (that they can picture owning) will influence their decision to buy or to return for another look. Although the total community probably has many benefits, prospects cannot take the whole project with them when they leave. They can take only one or two homes to which they can relate their personal interests and private motivations. Failure to attain that level of involvement during the initial exposure to a potential buyer can cost you the whole ball game.

If each morning you mentally select housing opportunities on which to concentrate your sales efforts, you will be ready to translate that preparation into action and quickly lead your prospects to the inventory you think matches their needs and qualifications. This means you will be able to use the time gained far more effectively when you are face-to-face with your prospects. You will also evidence greater confidence and enthusiasm, which will be reflected in your prospects' attitudes.

The salesperson who uses such mental exercises is like the baseball player who envisions the various pitches an opponent might throw and practices responses to each. The more times the player mentally plays the game, the more home runs the player realizes when at bat. The baseball player can then confidently look forward to the actual confrontation with the pitcher, and be mentally ready to handle anything. That is the way you should meet your own opportunities. Each day, be able to use your product knowledge with confidence and control, and focus your full attention on the specific needs of each buyer.

To help prospects visualize the benefits of owning a particular home or homesite, demonstrate the features in terms of the advantages of ownership. Too many sales associates assume their prospects fully appreciate what they see, or how a house has been designed, or what it will do for them when they own it. These sales associates say:

> *"Just look at our models. If you have any questions, I will be happy to answer them for you."*

The customer replies:

> *"Why are they priced so high? The lots are small and there is no landscaping. Your competition down the street has homes on much larger sites, and the recreation facilities are better."*

Every model home, every site, every inventory unit has characteristics worth demonstrating and dramatizing to qualified prospects. It is important even to know where to stand when you enter a room and how to position your prospects so they experience the full impact of the views, space relationships, and interior dimensions. Prospects should experience involvement with the living pleasures of each housing design, and it is up to the sales agent to understand and translate that feeling into words and emotions.

As Chapter 4 emphasized, certain rooms in a home have more sales impact than others. If there are excellent views, stimulating spatial relationships, or indoor-outdoor extensions of design, these should be illustrated in ways that excite interest and create a desire for ownership. Be able to accent these features in ways that trigger the emotional "hot buttons" of your customers. Help prospects achieve a maximum level of personal involvement, so that they can mentally and emotionally sense the benefits of ownership and the daily experience of living in the home.

On the prospect's first visit to your sales area, you want a favorable decision of some type. The first time a prospect is exposed to your properties, you want a decision—either a total buying decision or a partial buying decision. If you cannot close on a firm contract, at least achieve a mental commitment to return. Getting the customer to make such a commitment is vital to all of your sales objectives. Any degree of mental or emotional involvement achieved on first inspection will normally lead to greater involvement in the future. Perfecting your skills and knowledge to create these commitments will increase your own sales volume.

Controlled Information

One of the ways to achieve a degree of involvement with a prospect is to create a specific reason for coming back. This can be done rather easily by using controlled information. You should have sufficient knowledge about your products and community to be effective, but you do not have to tell a buyer everything you know at once. Telling everything not only takes too much valuable time, it also tends to eliminate the reasons you need to make further contact if the sale is not made on the first inspection.

When a prospect asks a question that can lead to further involvement, it is often wiser to hold your facts as an excuse to establish a future appointment. The kinds of information used for this purpose are those normally involving uncertainty. Maintain your credibility with a prospect and do not appear to be withholding information on purpose. Your need to check on these items should be believable to the customer. The categories most often used are:

- Estimated date of starting construction;
- Estimated date of completion;
- Possession date;
- Availability of specific materials;
- School enrollment information;
- Costs of optional charges;
- Availability of certain types of financing;
- Adjustments of any type;
- Availability of certain sites or units;
- Prices of new units;
- Availability of option changes; and
- Current lender qualifications for financing.

For example, if a potential buyer asks:

> *"Are there any problems getting my children enrolled in the parochial schools?"*

you might reply,

> *"It has been a few days since I last checked on their enrollment status. Let me verify that information. Could you possibly*

> *stop by around 6:00 tomorrow night on your way home from work? I can have the information for you at that time."*

Perhaps you know the exact situation, but such revelation at this particular time will not help you close a sale. You sense the customer is not yet sufficiently involved and time is running out for today's presentation. Whenever you can plausibly resort to verifying information as an excuse for setting up another meeting, it is logical to pursue this approach.

Appointment Cards and Calendars

The proper use of desk calendars and appointment cards can increase the degree of involvement you attain with your prospects. This in turn increases the number of be-backs and call-backs you create.

If you are successful in establishing a time when customers might be able to return, take the time to immediately record the appointment. By doing so in the presence of your prospects, you strengthen the commitment. If they see you write the appointment down, they tend to feel more of an obligation to keep the date. It is wise to have your calendar visible with your activity schedule shown. Better yet, give them your business card and note the appointment time on the back. At that time you might say something like this:

> *"I am reserving 6 p.m. tomorrow for you, Mr. Garcia, so we can have plenty of time to review this proposal and answer all your questions. Meanwhile, I will check on that information you requested. My phone number is here on the card; please call me if for any reason you cannot make it."*

Involvement of Others in the Office

It is even more effective to involve others in the office to further obligate the customer to keep the appointment. For example, you might turn to another salesperson and, in the presence of the customer, say:

> *"Joe, will you be here tomorrow night at 6:00 so I can set aside an hour or so to be with Mr. and Mrs. Garcia?"*

When Joe replies that he had planned to leave early but will stay to help cover the sales floor, you have involved another party and further committed the prospective buyer. This sense of personal commitment can be an important factor in controlling a prospect's attention.

Lot Holds and Reservations

One of the most effective techniques for obtaining a partial decision that can ultimately lead to a complete decision is to involve the prospect with a *lot hold* or *reservation* for a particular property. A lot hold is commonly accepted as an oral or nonbinding written agreement to hold a lot (or home) off the market for a limited period of time until the buyer can complete the purchase details. A reservation is a written agreement that allows the buyer to reserve a site for a specified period of time until certain things are accomplished. One is often used by builders when a firm sales agreement cannot be accepted due to any one or more possible factors—such as unavailability of final prices or incomplete subdivision filing documents. The buyers are not obligated to complete the purchase until they sign a normal sales agreement.

Even if the prospect's interest is only nominal, using a lot hold or reservation tends to increase the prospect's interest, as he or she begins to mentally picture ownership and use of the home. Sometimes builders and developers will not allow these contingency procedures, especially in fast-selling subdivisions. When used with discretion, however, such sales psychology has real merit.

The lot-hold or reservation approach should not be used as a crutch or as a substitute for closing with strength and confidence whenever possible. When you need to focus a prospective buyer's attention on one property and create a sense of urgency about making the total commitment, however, this approach can be valuable. Once the buyer has started down the road toward a decision, his or her will to complete the journey becomes stronger.

There are a number of ways to handle these partial buying decisions. You can actually complete a lot-reservation form, which identifies the specific property, the price, and the deadline for the final decision, or you can handle the reservation informally. Just putting a hold pin on a plot map can serve this purpose if you feel that filling out a document might put too much pressure on a prospect.

Where reservations might tie up valuable inventory, a practical technique is to provide the customer with a first right of refusal or a 72-hour notification if another buyer wants the same property. This kind of contract is frequently used when a purchaser must sell another house or arrange for termination of a lease before making a final decision to buy.

The act of putting a pin or tag on a plot map helps the customers feel they are making their own decisions, and it increases the sense of involvement that must precede the actual decision to purchase. A natural way to handle this is to say something like:

> *"Mrs. McGuire, would you like to put this pin on the lot you and your husband have tentatively selected, while I am completing the home estimate sheet for you?"*

Getting both spouses involved is wise. The wife in particular usually plays a major role in the homebuying decision. Her new home becomes real when she performs this simple act of putting a Sold pin or sign on the control map.

Log Books

When a number of sales personnel are working on the same project, a practical control can be accomplished with a *log book*. This book serves as a registry that officially logs all sales, reservations, and tentative holds, while sales agents are consummating their transactions. Only one book is used, and salespeople are required to check it before starting to write a sale. This device also provides an easy way to start the close. The salesperson merely says something like this:

> *"Mrs. Brian, let's check the subdivision control book to see if that lot is still available."*

This act begins to lead the prospect toward a decision and permits the sales associate to keep the customer involved in the sequence of events that precedes making the actual buying decision.

Ask the Prospect to Do Something for You

If you can involve the customers in doing something for you prior to a future engagement, this involvement can firm up a mental obligation. For example, you may ask them to pick up the latest price list from your competition because a new one has just been published, or to verify the financing offered by your competitor (when you know yours is better).

Tasks you might have a prospect do for you after leaving your subdivision include the following:

- Check prices on competition.

- Check competitors' financing.
- Return the checklist.
- Verify their mortgage balance.
- Check the condition of a sign outside the subdivision.
- Verify employment credits.
- Pick up extra brochures for your files.

MAINTAINING GOOD PROSPECT RECORDS AND PROFILE DATA

Without accurate and easy-to-use prospect information records, it is difficult to follow up the potential business you have generated. Figure 7.2 illustrates a typical prospect card used by new home sales personnel. The front side of this 5x7 card contains the essential information as to the customers' names, address, phone number, basic interests, and products they liked. The reverse side is used to record each call made or each subsequent visit to the sales area until the purchase is consummated or the prospect buys elsewhere.

One of the reasons the card works so well is that it can be easily carried in the coat pocket, while you work the sales floor, models, or on-site inventory. The sales agent can jot down essential facts before they are overlooked or forgotten. Most salespeople prefer cards to loose-leaf paper, which is difficult to transport and use under a wide variety of circumstances.

It is not enough to record names, addresses, and phone numbers. Also note what you talked about during the first visit; which model customers liked best; their motivations and personal interests as revealed through your qualifying conversations; and any other pertinent details needed later when you pick up the phone to call them. Often when you are busy on a high-traffic day, like Sunday, you may jump from one prospect to another without taking the time to record your notes while still fresh in your mind. Several days later as you look at your cards, you say:

"Now, who is that? What did we talk about?..."

The more details you immediately summarize on your prospect cards, the more effective your follow-up activity will be. Identify the little things that will help you trigger the next conversation. Names of children are as important as adults' names—if not more so. When you can refer to children by name, you win the parents' goodwill. Notations should be made of hobbies, likes, dislikes, and clues as to what

Figure 7.2. Prospect card.

```
Name _____  Salesperson _____
Address _____ Telephone _____ (Home)
                                      _____ (Business)
State _____ City _____ ?
                 Zip _____
Where did you first learn about _____ (development) _____
___ Friends  ___ Driving around  ___ Newspaper  ___ Magazines  ___ Other
To which newspapers do you subscribe? _____
If none, which do you usually read? _____
Lot preference _____  Model preference _____
Comments: _____
_____
```

Figure 7.2. (continued)

```
Urgency:  How soon? _____  Now _____  1-3 months _____  over 6 months _____
Income:   Qualifying income _____
Need:     How many bedrooms will you be needing? _____
Why moving? _____
What is maximum price you plan on paying? _____
Have you decided on this general area? _____ Yes _____ No _____ Undecided
Have you tentatively selected a home elsewhere? _____ Yes _____ No
   Where? _____
Follow-up date _____ Due-up date _____ Due-up time _____ Rating _____ Comments

       Why moving?    _____ Family      _____ Recreation    _____ Culture   Best time to call:
_____ Security        _____ Financial   _____ Privacy       _____ Love      _____
_____ Convenience     _____ Prestige    _____ Water         _____ Ego       _____
_____ Investment      _____ Other
```

may be the determining factors in making a homebuying decision. You never really know in advance which bit of information you will need to help you close a sale.

One way to retain prospect information on a busy day is to summarize your thoughts on a cassette tape recorder immediately following an interview. During slower periods of time, you can then retrieve this information and transfer it to your regular prospect control cards.

SELLING AGAINST COMPETITION

Suppose customers say they are first going to look at some other projects before making any decision to buy. How do you try to capitalize on this situation? One approach is to have a complete file of your competitors' brochures and to show the prospect you have already done the research for them. Another is to invite them to make comparisons because you know the quality and benefits of your merchandise will be evident to them when they make their inspection.

Some builders have developed a *competitive checklist* for prospects to use while shopping the competition. The benefits of their products are clearly identified in direct comparison to known competition, and the buyer is invited to look for these key factors when reviewing other housing products.

You can use the competition as a reason to follow up your customers. You might say something like:

> "Mr. and Mrs. Goodwin, here is a 'Homebuyers' Guide' that may prove helpful to you as you look at other new housing products today. We have provided a checklist of key items to evaluate and important questions to ask. Our quality features are listed in this column, and we invite you to check these same benefits in each home you inspect. When you are through today, I would like the privilege of calling to ask how our homes compare with others you see."

With this opening, you have set the stage for a phone call (preferably that same evening) and you have used *reverse psychology* in your selling approach.

FOLLOW-UP

Follow-Up Methods

Phone Calls. If a prospect does not return within two or three days after the first visit, make a phone call. After two or more days without follow-up, you begin to lose the impact of the initial exposure and the urgency of the original interest. You have many justified reasons for making a phone call to a potential buyer who has not returned to re-inspect property. Many of them are identified in this section.

When you pick up the phone, be prepared to follow through on your last conversation and to personalize your comments in a warm and friendly manner. Your first remarks should identify the reasons for the call and then follow with a direct question to force response:

> *"Mr. Benjamin, this is (your name) of (your company). When you were out to see our community last Sunday, you indicated interest in our Yorktown model. I have just learned that one of the finest sites for a Yorktown has just come back on the market due to the previous buyer's unexpected transfer to another city. I would like to be able to show that site to you and Mrs. Benjamin tonight. What time would be most convenient for you?"*

Direct Mail. Except for calls that lead to immediate appointments within 24 hours, all others should be followed with some form of personalized direct mail. Doing so doubles the impact of your phone conversation. A *handwritten* note is better than a commercial-looking letter or promotional piece. Figure 7.3 is an example.

Company Newsletters and Community Bulletins. Many builders and developers of new home communities publish newsletters or company bulletins that tell prospects and owners what has been happening in their new projects. These publications usually include a mixture of local community news, names of new owners, items about personalities in the community, and promotional information about new models, sales, and activities. If your company provides such house organs, you can put them to good use by seeing that copies of all new issues are mailed to those individuals you are still trying to influence. With each copy you should attach a personal note and relate specific items of interest for the particular individual involved.

Figure 7.3. Direct mail follow-up.

> Good Morning, Mr. Benjamin:
>
> Thank-you for visiting our new community last Sunday and for your interest in our Classic home series! During our phone conversation today, you asked about the list of options available with the 2-story plan. I am compiling them for you and will have them ready for your appointment Saturday at 3:00 P.M. I'm looking forward to seeing you then.
>
> Sincerely,
> Thelma Thoughtful

Opportunities for Follow-Up

New Information. Any new information is a legitimate reason for further contact with your old prospects, and you should promptly grasp that occasion to renew interest in your housing merchandise. Perhaps a salable house has come back on the market due to a cancellation, or new prices are anticipated, or a change in possession dates has been made, or a new model has been introduced. Whatever the reason, you can use it to rekindle the flame of interest and open the door to a sale once again.

Special Events. When you are unable to arouse interest and you need a reason to get customers committed to a return visit, you can sometimes make a customer a be-back by using an event that is about to happen soon. For example, you might have a special party or activity that is scheduled that week, and an invitation to attend the event gives you an excellent chance to secure another visit:

> "Mr. and Mrs. Jones, we would love to have you join our residents this Friday night for their annual amateur art festival held at the community clubhouse. It will give you an opportunity to meet some of our satisfied owners and discover how enjoyable life is for those who live at Quail Lakes."

In the process of meeting residents at special functions, customers can experience the benefits of living in the new community. This is one of the better ways to reinforce hesitant buyers and overcome their fears. Planned unit developments and leisure-oriented communities provide excellent environments for this kind of resident-prospect involvement.

It is wise to have a calendar of coming events that you can use to create incentives for customers to come back to the community. If nothing else, you can invite prospects to meet local owners through informal introductions that you structure. Some of the typical events on these calendars are the following:

- Art show;
- Block party;
- Dance party;
- Decorating contest;
- Gourmet cooking class;
- Grand opening of new facilities;
- Newcomers party
- New model opening;
- Open house;
- Pool party;
- Release of new sites;
- Swim meet;
- Sailing regatta;
- Tennis tournament;
- Wine and cheese tasting party.

THE IMPORTANCE OF HIGH-YIELD OPPORTUNITIES

Stone Institute studies reveal that there is a direct relationship between the time it takes to close a prospect from first inspection to contract date and the possibility of ever closing. The longer it takes to obtain a decision to buy, the less is the likelihood that a closing will ever occur. Some salespeople work on prospect cards that are six months old, while neglecting current customers. If you have new leads, pursue them while they are fresh. To let them "cool off" is to risk their never maturing. The longer a customer postpones the decision to act, the more likely it is that the justification will emerge for not taking the action.

A sense of timing is an important part of the process of helping people to buy a home. When the situation is ripe, a decision should be consummated. When the customer inspects the property and shows interest, it is essential to take action in a relatively short time span to bring that interest to fruition. Two to three days is usually the maximum time lapse from first contact to follow-up. If you do not hear from prospects, they should definitely hear from you. Create justified reasons for the call, letter, or visit. The day after the showing, it is appropriate to send prospects a thank-you note or some other literature as a means of sustaining the interest they have shown. Find ways to stimulate incentives to return to see the home or community.

Invest time with those who are closest to the decision point and whose motivations are still aroused, before they have time to begin doubting their instincts. When you run out of current leads, you can always spend time on old ones—but not at the expense of hot prospects.

To determine what is a reasonable time frame for closing new buyers, measure those you or your associates have successfully completed. There is a pattern for the majority of transactions—a week or two, perhaps a month on some prospects—between first visit and the date of signing purchase agreements. Occasionally, an adult retirement community or resort will have a longer time span than is normal for primary housing markets. These are the exceptions, however, not the rule. Research shows that most sales occur within the first ten days to two weeks of initial involvement. Check your own records and remember how important it is to use these critical days to advantage.

CONCLUSION

Effective prospect follow-up and successful be-back programs take personal organization and efficient time management. Most salespeople blame their lack of business on advertising, models, high prices, financing, or the market in general. While these may be contributing factors to sales volume, they are seldom the only reasons. The persistence of a professional new home salesperson in following up every prospect and creating sufficient involvement to generate more be-backs to the subdivision makes a great deal of difference in the sales results realized.

By studying and applying the ideas in this chapter, you will increase your capacity to close sales by increasing the number of be-back opportunities, which lead to sales. It is certain that your volume of sales is directly related to the number of qualified prospects you effectively involve with your homes and who return often enough to finally say yes. Remember, if you cannot obtain a total buying decision, try for a partial buying decision.

8: Closing the Sale

In the real estate sales profession, closing is the name of the game. Everything salespeople do is primarily designed to bring them to the point where they motivate prospects to purchase the builders' products. Everything in the business depends on the salesperson's degree of success or failure in closing buyers. No one gets paid until something is sold. The salesperson plays a vital role for builders, developers, Realtors®, and investors.

This chapter explores the many facets of closing homebuyers. Its goal is to add new dimensions to your closing skills. Before you read this chapter, you may want to evaluate your present closing skills. You can do so by playing the Closing Game, shown in Figure 8.1. Try playing the game again after you have read the chapter, to see how much you have learned.

THE RELATIONSHIP BETWEEN QUALIFYING AND CLOSING

The best qualifiers are invariably the best closers. The more you know about prospective buyers, the easier it is to close them. By quickly discovering prospects' motivations, abilities, and needs, you can capitalize on that knowledge to target for the right property, and close with emphasis on the buyers' dominant motivations.

The approach you use in closing should be predicated on the information uncovered at the beginning of your relationship with the prospect. Successful closing is really an extension of the other steps in the sales process: qualifying, selecting, involving, and controlling prospects.

Thus, the first step to sharpening closing skills is to improve your ability to qualify. The more experienced you are in this vital area, the

186 New Home Sales

Figure 8.1. The Closing Game.

QUESTIONS

So you think you're a *dynamite closer!* If you are, winning the Closing Game will be easy for you. Record your answers below each question, and compare your answers with those in the answer section. A score of 75 or better *WINS!* Good luck.

1. The prospect's repeated response to your closing questions is an emphatic "no." What do you do now?

    (a) Set up another appointment.
    (b) Try for another close.
    (c) Begin questioning the prospect to smoke out the unspoken objection.

2. If you get a *negative response* to your closing question, what should determine how many times you restate the proposition?

3. What is the most important *closing knowledge* you should have at your command?

    (a) Knowledge of the product.
    (b) Knowledge of financing.
    (c) Knowledge of the buyer's ability, timing, need, and urgency to buy.
    (d) Knowledge of the roadblocks to the sale.

4. Name the most frequently committed *closing sin.*

    (a) Not asking for the sale.
    (b) Not structuring the presentation toward the close.
    (c) Asking for the order too early.

5. True or false?

    "A salesperson should begin closing the moment the prospect enters the office."

6. You are well into your presentation when the prospect asks a question about a custom change that you are empowered to satisfy. What do you do?

    (a) Assure him or her immediately the modification can be made.
    (b) Haggle a while, looked pained, and then give in.
    (c) Pick up the phone and "call your boss" to find out.

7. Within the past 12 months, have you attended (or conducted) a training session or read a definitive book on closing sales?

Figure 8.1. (continued)

8. True or false?

    "60% of the time, salespersons *never attempt to close a sale*."

9. Is it good procedure to skip asking for the order and move right into *writing the contract?*

10. True or false?

    "It's too risky to ask a prospect to make a buying decision over the *telephone.*"

11. Is a *price concession* a wise closing technique?

12. Do you go into every sale with a *well-defined objective* in mind?

13. After completing a presentation that includes all the home's *features* and *benefits,* should you now ask for the order?

14. If a manager, do you observe your salespersons in action and make yourself available for closing assistance? If a salesperson, do you welcome such assistance?

15. True or false?

    "It's best to close *early and often.*"

16. If a manager, do you allow your salespersons latitude on prices and inclusions? If a salesperson, do you enjoy such freedom?

17. True or false?

    "Salespersons differ markedly in what they consider to be a close."

18. What should a salesperson do when the customer says, "I'd like to think it over"?

    (a) Show the benefits of living in the home now.
    (b) If there is a benefit to be lost by waiting, bring it up now.
    (c) If there is an added-value concession, mention it now.

ANSWERS

Give yourself five points for each question you answered correctly. Total possible score is 90.

Figure 8.1. (continued)

1. C. It is important to isolate the roadblock to the sale. This is best done through active questions.
2. Time is the consideration here. If it is a slow day, take the time to unwind the prospect and resell him or her on the merits of your offering.
3. C. Knowledge of these buyer characteristics is the most important function in the closing scenario. If prospects are properly qualified, they can be closed more easily.
4. Although not structuring presentations toward a closing and asking for the order too soon are barriers to effective closing, homebuyers rate not asking for the sale as the biggest mistake salespersons make.
5. True, the closing scenario begins with the approach function and continues into a closing posture as it moves toward the prospect's preference for a specific home.
6. C. Although you already know the answer to the prospect's question, picking up the telephone to call your superior is a classic and professional close.
7. Yes, if indeed you have. Nothing beats continual emphasis on how to get the sale done.
8. True. Shocking but true, surveys show that 60 percent of the time, salespersons avoid attempting to close the sale.
9. When you get a signal that the prospect has made a decision to buy, proceed immediately into the contract.
10. False. Many salespersons find that the telephone can achieve a closing commitment with effective follow-up. Then, the contract can be written face-to-face.
11. Yes, but only within parameters established by your company. Price concessions are sometimes vital in making the sale, particularly in a tough market. However, exercise caution, as some prospects can spot this tactic as the automatic giveaway.
12. You should; closing failures are created by not having a game plan in mind and keeping the prospect on the critical path to the sale.
13. Yes. This is a perfect time for a closing question. Too many salespersons get bogged down in financing complexities at this point, instead of using at least a trial close. Also, quick closing saves time.
14. Yes. Such techniques can increase closing efficiencies and serve as an educational guide for the salesperson.
15. True. Time is money, and delaying the sale may only raise unnecessary questions. Keep it simple!
16. Yes. Salespersons who have the power to negotiate exercise more sales power at the point of close.
17. True. There is no one close that is correct for a given situation. All salespersons have their own skills and rhythm.
18. C. This is the best choice. Even so, all three points are appropriate depending upon the closing scenario.

more proficient you will become in leading buyers to favorable housing decisions.

HANDLING THE DIFFICULT DECISION-MAKING PROCESS

When homebuyers start out looking for property, they can mentally choose from the whole world. They are not yet married to any particular subdivision or home. It is the salesperson's role to help them make a decision by first exploring where they are in the decision-making process and then focusing their attention on one or two homes available for sale. Usually, before customers will buy, alternatives must be overshadowed by one specific home they picture owning, and the doors must be closed to further investigation of other properties.

When you fail to effectively involve prospects with the merits of your community, neighborhoods, and homes, you leave the doors open for the prospects to pursue other products and areas before making a final decision. Most homebuyers look at several projects and many individual homes in different neighborhoods before making a final choice. It is essential, therefore, to gain the maximum involvement possible on the first exposure, to have a reasonable assurance of a return visit. Gaining such involvement was covered in the preceding chapter.

Another important fact is that every homebuying decision is ultimately a compromise. Buyers seldom, if ever, get everything they desire in a home. There has never been a perfect home, since economics and other factors limit what can be achieved in any specific situation. *The point to remember is that most homebuyers will compromise their specifications, but seldom their motivations.*

The Weighing Process

Any decision that requires a substantial monetary investment will be weighed carefully. This is certainly true of a decision as important as buying a home. For most individuals, their home represents the largest investment they will make in their lifetime.

The weighing process occurs in the prospect's mind, by balancing the benefits, or *plus factors,* against the disadvantages, or *minus factors.* When the prospect weighs the reasons in favor of buying against the reasons opposed to buying, the decision is based on which way the scale tips. No housing decision can really be made without the buyer going through this mental process. Before you can effectively close, you must be able to offset the prospect's fears and concerns with the perceived benefits of ownership. Remember, *the plus factors must outweigh the minus factors.*

Reinforcing all of the reasons why a prospect should buy, while minimizing the reasons against the decision, is a sound way to build a bridge to agreement, which leads to a closed sale. This means you should know how to interpret all of the benefits of your homes and their environments in ways that will motivate buyers to make favorable decisions.

The buyer always has alternatives open, such as:

- Buying another builder's new home;
- Buying a used home;
- Waiting until more property has been seen;
- Renting a home or apartment for an interim period; or
- Staying where he or she is now.

Unless the benefits of buying your home today can clearly outweigh all the disadvantages and alternatives the prospect is considering, you will be unable to close.

Trust and Credibility

Establish a solid platform of confidence with prospects. Abraham Lincoln once said:

> *"If you would win a man to your cause, first convince him that you are his sincere friend."*

The trust and credibility you gain with prospects in the initial stages of your relationship determines the degree of control you command in the final, closing stages. What you say, how you say it, and the degree of interest you show in your buyer's needs set the stage for your closing efforts.

So many salespeople sound insincere! They say things that sound contrived or false, and they give their prospects an uneasy feeling that they are being misled. This results in a lack of confidence and, in the majority of cases, to resistance to making a decision at all.

To easily lead buyers to a final decision and successfully close the sale, you must win their confidence and stay on their side throughout the entire process. Once prospects exhibit genuine interest in a particular home or homesite, the closing process begins by reinforcing all of the advantages and confirming each plank in the bridge to agreement. You need to establish a solid platform in your relationships with the people involved, so that *credibility and confidence* will hold the bridge together as you move to the closing point. Only by confirming each point of agreement and anchoring it solidly, one by one, will you be able to assure yourself of an opportunity to close. This concept is related to the one that says:

Make it easy for your buyers to make a decision!

Perceived Value

As Chapter 2 discussed, one of the determinants that tips the scales one way or another in the decision-making process is the matter of *perceived value.* Not all real estate values are necessarily perceived by homebuyers. As prospects look at homes, townhouses, and condominiums, they make judgments based on what they perceive or understand in terms of *their past experiences, their knowledge of your local market, including your competition, and their personal motivations as related to real estate values.* For example, many products are more expensive than the customers believe they should be. The actual costs of constructing a new home, developing land, providing amenities, and paying for the costs of services to deliver a finished product are frequently hidden from what a prospect sees and understands.

The values of a new home community may not immediately be evident, and they require explanation and reinforcement to be appreciated and accepted. A potential homebuyer can walk through a series of model homes and never recognize the merit of certain materials, methods of construction, or design features that were expensive to incorporate. Few homebuyers have the training or experience to know real estate values. What they learn usually comes from visual comparisons they make with other available homes in the marketplace or in contrast to present and past housing experiences.

This is particularly true when dealing with the newer and more complex housing environments, such as planned unit developments, cluster housing communities, and similar high-density recreation-oriented projects. When customers look at a townhouse, condominium, or tight-lot, single-family home in an open-space P.U.D., they may not readily see the values that are there. Square-foot costs or construction costs are often much higher than in typical single-family housing because they must include the costs of parks, playgrounds, natural open-space areas, clubhouses, tennis courts, and swimming pools. Unless these values are translated, the result normally will be a lack of interest, because costs related to values appear to be out of line with the buyer's expectations.

The competition plays a major role in this matter of perceived value. It might cost your builder much more to build a particular housing environment than it does your competitors because of a larger investment in land, land planning, engineering, development, utilities, amenities, and quality building materials. Unless your marketing approach and personal sales ability can adequately compensate for these increased costs as related to price, your prospects will gravitate to your competitors' products.

Influencing perceived values is one of the reasons why it is so important to know the competition. Unless you understand what prospects are seeing and perceiving, it will be difficult for you to emphasize the right points and influence the value differences as mentally interpreted by prospects. Knowing the pluses and minuses of your competition is one of the best ways to prepare for sales presentations that will effectively accent the added values of your homes and community.

Remember at all times that prospects are weighing the decision to buy or not to buy. Unless you can make them believe the values are really there in terms of their own motivations, abilities, and needs, you will find it extremely difficult to close. In making a major housing decision, the customer's instinctive resistance may prevent you from being able to overcome the minus factors that exist.

THE FOUR STEPS TO A SALE

The four steps to a sale frequently are summarized as: Attention, Interest, Desire, Action (the AIDA formula). The AIDA formula works well in every phase of the selling process, from qualifying to inspection to closing. In every instance, you must first have the prospect's attention before you can arouse interest. Then you must help convert the interest into desire, which, if well handled, will lead to action and thus a closed sale.

If you use your model homes to advantage, as well as all the other involvement tools discussed here, you should be able to easily gain the attention of any qualified prospect. To arouse interest, raise the level of involvement in specific properties and relate them to personal motivations of the prospect.

All successful closings are the result of increasing involvement, both emotional and rational. The more the buying temperature rises, the easier it is to obtain a positive decision. As the prospect pictures the benefits of ownership and anticipates the pleasures of living in a particular home or community, the accelerated response leads naturally to a positive confirmation.

To help prospects become involved, convert them from being *spectators* into being *participants.* Prospects should actively envision the benefits of ownership and enjoyment. Your words and phrases can be crucial in this phase of the selling process.

A professional salesperson learns to guide the customers' mental reactions through each phase of closing, and to maintain a personal attitude that is conducive to making a favorable decision. As your prospects' interest and enthusiasm increase to new heights, so should your own. Your emotional responses should closely parallel or gently precede those of your prospects. This helps set the stage for the close.

CLOSING TECHNIQUES

Master Your Own Fears First

Successful salespeople are always good closers. They know how to influence their buyers in order to lead them to the desired objectives. They are invariably individuals who inspire confidence. Why? Because they have learned how to harness and control their own fears and indecisiveness. How can you help a prospect to overcome fears when your own still dominate the scene?

It is amazing how many salespeople will not take command of the closing opportunities they are presented. Perhaps it is because they are afraid. Afraid of what? That their prospects will say "no"—or "yes"? Perhaps they are afraid of *themselves.* They are afraid to fail.

Some salespeople interpret a "no" answer as a personal failure, rather than as a professional challenge to continue selling. For this reason, many new home sales agents prefer to prolong the agony of endless inspections and be-backs, or worse, the lost sale, rather than to face the challenge of the closing session.

There is only one way to become a top producer in this profession. That is to have the courage and willingness to take command of the selling process so that you can help prospects firmly. They will seldom buy without moral support and assistance. If you are unwilling to assume this responsibility, you will be a failure to yourself, your buyers, and your builder. You will fail everyone who depends on you.

Assume the Close

The fundamental closing technique is based on the *assumptive approach.* This is more an attitude than a specific closing technique.

When you assume the close, you exhibit confidence that the buyers are going to buy, and you move steadily toward the closing event. Everything you do is designed to make it easy and painless for the buyers to say "yes" when the closing question is asked. Your positive attitude and steady progress toward the destination point help to guide them along the bridge to agreement, one step at a time.

If prospects raise a question or an objection, stop with them until it is resolved, and then proceed with continued confidence that they are going to buy this property—*today!*

Successful salespeople in this business radiate enthusiasm about their profession, especially during the showing and closing process. People who believe they will succeed usually do. Those who think they may fail generally find their own predictions become true in self-fulfilling prophecy. The assumptive technique is a positive attitude which infuses everyone around with the desire to take positive action. *Think success! Think positively! Think enthusiastically!*

A positive mental approach will appeal to customers and help them sell themselves on the merits of your proposition. Assuming the sale means acting and talking as though purchasing the home is a foregone conclusion. You know they are going to buy this property from you—today! That confidence infects your buyers, and, as a result, they develop increasing enthusiasm for your proposal—provided you make it easy for them to express themselves along the way.

Help Buyers Express Their Feelings

Unless buyers open up to you and feel free to express themselves, you may never hear the clues you must uncover, and the questions that must be resolved, before the final decision can be made. The most effective salespeople serve as sounding boards for their prospects' thoughts and emotions. They make it easy for prospects to talk about their reactions and ask questions. This is done by emphathizing with customers and reflecting genuine interest in each response they make as they are inspecting the property or discussing the pluses and minuses of ownership.

Be careful not to get in the way. Do not impose your own likes and dislikes on your buyers. Some sales associates tend to create more problems for themselves than they can resolve. Acting as a sounding board means merely reflecting what buyers feel or say and sharing their real feelings. That permits them to come closer to making a decision. In building the bridge to agreement, you do this in a positive way, one step at a time. Most buyers resist making major decisions and avoid situations that can upset their mental security.

In selling a new home, try to reduce the painful aspects of the sale by making it easy for the customer to agree with you and maintaining a relationship on which your final closing can be based. Help customers reach the big decision without having to say "yes" to the main issue or to think too hard about the pros and cons of buying. Try to eliminate fears before they are major hurdles. The sale should be the automatic result of a smooth, pleasant series of minor agreements and events which you construct into an assumed closing.

The conversation is kept on a plane of confidence leading the customer from point to point, without placing undue strain on the thinking processes. To maintain this feeling, never argue or disagree with a prospect. Instead, do everything possible to keep open a channel of communication and maintain a meaningful relationship that will allow you to close. *In essence, stay on the customer's side.*

Build Agreement

When a buyer has said "yes" many times within a short period, it is almost impossible for him or her to think negatively. The mind can be conditioned to a favorable decision by obtaining agreement on many minor points prior to the major question. Every nod, silent acceptance, or affirmative answer brings you one step closer to a signed purchase agreement. After many favorable responses, the buyer is usually helpless to reverse the trend when presented with the concluding question.

When buyers agree that the home has a cheerful kitchen, a superb view, an outstanding architectural design, they are unconsciously selling themselves on the merits of owning the property. You help them to create a pattern of positive thinking in which to frame the picture of possession. Your questions are actually positive statements with a question mark injected to confirm the buyer's attitude.

These kinds of questions are known as affirmative questions or *tie-downs.* Professional salespeople tend to use them automatically. They develop a particular manner of speech which works automatically as a closing technique. They usually tie their listener down after making a positive statement. The phrases they use to obtain mental agreement from the prospect include:

Don't you agree?	*Doesn't it?*
Isn't that right?	*Wouldn't it?*
Don't you?	*Don't you think?*
Isn't it?	*Wouldn't you?*
Aren't you?	*Aren't they?*
Can't you?	*Right?*

This is an easy way to control a prospect, *isn't it?* You can gently force them to nod their heads in agreement, *can't you?* And the result is a series of "yes" responses, which lead to an easy closing; *isn't that right?*

To develop an effective closing approach, use this simple technique whenever engaged in any conversation that offers an opportunity to practice influencing your listeners' responses. Build agreement on the things you know they have already accepted and where there is evidence of some potential agreement. At the same time, be careful not to challenge prematurely those areas in which you lack sufficient evidence of agreement, for that can have a negative effect on the buyer.

Where to Close the Sale

When you operate in a controlled sales environment with model homes and an adequate sales facility, the specific location in which you close the sale is not difficult to select. Unless there are extraneous factors that make it difficult to control the conversation, the best location would be in your own sales office, or in a quiet corner or room where you can proceed uninterrupted with the details. This is not always possible, however, especially if you are working on a high-traffic project and there are only a limited number of salespeople to service that traffic.

One of the most important points to keep in mind is that you must have control, no matter where you start to close the sale. Control is achieved in many ways. One way is by visual contact. Place yourself close to prospects, preferably seated, so that you have an opportunity to see their eyes, watch their expressions, and use your own communicative abilities to overcome the resistance you may experience during that period. This also means having a comfortable place where there is likely to be no interference. Certainly, the matter of physical comfort —the temperature of the room and environmental conditions—is a factor in how the buyer will feel during the final closing moments.

Most effective sales offices today are designed so that the closing area is more or less a conversational center, rather than a formal business office. It might have a round table and comfortable chairs in a pleasant environment so there will be no great psychological pressure on the buyers.

Avoid having distracting visual elements in the sales environment that could interrupt customers' thoughts or cause you to lose control. A cluttered desk is an obstacle course to a sales agent. When buyers are trying to make decisions, they should not be reading yesterday's newspaper, or your notes about another transaction, or any other information that could lead them away from your specific objective. It is best to have a clean and pleasant environment in which to close.

When you start to close, you should be able to finish in that same location. Your model homes or inventory can provide initial closing areas where the decision to buy is made on the assumptive basis. Sometimes you can complete the closing on-site at the property. Normally, return to the sales office where you have the necessary information and can provide the answers customers seek. It is unwise to start the close until you can carry it to a successful conclusion in a controlled setting.

Sometimes, you need an excuse to get your buyers back to your desk or to the sales area. This can be accomplished by having maps, brochures, or other information to give them before they leave. Once you reach the spot where the information is located and as you prepare it for them, you can begin the closing process using what is known as the *scratch pad technique,* or *summary close.*

The scratch pad technique is one of the easiest ways to get into the close without making it painful or obvious to the buyers what you are doing. Take a piece of paper—the back of a brochure or an estimate sheet—and begin to summarize the information you want them to take with them.

> "Mr. and Mrs. Smith, let's make a few notes about this particular home before you leave. Now the price is $86,000, and the initial investment would be $26,000, based on the amount you had planned for the down payment. That means the balance would be $60,000 at 14.5 percent. The monthly investments would include. . . ."

Figures 8.2 and 8.3 are sample home estimate sheets used by new home salespeople. These are a more formalized approach to the scratch pad technique. They are designed to allow the agent to list the price, options, or extras in a natural sequence and to provide a summary of the points agreed upon during the qualifying and inspection phases. They provide a natural bridge that leads to the closing questions.

AVOID INTRODUCING TOO MANY DECISION-MAKING SUBJECTS

As you will note on the sample home estimate sheets, a limited number of items are introduced on the forms. This helps to avoid the problem of having too many things for the prospect to think about

Figure 8.2. Sample home estimate sheet.

```
                            HOME ESTIMATE
                                       DATE _____

        PLAN NO.  _____
        LOT NO.   _____
        TRACK NO. _____
        BASE PURCHASE PRICE _____   $ _____
               Item 1 _____         $ _____
               Item 2 _____         $ _____
               Item 3 _____         $ _____
                     TOTAL PURCHASE PRICE          $ _____
        CASH PAYMENT REQUIRED:
               Down payment                   $ _____
               Closing costs                  $ _____
               Impounds, interest and prorations
                 (approx.)                    $ _____
                                  TOTAL    $ _____
               Less deposit paid              $ _____
               BALANCE DUE ON OR BEFORE _____, 19 ___ $ _____
        LOAN AMOUNT
               First _____          $ _____
                     (Interest)  (Term)
               Second _____         $ _____
                     (Interest)  (Term)
               TOTAL LOAN AMOUNT                   $ _____
        MONTHLY PAYMENT
               Principal and interest (First) $_____ (Second)$_____ Total $_____
               Current club dues                   $ _____
               Tax and insurance impounds          $ _____
               TOTAL MONTHLY PAYMENT               $ _____
                               _____
                                 RESERVATION
               I (we) wish to reserve the above property as of this date.
                             SIGNATURE(S) _____
        _____
                                OFFICE USE ONLY
                     Received by Inventory Control _____
```

Figure 8.3. Sample home estimate sheet.

```
                         HOME ESTIMATES

                                          Date _____
         Buyer _____       Phone _____
         Lot _____ Block _____     Addition _____
         Model _____ Elevation _____

         BASE PRICE                       $ _____
         _____            $ _____
         _____            $ _____
         _____            $ _____
         _____            $ _____
         _____            $ _____
         _____            $ _____
         _____            $ _____
         _____            $ _____
         _____            $ _____
         _____            $ _____
         _____            $ _____
         _____            $ _____
         _____            $ _____
         _____            $ _____

                    TOTAL                 $ _____
```

during the closing process. If there is a long list of options and extras or a variety of financing alternatives, you can lose control of the closing decision simply due to the confusion and indecision that can occur in the customer's mind. Customers can be overwhelmed by questions such as:

> *"Should we take this or that?"*
> *"How much more is it going to cost?"*
> *"Which style looks best?"*

The more the buyers have to think about, the greater the risk that they will decide to think it over or postpone the decision. That is why most of the professionals in new home sales consciously limit the areas of decision-making their buyers must consider. This can be done in a number of ways.

One way to avoid confusion is to not display all the options and extras in openly visible places if the selection is complicated. The lists of alternatives can be kept in controlled areas or in personal pricing binders not available for casual perusal by customers.

Another approach is to include a package of extras built into the total price. For example, rather than quoting a base price plus a fireplace, dishwasher, air conditioner, and similar options, the salesperson might say:

> *"That home, with fireplace, dishwasher, and air conditioner, is $86,500."*

In this manner, the sales associate assumes that the customer will want all of these items and avoids debating each option individually. This is often sound strategy when you are trying to make it easy for your buyer to make a final decision.

Another way to handle these choices that can become closing obstacles is to concentrate on the major decision of the specific home and site, leaving the minor elements for a separate discussion. For example, you might say to your buyers:

> *"Mr. and Mrs. Jones, let's make sure we have the right home and homesite you want. We can decide later on the other things you may want to include prior to construction. Once we have found the right location, you can take time to work out the little details you have in mind to personalize your home."*

In this way, you do not try to handle all of the minor decisions while the big one is being made. Later, after the major choice has been confirmed, the customers will have time to pick and choose minor items. The more you eliminate obstacles to decision making, the easier it will be to close your homebuyers.

THE CLOSING QUESTION

How to Ask the Closing Question

In order to close any sale, you have to *ask for the order.* That should seem rather obvious, but it is surprising how many salespeople fail to take this final step to closing a sale! The right to close is earned by all the steps that preceded, but you should capitalize on that right and not assume your prospect will say to you, "We'll take it!" It is true that once in a while that is what happens, but it is rare and certainly no way to program your sales career!

What the Closing Question Is

An affirmative response to a closing question can be transferred to the closing document. Real estate salespeople normally ask closing questions on one or more of the following topics: (1) the legal names the buyers desire to appear on the deed; (2) the nature of title arrangements, such as joint tenancy versus tenancy in common or community property; (3) the preferred date for possession; (4) the size of the down payment or initial investment; (5) the size and type of mortgage to be secured; (6) the size of the earnest money deposit; (7) one or more options or extras that are decided upon at the time of purchase; and (8) the investigations of any contingency that has to be resolved before the transaction can be completed.

Following is a list of examples of ways to ask these questions:

1. The legal names the buyers want to appear on the deed: *"How do you want your names to appear on the deed and other title instruments?"*

2. The nature of title arrangements, such as joint tenancy versus tenancy in common: *"How do you prefer to take title: in joint tenancy, tenancy in common, or community property?"*

3. The preferred date for possession: *"The home is estimated to be completed by June 1. Would possession on June 10 be satisfactory?"*

4. The size of the down payment or initial investment: *"The minimum initial investment for that model home would be $26,000. Would you prefer to use the minimum or to increase the size of your down payment?"*

5. The size and type of mortgage to be secured: *"Based on our discussions, it would appear that an FHA loan of $64,000 will meet your needs. Will that be satisfactory, Mr. and Mrs. Jones?"*

6. The size of the earnest money deposit: *"The down payment is $16,000. How much of that can you comfortably handle today?"*

7. One or more options or extras that are decided upon at the time of purchase (including elevation choices): *"Would you prefer the standard or deluxe fireplace for the family room in your new home?"*

8. The investigation of any contingency that must be resolved before the transaction can be completed (for example, the sale or trade of a used home): *"It will take us a few days to investigate the potential equity guarantee of your present home. When will it be convenient for you to have our Realtor® and appraiser inspect the property?"*

It is obvious that a positive answer to any of these questions automatically allows the salesperson to start writing the purchase agreement. *The sale is assumed once an approval or nonresistant answer is given.*

TYPES OF CLOSES

The Minor Point Close

One of the ways you can help to smooth the path to a decision is by avoiding the big question in favor of a minor question. As we have already emphasized, most people resist facing big decisions. The bigger the decision, the greater the tendency to avoid making it. By posing an easy question on a minor point, you can focus attention on some small element of the sale that, when answered, can lead to a close. Assume that the prospect has decided to buy and that now the only decision to be made is on some minor point or a choice between two of them. This assumptive attitude, coupled with an easy question, prevents a direct confrontation and lets the buyers feel that they made their own decision.

Most of the preceding examples of asking closing questions are applications of this minor point approach.

The Alternative Choice Close

One way to achieve an acceptance of your proposal is to isolate your closing question on the choice between minor alternatives. No matter which one is selected, the sale is confirmed. *"Which would you prefer"* is usually the best way to begin the alternative choice close:

> *"Which would you prefer in your new kitchen, the mahogany or birch cabinets?"*
> *"Which exterior elevation of that floor plan do you prefer, the colonial or the ranch?"*
> *"Would you prefer the sliding glass door to the patio or the French doors we show in the model?"*
> *"Which would you prefer, the finished recreation room for an additional $2,500, or to finish it yourself after you move?"*

This closing concept can be applied to almost any sales situation. It is an effective means of helping buyers negotiate that last hurdle before making the total commitment.

A True Story. A few years ago I had an opportunity to illustrate the power of this closing technique. In one of our new lakeside communities of semi-luxury, single-family homes, a doctor and his wife were having extreme difficulty in making a decision to buy a particular home. Our sales manager had, on repeated Sunday afternoons, tried to extricate the decision to buy, but without success.

On the third Sunday afternoon, I happened to be present when the couple returned for another visit. During previous discussions, the salesperson had informed me about their apparent dominant motivations and interests. The wife was impressed by the efficient floor plan and the fact that the main bedroom was located on the first level of the home and featured a private bath. The wife seemed more interested in the house than the doctor was, according to the salesperson's observations. The doctor was intrigued primarily by the fact that we featured a three-car garage. He had mentioned to our representative that the garage might be a good place for his power tools, which he used to pursue his hobby of making furniture and other things.

When the couple arrived that afternoon, I was introduced to them, and I took the occasion to see if a sale could be finalized. I said:

> *"Dr. Johnson, I understand you and your wife like our Victoria model."*

He replied:

> *"Yes, it is a lovely home."*

I suggested that I accompany them as they looked at the home again. We then strolled leisurely through the home and chatted about many things. I did not discuss the outstanding characteristics of the home because, by now, the Johnsons knew them better than I did.

We talked about their children, his profession, and her hospital volunteer work. Finally, we came around to discussing furniture making. It was easy to see that this was a real motivation in the doctor's life. After about 20 minutes of relaxed conversation inside the home, I said,

> *"Doctor, would you come with me for a moment? I have a question I would like to ask you."*

He followed me into the garage, where I strategically placed myself in the space the salesperson had indicated might become the doctor's workshop. Then I asked the following question:

> *"In designing this home, we had planned to install some extra electrical outlets for people like yourself who like to work with power equipment. Where would you prefer to have the 220 electrical outlet and power control switch—here or there?"*

The doctor thought for a moment and said, "Here." At that moment, when he chose the location, the sale was closed. We walked back to the sales office and wrote the purchase agreement. The position of the electrical outlet proved to be the minor point key in the entire buying decision.

Remember this story whenever you are having difficulty closing a sale. Find some point related to the motivations of your prospects, and try this approach. If the other items involved in the weighing process are balanced toward the positive side of the scales, the odds are in your favor.

Closing on the Buyer's Questions

Customers often give you closing cues. They ask questions that indicate they are either ready to buy or within easy range of taking the final step. Whenever prospective homebuyers ask you a question that you can convert into a closing opportunity, take the initiative to force the issue. For example, prospects might ask,

> "When will that home be available for possession?"

You might say,

> "That home is scheduled for completion by May 10. Would that date be satisfactory for you?"

In another instance, the customers might ask:

> "What kind of financing arrangements are you offering on this home?"

Now, instead of describing all the variables, convert the question into a closing opportunity:

> "The financing, Mr. and Mrs. Smith, depends on the size of your initial investment. How much were you considering for the down payment?"

In another example, the prospect asks:

> "Would the builder consider extending the master bedroom wall an additional two feet so that our king size bed will fit into that room?"

The salesperson could reply:

> "Mr. and Mrs. Jones, I have no authority to make that commitment, but I can take your proposal to the builder. Would you like me to include that adjustment in the purchase agreement?"

Obviously, you would use this approach only if you knew in advance that some flexibility was possible.

The key point is that you should take advantage of any question that can become a closing alternative. Do not just answer the question. Answer customers' questions with questions, and you will frequently close much more easily and sooner. As emphasized before, there is more money to be earned in this profession by knowing the right questions to ask than by knowing the right answers.

Closing on the Buyer's Objections

Sometimes an objection can also become a closing opportunity. For example, a buyer might say,

> "Your monthly payments are $200 higher than what we are paying now—and more than I think we can afford!"

Your approach to convert to a close could go like this,

> "Mr. Green, is that the only thing standing in the way of your buying this home today?"

If he says "yes," you then continue on the assumption you are going to make this the final objection:

> "In other words, you feel that the additional $200 a month is just too much to invest in the home? Is that right?"

You do this to help smoke out the real objections. There is little point in tackling an objection that is not a valid one. Conversely, if he again confirms that this is his only objection, you proceed:

> "Mr. Green, if I can prove to you that what appears to be $200 extra is actually a savings of more than $60 a month, you will have nothing to prevent you from confirming the purchase of this home, right? Now, let me show you why that is true . . . ."

Now on paper, and with good visual control, you summarize the facts to dramatize your point:

> "Where you live now, you are paying rent of $550 a month. Is that right? None of that rent gives you any tax benefits? It is a 100 percent lost investment in terms of your income tax. However, here, where the payment is $750 a month, approximately $700 each month will be a tax deductible expense. In your tax bracket, that is about $210 in savings each month. In addition, $50 a month is forced savings going into the principal amount of the loan and reducing the balance you owe. Thus, your actual equity at today's prices is increasing by that amount

> *each month and accelerating year by year. This means you are saving $260 of that $750 each month, and your net cost is only $490, or $60 less than you are paying now.*
>
> *"What's more, your home will appreciate in value each year, and when you decide to sell, you will get all or a substantial portion of the $490 a month back in the form of real gains in value and equity. Some homebuyers have been able to live virtually rent-free based on these combinations of ownership benefits.*
>
> *"Now that answers your question doesn't it? How soon would you like to make the move?"*

This is an example of converting a seeming objection into a power close. Of course, you should know your facts well enough to make a convincing presentation. It is also important to remember that this closing technique works only on those objections you know you can answer; otherwise, they may become *final* objections! In the preceding sales process, you should have built bridges to agreement, so that now you do have the right to ask for a decision once the objection is satisfactorily answered.

Third-Party Stories

Because of the tension that often arises when closing a sale, buyers may extend objections, difficult questions, and excuses for not making a buying decision now. The truth frequently is that they are beginning to feel mounting psychological pressure as they head toward a final decision point. It is important to ease their discomfort and make them realize that their feelings are perfectly normal.

As Chapter 5 illustrated, this is a good time to tell them a third-party story. Use the key words *feel, felt,* and *found.* Following is an example:

> *"I know how you* feel, *Mr. and Mrs. Baxter. It is perfectly normal to* feel *this way. Mr. and Mrs. Harvey* felt *the same way before they bought their new home from us. They are the lovely couple who will be living across the cul-de-sac from you. They told me the other day that now that they have bought their new home they have* found *so much pleasure in picking the furnishings and making their plans that they are truly excited about the whole experience!"*

Just as in handling objections, the use of true third-party stories can help you overcome buyer resistance during the final closing session. It is easier for customers to be objective about other people's reactions and experiences than about their own. By using appropriate true case histories, you can educate and motivate your prospects at the same time. To prepare yourself for these difficult moments, index all the examples, situations, and case histories that may be used to help resolve these difficult closing obstacles, and refer to them in your quiet moments when you are not working with customers.

BODY LANGUAGE AND BUYING SIGNALS

People unconsciously communicate their reactions and feelings in a variety of ways. Positioning oneself in relationship to another can reveal inner thoughts and feelings. Facial expressions, hand movements, and actions can say more than words in many cases. Knowing how to interpret these nonverbal means of communication is a critical selling skill.

Some of the body language signs that indicate you are on the right track and headed for the close are when customers:

1. Relax their position—especially when they open up their hands.

2. Assume a more pleasant expression.

3. Uncross their legs.

4. Evidence an unusual sparkle of interest in their eyes.

5. Lean toward you as you proceed.

6. Pick up the contract or some other related document and begin reading it.

7. Smile favorably at each other during key sales points.

8. Show agreement by nodding heads as you make your sales points.

9. Draw closer to you in the physical setting as well as in body positioning.

Some of the nonverbal signs that people exhibit when they are under tension or losing interest are:

1. Tightening fists or clenching them in constant movement.
2. Rapping the desk or arm of chair with rolling motion of fingers.
3. Moving chairs away from you or moving their bodies.
4. Crossing arms suddenly in a locked position across the chest.
5. Shifting eyes from object to object rather than looking at you.
6. Failing to nod head when you are seeking agreement.
7. Frowning at one another or passing silent messages indicating concern.
8. Standing up or shifting uncomfortably in the chair.
9. Putting hand in front of mouth (often a sign of retreat).
10. Looking at watch.

These are just a few of the common body language signals people will send during the closing process. Reading them accurately and understanding their meaning can help your sense of timing and control.

RELIEVING BUYER TENSION

When you become aware that your prospects are becoming increasingly tense, do or say things to help relieve that emotional pressure before continuing the closing process. Empathy is vital in these critical moments. Reach for your prospects before their tension becomes a negative element. For example, express awareness of their fears or concerns by saying, "Mr. and Mrs. Smith, I sense something is bothering you. Am I right?"

Usually such a direct and forthright approach will disarm the prospects, and they will then vent their feelings. Once the steam valve has been tapped, it is normally easier to get back on track again. Hidden fears or objections will gradually erode confidence in making a favorable decision if not released soon enough. You cannot solve anything that does not surface so that you can evaluate and tackle it objectively.

Most professional real estate salespeople also have learned to use humor as a leveler. It helps people to relax. Humor should always be in good taste, and never directed at the customer. Poke fun at yourself, your builder, and other situations, and you will have customers laughing with you.

Sometimes a simple act like dropping a pen or a piece of paper can temporarily take the tension out of a closing session. You can also physically move buyers to an exhibit or another room and change the environment. Doing something together that involves physical response tends to take buyers' minds off the stressful closing process.

Another way to handle tense moments is to change the subject purposely to something lighter and easier to discuss. If customers have children with them, a discussion centering on their offspring is often a good way to help them feel more comfortable. Having them talk about themselves is always a positive move.

Most of all, it is how you conduct yourself that counts. Your own attitudes and actions will be mirrored by your prospects. Do not become so serious and cold that you do not warm up your customers. To cultivate your buyers during closing sessions, try to be as comfortable and as reassuring as possible. You are the catalyst for the emotional vibrations that are generated in the sales environment.

Keep Customers Busy While Writing

Pre-arrange some activities to use at the stage of writing the purchase agreement. Buyers can be kept busy filling out forms or choosing minor items that will take the pressure off the final moments of preparing sales contract and obtaining signatures. This is one of the more critical phases of closing. If buyers watch you write the agreement and have nothing else to do, they may begin to express their nervousness by requesting the whole thing to finding another excuse to postpone the decision. One of the best involvement tools for this purpose is a *buyer profile sheet*. It is a research questionnaire that provides practical data to the marketing staff and gives the husband or wife (or both) something physical to do during the contract preparation stage of closing. Figure 8.4 is an example of a typical profile form.

Involve Others If Necessary

Sometimes it is a good idea to involve someone else in your sales office who might be able to reinforce your customers' interest and help them take the final step. For example, you might call out to another salesperson to verify that a certain lot or home is still available. That sales agent can then respond affirmatively, adding some appropriate comment that gives the prospects confidence that they are making the right decision. If you have a sales manager in the office, or if your builder is close by, introduce your prospects to "the boss." This is a good way to impress them and make them feel important. If you need help at this point, a well-worded question can clue your manager or associate as to what to do or say.

Once in a while, it is advisable to turn customers over to someone else who can carry on for you. A turnover system is often used in other product selling situations, and it has its application to this business as well. Perhaps the manager or an associate knows more about the financing details, construction options, or other items than you do. If that input is essential to the sale, seek needed advice and assurance rather than risk losing the sale. Personality differences also are sometimes a consideration. When you seem to be unable to win a meaningful relationship with your prospects, it may be in your best interests to introduce someone else whose approach could make the difference between success and failure. Never let your ego stand in the way of success.

THE SALESPERSON'S APPROACH

Maintain Control

Ultimately, your ratio of closed sales to the opportunities available will depend on how effectively you gain control of prospects and the sales environment. The more thoroughly you learn the art of controlling the sales conversation, the easier it will be to help prospects make favorable buying decisions.

You have to *create a climate of acceptance* before you can close your customers. Throughout the qualifying and closing phases, *command and maintain attention,* or you will lose control. Your purpose is always to *build a bridge to agreement,* by nailing down one plank at a time.

The real key to control is *asking the right questions,* because you can close only when you have enlisted the thoughts and emotions of your potential buyers. The kinds of questions suggested in this chapter should be practiced and perfected with every opportunity. These are only examples—you will undoubtedly have many others to use in your own sales conversations.

Whenever you seem to be losing control of your prospects, try some of the suggestions given here. Involve clients in visual displays, or encourage them to talk about their own interests. When outside influences interrupt the flow of conversation, pause for a moment, relax your buyers, then regain control by re-indexing the last few points on which you have reached agreement. Try to set up your final closing effort in a controlled environment, not easily interrupted, to ward off

Figure 8.4. Sample buyer profile sheet.

```
                        BUYER PROFILE FORM
                                              DATE OF
COMMUNITY _____     CONTRACT _____
BUYER NAME _____     DATE _____
                                              NO. IN
BUYER NAME _____     HOUSEHOLD _____
SALES REPRESENTATIVE _____     MANAGER _____
------------------------------------------------------------------------
HOME PURCHASE INFORMATION
Site location _____ Model/Type _____
Price _____ Additional Items _____
Initial investment _____ Mortgage amount _____
Trade or contingency _____
Other notes _____
------------------------------------------------------------------------
PREVIOUS RESIDENCES
Current address _____ Phone _____
City _____ State _____ Zip _____
Years there _____ Type _____ Own _____ Rent _____
Prior address _____ Years there _____
City _____ State _____ Own _____ Rent ____
Type _____ Reason for move _____
Number of prior residences _____ No. owned _____ Rented _____
------------------------------------------------------------------------
PROFESSIONAL DATA
Head of household _____ Position _____
Name of company _____ Location _____
Years associated _____ Years in profession _____
Other professions in family _____

Estimated total annual family income: $_____
Age of head of household _____ Age of spouse _____
------------------------------------------------------------------------
SCHOOL INFORMATION
                                       Number of children at home _____
Pre-school (under 5) _____ Elementary (5-11) _____
Junior high (12-15) _____ Senior high (16-18) _____ Older __
Notes (special needs) _____
```

Figure 8.4. (continued)

RECREATIONAL INTERESTS

		Fishing _____	Other: _____
Golf _____	Hiking _____	Surfing _____	_____
Tennis _____	Skiing _____	Bicycling _____	_____
Swimming _____	Boating _____	Gardening _____	_____

SOURCE OF INFORMATION ABOUT HOMES

TV _____ Other: _____

Referral by owner _____ Newspaper ad _____ _____
Referral by others _____ Radio _____ _____
Signs (billboard) _____ Direct mail _____ _____
Signs (on-site) _____ Publicity _____ _____

HOUSING RESEARCH

Did you consider used homes? _____

Months looking _____
Did you work with a broker? _____

Number of projects investigated _____
Number of homes seriously considered _____

Number of homes inspected _____
Other notes: _____

MAJOR CONSIDERATIONS   (Please identify the major reasons you selected our homes and this model site):

_____
_____
_____
_____

© Copyright The Stone Institute, Inc.

negative influences that could adversely affect your objectives. Constant awareness of customers' reactions and a sensitivity to their inner feelings will help you to work in a way that relieves emotional pressure. Your own responsiveness is your best safeguard against losing control in the critical moments of leading prospects to the closing point.

Work from Strength

Some salespeople approach buyers with hesitancy and fear. They deal from an inferior position and thus lose the customers' respect and the control needed to realize success. They always seem to be in retreat. People admire and respect strength. This does not mean physical prowess, but character and self-control. People who are straightforward and sincere and who possess high self-esteem are attractive. They give others confidence to offset their own doubts and fears. In the presence of such people, others are more willing to do positive things.

Do not retreat from your buyers. Stay with them. When they challenge you to make concessions that you know you cannot, be open and honest:

> "Mr. Kline, I would like to do what you ask, but it is impossible. You see, we have carefully designed our homes to provide an outstanding value. If we were to make the changes you suggest, the costs would be prohibitive for you and other buyers as well.
>
> "Here is what I suggest: Why don't you live with the home the way our architects and planners have designed it, at least long enough to see if you really want the changes you suggest? Afterward, if you decide to make them, we will have one of our subcontractors handle the matter for you on a separate basis. This way, we can protect the price and values for you and other homebuyers."

Making unauthorized concessions weakens your position with your builder as well as with your buyers. Owners in a new community talk to each other. If you do something for one and not another, you and the company will ultimately pay the price in dollars or goodwill (which amounts to the same thing).

INITIATING THE CLOSE

The Importance of the First Step

The first step, on the journey to a sale, is always the most important. Unless that step is taken, none will follow. Therefore, obtain either a total buying decision or a partial buying decision from the prospect, as recommended in Chapter 7. A partial buying decision can be just an appointment to return for another inspection. It can also be a lot hold, a 24-hour reservation, a contingency agreement, or a first right of refusal.

Whenever you sense you cannot carry your customers to the ultimate goal in one single visit, do the next best thing. Extract some type of decision that begins the process of involvement, which may lead to a final commitment. Within your company policies, use your discretion as to the form of involvement that will be most practical for all concerned. The lot hold or reservation is undoubtedly the most popular means of achieving this objective. Merely pinning a name on a homesite can make the buyers feel they have really purchased a new home. The mental commitment is actually more important than the written document, since people often cancel sales they did not fully believe in or accept at the inception of the transaction. Mentally moving customers into one home on their first visit is one way to be sure of having a second opportunity to complete the sale.

Using Log Books to Start the Close

In most new home communities, there is an official master sales log book or site control plot plan that is used to record all sales, reservations, holds, and available inventory. When a number of salespeople are working the same project, this procedure is necessary to avoid mistakes or duplicated sales. If you have such a master inventory control device, you can use it to start the close. You might say something like:

> *"Mr. Johnson, let me check the subdivision control book to see if that homesite is still available...."*

This gives you an excuse to go to the room or place where you want your prospect to be for a trial close—and your statement is part of the assumptive attitude that may lead to a favorable buying decision.

CONFIRM AND REINFORCE THE BUYER'S DECISION

Perhaps you have discovered what many new home sales agents soon learn—*the people you close too fast are usually the first ones to cancel out.* Fast closes often result in cancellations or frustrating situations. The after-buying blues set in because the mental plus and minus evaluations have not yet occurred. Buyers go back to their old homes or apartments and say:

> "What did we do? Are we sure we did the right thing? We really haven't seen very many homes yet. How do we know if that was the best buy? That salesperson sure fast-talked us into that one! Let's call and say we have changed our minds!"

If financing is involved, customers can arrange to disqualify themselves by the way they handle mortgage processing. Meanwhile, a valuable home or site is tied up when it could have been sold to someone else. To avoid these problems, take some additional steps following a fast close to lessen the psychological impact of after-buying blues.

Tell Them What to Expect

Once you have secured a quick buying decision, reassure new homeowners of the wisdom of their decision. Recapping the benefits and motivations that triggered the sale in the first place reinforces the factors that justify the big step. This is like renailing the planks in the bridge. You want to be certain it is strong enough to withstand the pressure of buyers' remorse.

Even more important, tell them what to expect:

> "Mr. and Mrs. Cox, you have made a wise decision. However, I know you are going to feel like most new homebuyers when you go back to your apartment tonight. You will probably ask yourselves whether you made the decision too quickly, or you may have other questions that we failed to cover adequately today.
>
> "This is perfectly normal, and permit me to assure you that it is the way most buyers feel at the beginning. Please do not worry about this, however, because you have selected the best home at the lowest price, and it truly fits your needs. If tonight you should have any questions, please call me, and we will talk about them, so you can get a good night's sleep. Here is my home phone number."

In this way, you tell the buyers in advance that most buyers have these reactions. Then, when they experience doubts, it should not come as any great shock. Also, your willingness to remain psychologically close to them during this stage will give them added mental security. Carefully reinforcing customers' confidence can prevent many of the cancellations and problems that might otherwise occur.

Keep Buyers Involved After the Sale Is Made

There are always a multitude of things to do once a new home sale has been made. There are construction orders, color selections, material selections, mortgage applications, credit reports, change orders, utility orders, *ad infinitum*. The work just begins when you sell a home. If the sale has been made very fast, it is often wise to delay completion of these other items until a second appointment the next day.

Equally important is to keep buyers involved and happy with their purchase. If left to their own isolated worlds without weekly contact, they can begin to lose interest in their new homes. To avoid communication problems and lost sales, program your daily activities to include follow-through time with all of your unclosed sales—those who have not completed title or possession to their new homes.

Hearing from you weekly can be comforting to your buyers. Besides, it is an effective way to gain referrals. Ask buyers if they know other people who might also be interested in your development, and you may uncover additional names of friends, relatives, and acquaintances. This will be covered in more detail in Chapter 9.

Some salespeople drop occasional notes to their buyers to report the progress of construction on their new homes. A clever idea is to give the buyers a photo album, when the initial agreement is signed, with the first picture taken on their new site. Each week, during construction, send them a photograph of their house as it progresses through the various stages.

The more interest and involvement you achieve during the long period from signing a deposit receipt to the occupancy and settlement date, the better your chances of avoiding misunderstanding and of building a solid base for future referrals.

9: Opportunities Through After-Sales Service

In real estate sales, many things can go wrong between the time a buyer signs a contract for a new home and the time he or she finally takes delivery. You cannot control the weather, the money market, the labor supply, the construction department, or the materials suppliers. You *can* control your own actions and attitudes. This chapter describes ways you can help customers after a sale has been made.

If any matter appears bound for trouble, you should head it off at the pass. Let the direct approach be your first approach. It is far worse to brush something under a rug and hope it will go away. In most cases, it will not go away, it will only get worse.

GENERAL FORMS OF AFTER-SALES SERVICE

Listening to Customers

Let buyers vent their disappointments and their frustrations; the act of expressing them relieves some of the tension. Maybe you cannot change what has happened, but you can say, "I understand your feelings, and I appreciate the inconvenience and the trouble this has caused you and your family."

Human understanding acts as a salve on the frustrations of life. Saying "I care" helps people over the emotional hurdles of accepting disappointments or delays. Your ability to understand this and to appreciate the significance of emotional involvement as it relates to the final conclusion of the sale is crucial.

KEEPING BUYERS INFORMED

There is an old saying that no news is good news, but that is not necessarily true in your relations with homebuyers. When buyers are told that their home is going to be delivered at a certain time, but the completion date is postponed again and again, they become frustrated and unhappy. The outlets they find for this frustration may be harmful to you and your building company.

The sales department should try to coordinate move-in dates with production scheduling in a way that reduces, if not avoids, the chance of problems. If you think the construction people are being unrealistic when they tell you a house is going to be finished on a certain date, add a few days and tell the buyer the home will be ready around that date and not to count on anything earlier. That is better than having the buyer discover that he or she is not going to get what was promised. Even though the buyer may be hooked and unable to change his or her mind, he or she will become an irritated buyer who will work against you from then on. It is far better to promise less and deliver more than to do the opposite.

Learning to anticipate problems before they occur lessens the impact of the variables that are beyond your control. Suppose, for example, that you sold a home to a buyer who expects it to be delivered in 60 days, and a week later you learn that it is not going to be ready for at least 90 days. Do not wait until 60 days have passed before telling the buyer. He or she may be able to make arrangements to extend the lease on his or her present home or to renegotiate the possession date on the home he or she is selling. The buyer certainly would prefer prompt information to dealing with the shock of discovering at the last minute that the home he or she expected to move into will not be ready for another 30 days. At this point, the buyer has neither the time nor the patience to make adjustments.

Some salespeople believe that the only way to make a dollar is to take it from someone else with no regard for the other person's interests. Selling has always attracted people who are willing to manipulate others for their own personal benefit. Nevertheless, honesty and integrity are basic to true success. If you gain the buyers' confidence and trust, your interest and sincerity will be rewarded with referrals.

The average person is far more sophisticated and educated than many salespeople tend to believe. Today's customers live in an age of communications. The public is more knowledgeable about the environment, housing, and related factors than any preceding generation. Level with customers, and give them the information they need, couched in positive terms that will sustain their confidence. If you fall into the trap of giving them generalized statements or exaggerations, you will only end up in trouble later on.

If you do not know the answer to a question, bluffing is the worst thing to do. Instead, say something like:

> *"I would like to verify that matter for you, Mr. Jones, before I give you an exact answer. There may be new conditions, and I am not absolutely certain that the information that I have at this point is really up-to-date."*

THE PURPOSE OF AFTER-SALES SERVICE

Once you have made a sale by obtaining a purchase agreement from a qualified prospect, you have accomplished your first objective. Now you must pursue other, equally important objectives. Having a signed agreement does not assure you of a closed transaction. Many things can occur to disrupt your prior efforts and cancel the sale you thought you had made.

There are three major objectives on which you should concentrate after you have obtained an agreement to purchase from a prospect. They are:

1. To prevent cancellations;
2. To build more referrals;
3. To reduce new-resident blues.

These objectives are intertwined. What you do to achieve one helps you with the others. The little things you do right make the big difference in this business. For example, an awareness that after-buying blues do occur prior to move-in should accelerate your interest in reducing or avoiding them. Although the preceding chapter touched on this subject, it deserves a more intensive analysis.

SPECIFIC WAYS TO PROVIDE AFTER-SALES SERVICE

Anticipate After-Buying Blues

One of the more common reasons for incomplete sales is known in the trade as *after-buying blues* or the *buyers' remorse syndrome.* It is the result of the emotional experiences following the decision to buy, which lead to doubts and indecision. This reaction usually occurs after the impact of what buyers have done begins to set in. The buyers replay all the concerns they probably felt during the sales process. Unfortunately, however, you are not present to answer their rekindled objections and personal doubts. The buyers are alone or with their own third-party advisors.

The result can be a desire to retreat from the commitment the buyers have made with you, and a cancellation may follow.

Why does this happen, and how can it be prevented? The principal answer to the first question is to recognize that the sale is not completed by a mere signature on a piece of paper. The only sale that really counts is the one buyers have accepted (in their own minds) and are completely prepared to consummate. The bridge to the sale may not hold up under the emotional pressures of the buyers' private review, if the foundation for that bridge was not solidly constructed when the buyers were with you.

A good example of this is the case of a buyer being closed before the salesperson has adequately presented the full message and the buyer has completely perceived the values. Prospects who sign purchase agreements too quickly often cancel just as quickly. When they leave your sales environment to return to their own location, they begin to evaluate the justification for the decision without the full benefit of your presentation to reinforce their own weighing process:

> *"What did we do? Are we sure we did the right thing? You know, we really haven't seen as many homes as we anticipated investigating before we made that decision. Do we really know if it was a good value? That salesman sure talked fast, and we really did not have a chance to ask many questions. Why don't we phone him and tell him we changed our minds?"*

During this period, prospects often seek advice from their close friends, relatives, and associates. That third-party advice, as already emphasized, can be detrimental to your objectives. Prospects' own consultants may say things that interfere with the sale, because of the third-party advisors' own feelings. Sometimes people will make negative comments about the purchase of the home because they believe they could not afford one themselves, and they are too envious to see their friends owning a new one. Others are people who have looked upon themselves as mentors, patriarchs, or protectors and are used to giving advice. They like the role, and when they recommend that their student not do something, and the student complies, they have a sense of power or a feeling of control. However honest third parties' objectives may be in giving advice, the prospective customers are subject to the ego pressure of justifying their decisions to others. Unless they really believe they have made the right decision, they can bend under that pressure.

Also, there are many ways buyers can disqualify themselves from a purchase. Almost all sales are made subject to financing or mortgage approval. If buyers don't want to be approved, there are fairly easy ways for them to arrange for the information on their loan application to disqualify them. It is equally important to remember that during the period of time they are going through this mental process, you have tied up a piece of property that could have been sold to someone else and on which your company and you are depending to maintain sales objectives. You can do a number of things to help cope with the buyers' remorse syndrome.

Prepare Buyers

As Chapter 8 emphasized, once you have secured a decision, particularly one that comes too easily, it is in your best interest to take some additional time to reassure the potential new homeowners of the wisdom of their decision. By going back and covering the key points that led up to the decision and reinforcing the benefits and the motivations that preceded the sale, you can often help buyers justify their actions, so that they can withstand the pressure of second thoughts or outside opinions. For example, you might say:

> "Mr. and Mrs. Hamilton, I want you to know you have made a wise decision. The home you selected is the last one in that current series available at today's prices, and it is a choice location. You're going to be extremely pleased with the benefits of living in our new community and in that particular home.

> "However, I know that you are going to be like most of our new buyers. When you return to your present residence tonight, you will probably begin asking yourselves whether you have made the right decision, or you will have other questions that we may have failed to cover adequately in our conversation this afternoon. I want you to know this is perfectly normal, and I want to assure you that it is the way most buyers feel at the beginning of the new home buying decision. Please do not worry about this, since you have made a good choice. You can rest easy with the knowledge that your new home is an excellent value. Here is some additional information I would like

you to take with you that will answer other questions. Should anything arise that you want to review with me, please do not hesitate to call me at any time. Here is our office number, and here is my personal home number."

If buyers are prepared for the reaction they will probably experience, it will not be as great a shock to them when it occurs. You also enhance your own credibility by telling them what to expect and letting them know that it is a normal human reaction. Your willingness to support them during this critical stage gives them added mental security. Carefully reinforcing customers' confidence levels can prevent many of the cancellations and serious problems that might otherwise develop following the execution of the purchase agreement.

Keep Prospects Involved

Once the buyers have left your environment and gone to their own worlds, they will be subject to all kinds of pressures. They need to be involved in the mental process of moving into the new home and thinking positively about it, so as not to lose interest in that decision.

Handouts. First of all, get the buyers involved at the point of sale. When you tell them what to expect, also give them things to take with them to review. Possible handouts are checklists of things they now should do in preparation for the completion of the sale. Others are pre-move-in guidelines; information about the activities or a schedule of events that are occurring in your community; answers to a list of questions that are frequently asked (these are sometimes prepared by the salespeople and at other times by the company); and additional information that you want them to have as part of the reinforcement package.

Regular Follow-up. Program your daily activities to include enough time to follow through with all unclosed transactions. *If a buyer does not hear from you, the silence can be risking the sale.* You need contact with buyers to maintain their interest. At the minimum, this should be once or twice a week during the pre-closing period. The really hesitant buyers and those with serious doubts should be contacted almost daily.

Follow-up Paperwork. Another way to keep buyers involved is to postpone some of the paperwork that you could have done on the day of the sale, and to find a good reason to get the buyers back the next day or within a relatively short span of time. Making color selections and coordinating elements to go into the home can fit into this category. So can the completion of financial qualification forms, buyer profiles, and the documentation that must be submitted with the sale. During this same period of time, you are targeting for your other objectives—building referrals and reducing new-resident blues. It is a good way to increase your opportunities for additional business. Simply asking buyers if they know people who might also be interested in living in your community or who would like to take advantage of the homesites you have left at a certain price will give you the open door to discussion that may lead to additional sales.

Handwritten Notes. The personal touch is also useful. This includes dropping buyers handwritten notes on the progress of their home while it is under construction or sending them information about people and events in the community. If you sell the home adjacent to the one they bought, that information would be of interest to them, and it keeps them involved in the idea that your community is not just one home. It is a neighborhood of people who have common interests and who will enjoy improved lifestyles together. The more interest and involvement you can develop during the long period from signing a contract to the date of occupancy, the better your chances of completing the sale without problems.

Give Reliable Scheduling Information

There is a tendency in the business to want to promise the moon and then deliver less:

> *"Oh, yes. Your home will be done on time. We can get you in by (specific date)."*

Then delays occur, and you are fudging a little bit to cover your original comments. When things do not go as expected, the potential resident becomes unhappy and then looks for other reasons to be disappointed. When buyers are given accurate information and then kept up-to-date with what is really happening, they feel confident about the decision and the company. Do not promise things you cannot deliver. In fact, it is wise to go the other way. Hedge your bet a little. Give people a margin for error. For example, you might say:

> *"We believe that this home is going to be completed by (date). That's our current projection, but you must allow for the fact*

> *that there are always potential delays caused by subcontractors, weather, and delivery of materials, so please give us a little freedom in that regard. The outside date that we would shoot for at this point might be (and give them that date)."*

Your production schedules should be based on a realistic projection, but they do change from time to time. You cannot control all of the sources of materials, supplies, and activities of subcontractors. Even the most carefully made plans can go astray.

To win, you need more than just the sale, but also your buyers' belief in you and your company. It is certainly more pleasant to work with people who are satisfied than with those who are constantly upset. New-resident blues and referrals, even if you close the sale, can be adversely affected if you have not given your customers all that they expected. They certainly would not want to put their friends into the same situation. They may feel as though they have been hooked and cannot change their minds, but they are irritated. That irritation can be transmitted like a disease to others. Customers that become dissatisfied residents can upset other people who have not yet bought or who are already living in the community. There is an old saying, "Promise less and deliver more, and you will win your customers' loyalty."

Anticipate Problems

By anticipating the variables that seem to be beyond your control, you can lessen them. For example, if you sold a home to a prospect who is going to be making some adjustments, and you know that those adjustments have to be processed in order to be accepted by the company in time to put them into effect, you need to personally supervise seeing that those changes occur and to let your buyers know that you are working on their behalf. Do not wait until it is too late to make the changes. Do not let paperwork drag. If you know that the delivery schedule will change after the sale is made, do not let the buyers discover it several weeks later, after they have made their own moving plans. Get on the phone or drop them a letter and let them know now that there has been an unanticipated problem. If the buyers have to make arrangements to extend their occupancy in their present location, or if they have to renegotiate something, it is easier to do that in the initial stages of the process than it will be later when they are firmly committed to the dates you have specified. It is extremely unpleasant to deal with the shock of having buyers discover, at the last minute, that the home they had planned to move into will not be ready for another

30 days, and that they have to live in a motel or stay where they are. At that point, you will have upset clients and unhappy residents.

Be Honest at All Times

Many salespeople believe that the only way to make a sale is to tell the buyers anything they want to hear, just to get the order. Selling is a profession that has attracted people who are quick to manipulate and to profit from susceptible buyers. Honesty and integrity are basic to real success, however, and are qualities of all professionals. Once you gain the confidence and trust of the buyers with whom you work, you can do almost anything, and they will believe you because they know that you try and are honest. You will be rewarded for your interest and sincere efforts. This builds referrals and opportunities for the future, to say nothing of reducing the friction that can be created when you do not follow through or when you make statements that cannot be supported.

The average prospect with whom you work today is far more sophisticated and educated than most salespeople tend to believe. You are working with people who live in an age of communication and knowledge. The public receives information from a variety of sources, and housing facts are available not only from personal inspection but from all of those who are trying to protect the public in this consumer age. Never bluff! If you do not know something, and customers want an answer, tell them the truth:

"I do not know, but let me check on that, and I will get back to you with the information."

If you fall into the trap of giving people generalized statements or of making exaggerated comments, you will end up with difficulties later.

Make Your Role Clear to Buyers

While your primary loyalty must be to your builder, also recognize that it is vital to maintain working relationships with your buyers. Make them feel they have a friend in the company who is their link to the builder. At times, this can place you in a position of seeming to protect their interests instead of those of your company; you must know the difference. It is the way buyers perceive your actions that really counts. Try to avoid being placed in the awkward position of defending the company against the buyers' interests. In the event that the building company, for some reason, does not perform well on something, you should be able to provide a sympathetic ear to the prospects without generating a lack of confidence in you or the developer. Never speak for management, however, because you are in sales. It is not your responsibility to talk about or judge what is done in production or in other avenues of your builder's operations. You are there as a communicator and a representative of the company to help the customer buy a home.

Recognizing that you personally have no responsibility for repairs, warranties, and property conditions, do not imply that you will handle these items yourself, and do not get involved in trying to resolve all of the issues. Other people in the company have that responsibility. Make clear to the prospects the nature of your role and the limitations of your authority. Matters that are handled by the building department or the customer service department should be directed to them. Those that are a matter of sales management should be directed to the sales manager. Admittedly, this puts you in a difficult position from time to time, but it is important to keep the customers' goodwill while earning respect for your company. Whenever a prospect is unhappy or disappointed, your role is to be a shock absorber, a good sounding board.

Communicating with unhappy buyers can be trying. It is certainly trying for everyone else. Few subcontractors, suppliers, and other people working in the building profession are public relations people, and they may not know how to communicate well with buyers. If you have to be a shock absorber, be a good listener. Let the buyer fully vent his or her accumulated emotions, and do not fall into the trap of acting defensively or negatively just because people are upset. Avoid making statements or comments you cannot support and will probably regret later. Try to build a solid bridge between your buyer and your builder.

There are, of course, exceptions to this rule. Everyone has met people who cannot be satisfied under any condition. These people are emotionally upset and disturbed at all times. They seem to spend their lifetimes finding fault with others. Something else is wrong in their lives. Do not try to be a psychologist or psychiatrist. When in such difficult situations, your best course of action is to respond firmly or to ignore the troublemakers, after a reasonable effort to try to ameliorate the problems involved. Sometimes the best answer is to turn them over to someone else, such as a manager or a third-party representative in the company. Your status as a professional should allow you to develop and maintain attitudes that are based on understanding; doing so will give you confidence to tolerate conditions you cannot change.

Some situations involve personality conflicts. These happen just because people are different. If you reach an impasse with someone, perhaps the injection of another personality will help. Try to avoid, at all costs, being the emotional punching bag for the frustrations of others. You need to maintain a positive mental attitude, and you need to concentrate on new sales and new programs and to solve the problems involved in normal, day-to-day sales activities. If you think you are losing control, talk it over with your fellow associates or with your manager.

Follow the Progress of Undelivered Homes

Although you do not have a direct line of authority with production, keep abreast of what is occurring in each of the sales you have generated. That includes knowing the status not only of the paperwork but also of the property your purchasers have bought. Although it is not your responsibility to see that the home is built or to make any adjustments or changes therein, it *is* your responsibility to know what is going on. After a sale has been initiated, there must be an open communication line with the buyers until they take possession and afterward—to make sure the buyers are happy and satisfied. The buyers will turn to you for information, and they are justified in expecting you to know the status of the home they have purchased.

Each day, or at least once a week, check the production schedule. If the home is in its early stages, look to see if the things that have been ordered as options and extras or changes have been installed. If you spot something that is out of sequence (according to the original projections), report it through the proper channels. Do not negotiate or talk directly with the subcontractors or the people in production unless you are authorized to communicate with them. Personal inspection and watching what is happening is in your best interest and that of the company's. If you are poorly informed, you cannot keep the buyer informed. If you do not know what is happening, you cannot influence some of the things that later may become issues. Do everything possible to avoid misunderstandings.

Also important is doing little things that people may not expect you to do. Someone once said, "Service is the only rent we pay for the space we occupy on this earth." When you go the extra mile and do the things that are not expected, you indicate that your interests are not just monetary or perfunctory. You are thinking ahead to fulfilling their needs. The benefit of this approach is that people will want to return that consideration. In a well-managed company, the lines of communication are fairly well-defined. Production personnel know their roles, and you should know yours. Sometimes, however, it is necessary to short-circuit these lines of communication when there are emergencies that must be attended to immediately.

It is wise to know the people with whom you are supposed to have contact and working relationships. Many little items can be handled without going through a lot of lengthy paperwork. Often, if you take time to make a major report on something, by the time it is received, it is too late to change anything. Do not violate any policies and procedures of your company, but learn how to communicate and coordinate with managers and production people who are fulfilling their assigned roles. Alertness can increase the organization's efficiency and improve customer relationships.

MAINTAIN GOOD CUSTOMER AND SALES RECORDS

Keep a file folder for every site and homebuyer with whom you are working. The building department will have its own system for following through on production schedules, but you need to have, at your fingertips at all times, a record of the transactions on which you are working. This is one way to avoid problems and to be ready to answer questions that arise.

Good records are memory joggers. They help you keep track of things that you would otherwise forget. At least once a week, check on each of the sales you have in progress. In some critical cases, sales need to be checked every day. If file folders are not up-to-date, you will drop behind in your capacity to communicate with buyers and to watch the details that make the difference between a smooth transaction and one that is complicated.

You certainly need to maintain records on the people who are of personal interest to you—not just their names and addresses, but the ages of children, their hobbies and interests, their motivations, details you know about them that will be important in the conversations you have with them. This is the extension of your prospect card into a permanent client referral system. Once buyers become residents in the community, they are more than just normal customers. They are now a solid source of referral business. The more you develop your records as a permanent resource for business opportunities, the easier it will be for you to stay on top of your business. By following these procedures, not only will you avoid problems, but you will also establish friendships with your buyers.

BUYER INVOLVEMENT

There is often a long road between the point of sale in a new home transaction and the final delivery of the home. Many things can happen in the course of the weeks or months of the transition, and any one of these periods of time can cause the buyer to lose interest. Cancellation rates and dissatisfaction go up in inverse proportion to how much people feel a part of the community and the degree to which they are kept informed and involved.

If homebuyers are local residents in the neighborhood or community where you are operating, they probably will be out looking at the home themselves, once a week or more often. That is good. You want them to see their property under construction—not necessarily to walk through it during the dangerous stages of construction, but you want them to have the personal interest that assures you they are not just sitting somewhere waiting for a date to close. It is unusual for anyone to remain isolated from property when he or she has made the decision to move.

Of course, some buyers do come from other states and outlying areas. They may be unable to see the property on a regular basis, but they do expect to be kept informed by phone or mail. In your community, maintain weekly or monthly newsletters or personal notes that can be mailed to customers. Whatever your builder is offering should be supported and supplemented by whatever you can add to it that is of personal interest to your buyers. News articles in the local paper about events that would be of interest to the potential new residents are of help. Notes about people who have moved into the same community or a list of community events that are scheduled for the next few months are excellent items to forward to customers.

Personal letters and newsletters should radiate friendliness and warmth to future homeowners. Involve and interest them in community activities. Encourage them to come to your community and to become part of it while they are still waiting for the completion of their home. If you have a package of amenities, take advantage of recreational facilities such as swimming pools, tennis courts, golf courses, lakes, or whatever you have as elements of common interest. Urge customers to attend special events that are sponsored, giving them a chance to mix with resident owners and feel they are a part of the community before they have taken possession. If they meet and know new neighbors who are satisfied residents, they may also begin to feel that they will not be isolated when they live there. This is particularly true of senior citizens, who are leaving roots and friendships they have established over years in their former location. For them, new-resident blues are partly the result of being uprooted or of feeling a loss of identity with people and things that were important to them in their prior residences.

HELP WITH THE TRANSITION TO A NEW HOME

Even though moving is a change to something better, it is a challenging experience for anyone. This is particularly true if the new property is a primary residence and not just a vacation home. Being uprooted is uncomfortable. When the pattern and fabric of life are disrupted, people become irritable. Anything you can do to help buyers make the transition, with a minimum of disruption in their lives, will be greatly appreciated by them and will assist you in the objective of keeping them satisfied residents.

Pre-move-in kits and support documents are a good way to help buyers organize their move. These kits can be relatively simple. The company you work for may have one. Even if your company tries to provide you with as much as is necessary in the follow-through procedures of sales processing, create and use the things that you find important, subject to your manager's approval.

A moving kit typically includes the following items:

- Inventory forms for furnishings;
- Labels for furniture packing;
- Change-of-address cards;
- A checklist of things buyers should know about the new community;
- A community directory with names and addresses of business services such as electricity and water;
- Background information on the community;
- List of the churches and other houses of worship, social clubs, and other organizations;
- Information on schools and guidelines for registration in those schools;
- For out-of-state purchasers, special information, such as a drivers' license booklet

Figure 9.1 and 9.3 illustrate typical checklists for moving. Figure 9.2 shows a change-of-address card, referred to in Figure 9.1.

Figure 9.1. Sample checklist for moving.

Checklist to Organize Your Move

Prior to move
Prepare inventory of belongings. Obtain moving cost estimate. ☐
Throw out items you do not need or want to move. (Call charities).☐
Obtain moving cartons and other necessary supplies. ☐
Give local post office your forwarding address; obtain change-of-address ☐
cards and send to magazines, insurance companies, friends. ☐
Arrange with principal of your children's school for transcripts of
grades to be sent to new school. ☐
Obtain medical records (shots, eyeglass prescriptions, dental records, etc.).☐
Obtain birth and baptism records (if applicable). ☐
Request meter readings of gas, electricity, water. Cancel telephone,
milk delivery, diaper service, newspaper, and other services. ☐
Ask Realtor® in new area about fees or deposits required for
utility installation. ☐
Remit the utility deposits required with information as to when and
where you will want the same services reconnected. ☐
Transfer your bank account and charge accounts. ☐
Transfer fire insurance on personal possessions, so they will be covered
at your new home and en route.☐
Arrange for sufficient cash to cover cost of moving services and expenses
until you make banking connections in your new community.☐
Have your refrigerator and other appliances serviced for trip. If car and
other possessions are not fully paid for, obtain permission to move them.☐
Notify your church or synagogue, service organizations, and clubs of
your move. ☐
Arrange for transfer of jewelry and important documents that movers
will not take. ☐
Pack items that will be needed for first days in new home.☐
Arrange for babysitter for moving day.☐

On moving day
Be present on moving day to answer questions and attend to any over-
looked items. Be sure you are familiar with the moving company proce-
dures, and sign necessary forms and authorizations. ☐
Verify mover's final inventory of your belongings. ☐
Leave keys and forwarding address with Realtor®☐

When you arrive at your new home
Obtain certified check or cashier's check necessary for closing real
estate transaction.☐
Check pilot light on hot water heater, incinerator, and furnace. Call gas
and electric company if adjustments are necessary.☐
Notify post office of arrival and ask for mail they may be holding.☐
Register car within five days after arrival in state, or a penalty may have
to be paid when obtaining new license plates. Have new address recorded
on driver's license. ☐
Visit city offices and register for voting.☐
Arrange for bicycle, pet, and other licenses.☐

Figure 9.2. Change-of-address card.

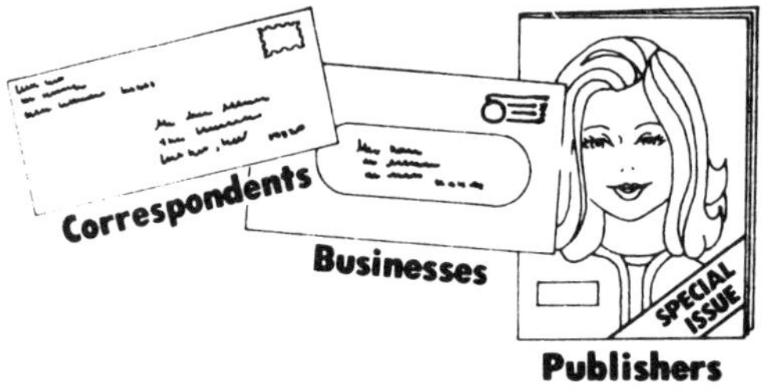

Figure 9.3. Sample inventory checklist.

Household Inventory				
The following is an inventory sheet for recording your household furnishings and personal inventory. It is important that you have a record of your possessions and their value. We hope this form will be helpful in compiling this record.				
Article	Number	Year bought	Cost	Present value
Living room				
Chairs				
Tables				
Davenports/couches				
Rugs				
Carpet				
Lamps				
Pictures				
Mirrors				
Piano				
Organ				
Radio				
Clock				
Curtains				
Draperies				
Fireplace fittings				
Vases				
TV set				
Record player/stereo				
Records				

Total living room _____

Figure 9.3. (continued)

Article	Number	Year bought	Cost	Present value
Family room				
Chairs				
Tables				
Desks				
Sofas				
Rugs				
Carpet				
Lamps				
Pictures				
Radio				
Stereo				
Mirrors				
Clock				
Bookcases				
Curtains				
Draperies				
TV set				
Bar				
Ping-Pong table				
Pool table				
Games				
			Total family room _____	

Figure 9.3. (continued)

Article	Number	Year bought	Cost	Present value
Dining room				
Table				
Chairs				
China cabinet				
Buffet				
Server				
Tea cart				
Rugs				
Carpet and pad				
Curtains				
Draperies				
Mirrors				
Dinner sets				
China				
Glassware				
			Total dining room _____	

Figure 9.3. (continued)

Article	Number	Year bought	Cost	Present value
Bathrooms				
			Total bathrooms	_____
Bedroom 1				
Beds				
Springs				
Mattresses				
Chests				
Vanities				
Dressing tables				
Clocks				
Rugs				
Carpets				
Lamps				
Pictures				
Bedside tables				
Curtains				
Draperies				
Radios				
			Total bedroom 1	_____

Figure 9.3. (continued)

Article	Number	Year bought	Cost	Present value
Bedroom 2				
Beds				
Springs				
Mattresses				
Chests				
Chairs				
Vanities				
Dressing tables				
Clocks				
Rugs				
Carpets				
Lamps				
Pictures				
Bedside tables				
Curtains				
Draperies				
Radios				

Total bedroom 2 _____

Figure 9.3. (continued)

Article	Number	Year bought	Cost	Present value
Bedrooms 3, 4, 5				
Beds				
Springs				
Mattresses				
Chests				
Chairs				
Vanities				
Dressing tables				
Clocks				
Rugs				
Carpets				
Lamps				
Pictures				
Bedside tables				
Curtains				
Draperies				
Radios				
			Total bedrooms 3, 4, 5	_____

Figure 9.3. (continued)

Article	Number	Year bought	Cost	Present value
Kitchen				
Refrigerator				
Range				
Deep freeze				
Floor covering				
Curtains				
Chairs				
Tables				
Utensils				
Dishes				
Supplies				
Radios				
Dishwasher				
			Total kitchen	_____
Laundry				
Washer				
Dryer				
Ironing board				
Tables				
Electric irons				
Dehumidifier				
			Total laundry	_____

Figure 9.3. (continued)

Article	Number	Year bought	Cost	Present value
Lawn furniture				
Chairs				
Tables				
Couch				
Glider				
Swing				
Gym set				
Barbecue				
Total lawn furniture _____				
Machinery and hand tools				
Sewing machine				
Vacuum cleaner				
Woodworking equipment				
Power tools				
Hand tools				
Total machinery _____				

Figure 9.3. (continued)

Article	Number	Year bought	Cost	Present value
Garden tools				
Lawn mowers				
Wheelbarrow				
Hand tools				
Garden hoses				
Total garden tools _____				
Clothing				
Men's				
Women's				
Children's				
Total clothing _____				
Linens				
Sheets				
Pillow cases				
Blankets				
Bedspreads				
Tablecloths				
Napkins				
Luncheon sets				

Figure 9.3. (continued)

Article	Number	Year bought	Cost	Present value
Linens (continued)				
Towels				
Washcloths				
Bath mats				
Total linens _____				
Jewelry				
Watches				
Rings				
Necklaces				
Bracelets				
Brooches				
Total jewelry _____				
Silver				
Hollowware				
Silverware				
Tea set				
Trays				
Total silver _____				

Figure 9.3. (continued)

Article	Number	Year bought	Cost	Present value
Personal belongings				
Sports equipment				
Guns				
Luggage				
Stamp, coin collection				
Bicycles				
Toys				
Musical instruments				
Furs				
Total personal belongings _____				
Summary of valuation				
Living room				
Family room				
Dining room				
Bathrooms				
Bedroom 1				
Bedroom 2				
Bedrooms 3, 4, 5				
Kitchen				
Laundry				
Lawn furniture				

Figure 9.3. (continued)

Article	Number	Year bought	Cost	Present value
Summary of valuation (continued)				
Machinery and hand tools				
Garden tools				
Clothing				
Linens				
Jewelry				
Silver				
Personal belongings				
			Total value _____	

Move-in Procedures

Some building companies have well-organized procedures for checking out a property to a buyer and making the formal arrangements to turn it over for occupancy. Others work on a loose and informal basis. No matter what your company's policies may be, the coordination of details surrounding the actual transfer of title and occupancy of the home is crucial to maintaining good relationships with the new owners. This is the moment of truth; all the things you have been doing are focused on the actual transfer of the property. Improperly handled, it can sour a buyer on your operation and undo all the good things you have done in the past.

Formalize the move-in procedures to include at least a checklist of things that should be done by construction, by sales, by management, and by any others who are involved in this transfer. The construction superintendent should pre-inspect the property before the buyer inspects it in a completed state for the first time. Often the home is not really finished; minor things may still have to be done. Because the buyers are concerned about their new home, they can become irritated, especially if they are shown the property in a condition that they cannot reasonably accept.

If the construction superintendent walks through the home a few days before and makes note of the things that need correction, it can save a lot of time and frustration. The less you have to put on the list of items to be attended to after the buyer's inspection, the better will be your working relationship with that new resident.

Commonly, one representative from sales and at least one representative from construction are present for the buyers' inspection. Some builders think, perhaps justly so, that having any salesperson present may create more problems than it solves, and at times this can be true. In any case, someone representing the company should carefully go through the home with the buyers and do the following:

1. Introduce the buyers to the property in a gracious way to make them feel that they have just become the owners of a truly fine product that they can be proud of.

2. Tell them about all the warranties and the operation and maintenance of the home. (An example of a printed warranty is shown in Figure 9.4.) This will help give the buyers a feeling of confidence and understanding of the property. Knowing which things are the builder's responsibility can prevent service complaints and frustrating callbacks that are expensive to the building operation. It is a good idea to use a

Figure 9.4. Sample warranty.

WARRANTY

1. For good and valuable consideration, Seller hereby warrants to Buyer that the new home located on the herein described property was constructed in substantial conformity with the plans, specifications, construction work order, selection sheet, and authorized changes or variations thereto forming a part of that certain Purchase Agreement dated _____, 19____, entered into by and between the Seller and Buyer. The new home, upon delivery to the Buyer, was structurally sound and free from substantial defects in material and workmanship not common to the grade and type of materials used in it. Seller shall replace within one year from the closing of the above described Purchase Agreement or before resale by Buyer, whichever date is earlier, provided, however, that this Warranty shall apply only to such instances of substantial nonconformity or defects as to which the Buyer shall have given written notice to Seller on that certain Certificate of Occupancy of even date herewith addressed to Seller and executed by Buyer or by subsequent written notice delivered to Seller within one year from the possession date as described in the above Purchase Agreement.

2. The home, located on Lot _____ in _____ has been inspected and approved as meeting the requirements of the local Building Department.

3. Seller does not hereby warrant or assume responsibility for (a) damage due to natural wear and tear; (b) defects that are the result of characteristics common to the materials used; (c) loss or injury caused in any way by the elements; (d) conditions resulting from condensation of, or expansion or contraction of, materials; or (e) other conditions beyond Seller's control.

4. This Warranty is the only warranty made or authorized by Seller with respect to the above new home, and is in lieu of all other warranties, made in the past or to be made in the future, expressed or implied, of merchantability, fitness for intended purpose, or otherwise, and of all other obligations or liabilities on Seller's part, whether with respect to material or workmanship in the new home, damage to the Buyer or others, or to his, her, or their effects, or otherwise for consequential damages. Seller makes no warranty beyond the time above stated, even though the claimed defect does not become apparent within such time.

5. This Warranty is not transferable and is exclusively for the protection of the original Buyer whose signature appears below.

In witness whereof, Seller has caused this Warranty to be executed this _____ day of _____, 19____.

_____   _____
Owner   Seller

form, such as the one shown in Figure 9.5, to have the buyers acknowledge that they were given this information.

3. List all the items that need to be attended to before the buyer takes possession or that must be completed within a specified time afterward. Companies usually have a standard form for this; an example is shown in Figure 9.6.

4. Resolve any misunderstandings that may have occurred on such things as options, extras, and color choices.

Some companies have two inspections by the buyers: one a week or so before the date of occupancy, at which time the list of things to be done is made, and the second a day or two before the planned move-in date.

This period—crucial with respect to the buyers' personal interest in the home—should be handled with great delicacy, and the individuals who do the inspection work should be oriented to public relations. Construction people do not always understand this and may say and do things that upset the buyers. Everyone should be aware that getting the buyers off to a good start is invaluable to the total marketing effort, for referrals can occur only when the buyers are satisfied that the company is genuinely interested in them and their new home.

Many builders provide buyers with a copy of the National Association of Home Builders' booklet, *Your New Home and How to Take Care of It*, at the time they take possession. This publication introduces the buyers to their home and all the various items in it—such as the foundation, roof, and floors—and describes how to maintain and repair the home. It also discusses when the owners should repair something themselves and when they should contact the builder or another professional. The booklet is an excellent, thorough introduction to homeownership. It is available to builders and developers through the locally affiliated homebuilders' association serving your community. Again, providing information of this type contributes to the buyer's confidence in you.

The following excerpt from the first part of the booklet illustrates the kind of information you could give buyers to assist them in settling into their new home. The booklet is necessarily unspecific about contractual obligations; such details must be provided in each case by the building company.

> "After you have taken title to your new home, inspect it thoroughly before moving in. See that everything has been com-

pleted as agreed upon. You will be satisfied and the builder's contractual obligation will be met.

"*If you discover that minor repairs are needed, notify the builder immediately—in writing. Telephone calls, oral statements, and rough memoranda can go astray or be forgotten.*

"*The best way to handle your initial service problems is to make a list of all such items and turn it over to your builder at the end of a specified period—perhaps six weeks after you move in—or at some time agreed upon by you and your builder.*

"*Sometimes adverse weather conditions or temporarily unavailable material or labor may cause a delay in doing the jobs on your list. When this happens, your builder will explain the reason for it.*

"*Some of the service problems that may arise while you are living in the house will legitimately be your responsibility or that of the manufacturer and subcontractor who made or installed the various parts and equipment.*

"*Should your home ever require major repairs, consult your builder for advice or call a specialist in the type of repairs needed. In most cases, major repairs should be left to the professionals.*"*

Coordination between Marketing and Production

Failure to adhere to your company's policies and procedures may result in confusion and, ultimately, costly errors to the company. Keep communications with other departments open and friendly. This will serve to reduce some of the problems that can occur when lines of communication are closed.

Often, the marketing director and production manager meet regularly at the executive level to communicate and actively administer related functions of the company. It is recommended that production superintendents and on-site sales associates inform each other of their activities daily (or as often as possible). This can be done briefly in the morning or at a more convenient time during the day. The sales associates and superintendents can discuss potential move-ins, study change orders not yet processed, and review inventory and other matters affecting both operations.

*"*Your New Home and How to Take Care of It,*" National Association of Home Builders, Washington, D.C., pp. 6 and 7.

Figure 9.5. Sample buyer acknowledgment of information received.

HOMEOWNER REPORT

CERTIFICATE OF OCCUPANCY AND ACCEPTANCE

Date _____

Homeowner _____

Address _____

Subdivision _____ Lot number _____

Escrow closed _____

I have been shown the location of lot lines, electric circuit main panel, water meter and shut-off, plumbing fixtures, water shut-offs, sewer cleanouts, and other important items.

I have been instructed about the operation of all mechanical equipment.

I have inspected the condition of the plumbing fixtures, tub/shower walls, cabinets, countertops, floors, walls and ceilings, windows and doors, and exterior improvements.

I have found everything to be satisfactory except the following, which will be corrected, as well as other future items, per the one (1) year warranty agreement.

_____

_____

_____

_____

I hereby accept the Homeowner Move-In File with one (1) year warranty and other important items, and the house keys.

Date _____

Builder _____ Owner _____

_____   _____

_____   _____

Figure 9.6. Sample form for listing needed repairs.

CUSTOMER SERVICE WALK-THROUGH INSPECTION					
Buyer _____ Home phone _____ Date _____					
Lot # _____ Community _____ Address _____					
Best day or time for repair _____ Key location _____					
ITEM	LOCATION	DISCREPANCY		ACTION	ORDER NO.
Electrical					
Carpentry					
Floor covering					
Tile/sheet goods					
Carpeting					
Painting					
Miscellaneous					
Chips:		Yes	No		
Kitchen sink					
Bathroom (hall/ master)					
Range					
Range hood					
Tub					
Shower					
Countertop					
Windows cracked					
Screens missing					
Yard regrade					

UTILITIES CLEARED _____
Other than the items listed above, the house is satisfactory.

_____ _____
Representative   New Homeowner

Certainly, it is to the sales associates' advantage to know as much as possible about construction, land development, siting criteria for new homes, and other related matters affecting sales. Sales associates should take time each week to review all unsold inventory and refer items needing attention to on-site superintendents. At the beginning of each day, the superintendents and sales associates should touch base to discuss what has happened that may affect each other's operation. Everyone should appreciate the company's overall objectives, which are to sell more homes and to properly service customers. No one should seek to build empires or protect personal positions at the expense of these objectives.

Pre-Move-in Inspection Procedures

The pre-move-in, or walk-through, inspection is often conducted by a color coordinator, who helps purchasers select colors, carpets, and other optional materials prior to the date of occupancy. Having a color coordinator present property to the buyers tends to eliminate some of the problems that arise during this inspection process. At times, the color coordinator is not available, and an alternate is assigned to fulfill this role. This is a good time for completing an inspection form, such as the one shown in Figure 9.6. Any alterations that must be completed prior to or following move-in are noted. The customers, production department, and color coordinator all receive a copy of this form.

When emergencies arise, sales associates should contact the marketing department for advice regarding the steps to be taken to meet pre-move-in requirements.

Move-in and Utility Connection Procedures

It is crucial to expedite move-in procedures for a new resident. One way to do so is to present a checklist, such as the one shown in Figure 9.1, to the purchasers to help them make the transition.

Also take care of connecting utilities at the point of sale or shortly thereafter by obtaining the purchasers' authorization to do so. Two to three days prior to scheduled move-in, your company can ask the utility companies to turn on the gas, electricity, and water and forward the bills to the new owner.

On the date of move-in, the sales associate should try to be present to welcome the new residents. Perhaps a gift of some kind will make the move to the new home a more pleasurable experience for the buyers. Decreasing new-resident blues will add to the owners' satisfaction and ensure the future referrals so important to you and your company.

Rental Agreements

In an emergency, it may be necessary to let purchasers occupy a home before the final title transfer has been processed. In many firms, it is the marketing director's responsibility to screen each request for making a move-in prior to final settlement. The marketing director reviews the buyers' credit application and confirms their statement that all monies have been received and steps taken to close the sale. If the credit application seems to be in order, the marketing director then checks with the loan processing department and mortgage company for their observations. At that point, a rental agreement may be prepared, with the marketing director's authorization. Each company has its own procedures and regulations related to rental agreements.

The Homeowner's Warranty Package

Your company undoubtedly takes great pride in the quality of its homes, customer services, and warranties. Its warranties express its confidence in its products. On the date of closing the transaction or at move-in, whichever is most appropriate, give new residents an owner's warranty package. This package could include items such as the following:

- A copy of the booklet *Your New Home and How to Take Care of It*, by the National Association of Home Builders;
- A policy statement of your service department;
- An inspection form such as the one shown in Figure 9.6;
- A form for the new owner to fill out to request service after delivery of the home, if the owner discovers that something needs to be repaired;
- Move-in information, containing a list of important phone numbers;
- A warranty statement;
- A warranty certificate.

NEW RESIDENT ACTIVITIES

Make your new buyers feel at home as soon as possible. This is everyone's responsibility, particularly that of the sales associates, who meet and work closely with the buyers.

Ways to make your buyers feel at home include a newsletter for residents in each community, which can be published once a month or more often. A newsletter is a way to communicate with residents on an ongoing basis, so they begin to experience a sense of community. Bulletin boards on which community events and related resident interests can be displayed are also helpful. Some projects have homeowners' associations, which sponsor activities that can be promoted through the sales offices, as well as by association officials.

WELCOMING BUYERS TO THE COMMUNITY

It is definitely appropriate to say "thank you" to your new resident buyers after they have completed the sale and taken possession of the home. One of the better ways to do this is to give your buyers some type of a gift of appreciation. A personal approach works best.

The following is a list of appropriate gifts that can be given to buyers:

- Stationery with buyers' names, new address, perhaps phone number;
- Door nameplates;
- Door knockers;
- Mailbox identification labels;
- Plants for patio or yard;
- Gift certificates to a nursery;
- Complimentary dinner tickets to a local restaurant;
- Wine and cheese assortments;
- Champagne to celebrate the move-in;
- Gold-plated house keys;
- Valuable-papers box or folder;
- A year's subscription to a local newspaper or some publication of local interest;
- Some attractive ornamental piece for fireplace, mantel, etc.;
- A bulletin board for use in kitchen, den, or garage;
- Fruit basket;
- Personal gifts selected for specific individuals.

Remember, when you take the time to deliver a thank-you gift personally, you add to its value. This shows your buyers special attention and sets the stage for referrals that can result directly from that contact.

Provide new residents with a list of names, addresses, and phone numbers of all warranty subcontractors, together with a list of community services, and the names and phone numbers of emergency services such as ambulances, fire, and police.

Your company's programs may vary from others', but you should personally have a list of things to do that are applicable to your project. After all, those buyers are your buyers as much as your builder's. When they move into the home, you want them to feel they are welcome residents of the community. Arrange to send them a personal letter or note and invite them to attend some event in the community. Host them by introducing them to neighbors. You have two purposes in doing this. One, of course, is to make them feel at home; the other is to win their confidence in establishing a basis for future referrals and additional sales opportunities. If you want more referrals, you must earn them with the interest and attention you show to buyers.

If you have buyers' respect, confidence, and friendship, ask for those sales opportunities. You know that people have friends and relatives who helped them move and who are interested in their move. You also know that they may have housewarming parties and other events that become a chance for their friends to see where they live. Use referral cards that list the date; buyers' name, address, and phone number; basic information; and notes. On the reverse side of the card, maintain a follow-up record, which provides notes about all contacts, mailings, and other items of interest.

Develop your skills in obtaining referrals by doing the projects listed in Figure 10.7.

SUMMARY

In the business of selling new homes, many things can and often do go wrong between the time the buyer signs an agreement to purchase and the time he or she is actually given possession of the property. You may be unable to control many things such as weather, the money market, labor supply, and construction. You *can* control your own actions and attitudes, and you can reduce the pressure on the buyer, in order to avoid cancellations, to build referrals, and to reduce new-resident blues.

If anything appears headed for trouble, try to head it off at the pass. The direct approach is the best approach. It is far worse to try to brush something aside and forget about it, hoping it will disappear, than to hit it head-on. Things only get worse when you ignore them.

Figure 9.7. Referral projects.

1. Buy an index file with 3x5 cards and develop a system of staying in contact with your prospects, sellers, and friends.
2. List all the people you have ever met, or known before you entered the real estate business, and put them in your referral file.
3. To each person in the file, send a personal handwritten note to advise them you are in the real estate business and to re-establish your contact.
4. Buy a quantity of small remembrance cards of various types and put them in your desk drawer where they will be quickly available for use when the occasion arises.
5. Consider designing some type of personal note pad or form that personalizes your own memos to clients and friends. Use it for the frequent handwritten notes you will send to various individuals.
6. Practice saying thank you personally and in writing whenever anyone does something for you, such as referring a customer to you, or a listing contact.
7. Discuss with fellow salespeople and your broker various ways they have found successful in building a referral business.
8. Review your known centers of influence and ask yourself these questions:

    a. Am I staying in touch with each of them so that they will think of me when the next real estate deal comes along?
    b. Have I sent them written notes and messages to thank them for past business and expressed interest in their activities?
    c. Have I used gifts and other items to cement my personal relationships with these key people?
    d. Have I performed professional work that is worthy of their consideration?

9. Practice improving your memory for names and faces. This is a vital aspect of selling, and the more effectively you recall people's names, backgrounds, and interests, the easier your task of cultivating them will be. Memory courses are available in many areas, as are excellent books on the subject. Ask those who seem to be able to do a superior job of remembering names how they achieve their proficiency in this area of personal performance.
10. List the things you can personally do to improve the quality of your real estate activities. Nothing will bring you more business more quickly than the improvement of your professional services to the public.

The ability to understand and appreciate the significance of the emotional involvement present in the conclusion of a new home transaction is an important part of your role as a professional in new home sales. This is not an easy business, and that is why there are so few who are qualified to work for builders and who are successfully earning a high income.

Closing takes a great deal of patience and understanding; it is more than signing a contract. It is getting a satisfied resident into the community, one who leads you to more satisfied residents. When you leave a community with residents who are happy in their purchase, you have left behind a success you can use as a credit to your company and to other salespeople. This is accomplished by moving forward on the platform of credibility and confidence, which you and your company have built together.

10: Managing and Marketing New Homes for Builders

Although the major portion of this book discusses the basics of selling new homes for builders and developers, it seems appropriate to devote a chapter to the subject of how to manage and market builders' properties effectively. It is impossible to cover this topic completely here. Therefore, this chapter is intended only to be a brief summary of the essential facts for those who are in a management or marketing role, either directly associated with the building company or as an agent for that organization or individual. The purpose of this chapter is to establish guidelines for the individuals who represent sales management: the listing agents and the marketing directors who are involved in the selection, training, and development of sales personnel, as well as in formulating marketing strategies for their builder/clients.

As a prelude to the other topics discussed in this chapter, it is important to first identify the management structures that a builder can employ to meet sales and marketing objectives. Many building companies prefer to have their own full-time sales managers, salespeople, and marketing specialists. Larger organizations, in particular, tend to prefer the in-house sales system to employing outside brokerage companies. They usually justify this choice by citing the following three major advantages:

1. Maximum control of their sales and marketing functions with no competition for the attention and interest of the salespeople or managers involved.

2. Lower cost per housing sale, based on commission structures and budgetary expenses.

3. The confidentiality that arises from using the company's own people, who are not involved in any other operations where the education and knowledge they gain might be used to a competitor's advantage.

Often, other reasons are cited, but these are the most frequent ones given by the hundreds of companies who use their own sales and marketing personnel.

A large number of builders and developers have successfully employed the services of real estate brokerage companies, or individual agents within those enterprises, to represent their new housing projects and communities. The advantages these firms perceive include the following:

1. Reduction of fixed overhead and variable expenses that are incurred for in-house sales staff and sales managers. Brokers and agents work usually on a contingent fee basis; that is, they get paid only when a home is sold and/or closed, rather than in advance. The builder is thus able to keep sales costs in line with projections.

2. Increased exposure to markets and prospective buyers that the builder alone might be unable to reach. This is particularly true when dealing with buyers in special categories, such as those who are tied to an equity in an existing property or who are transferred from another city and need orientation to the general market before purchasing.

3. The broker's access to a larger pool of sales personnel than a builder can have on his or her own team at any given point in time.

Other advantages are often discussed, but these tend to be the major ones influencing builders who choose to work with brokers. It is appropriate at this point to evaluate the role of outside brokers in representing builders' merchandise and to review guidelines for their involvement. This chapter is equally applicable to in-house and outside representation. However, since many readers are real estate brokers and salespeople, working with builders, who desire to improve their management skills and opportunities in the new housing field, it is in their best interests (and that of the profession) to look at the ways a real estate company can effectively represent builder/clients.

THE ROLE OF THE BROKER IN BUILDER SALES MANAGEMENT

Few real estate companies specialize in new home sales representation. There are exceptions. Some companies are totally devoted to marketing and selling new homes for builders. These are unusual entities in the profession, and they tend to be limited to major metropolitan markets where the volume of activity justifies this degree of specialization.

Residential resale personnel make their living by working on any opportunities that come their way, particularly the marketing and sales of existing homes. As Chapter 1 identified, there are some unique differences in the skills required to sell new housing versus resale properties. For that reason, many brokers and salespeople tend to confuse their roles when working with builders, and operate on somewhat the same premise as they do when working for an individual client who has a pre-owned home.

Some brokerage companies, however, have realized not only the opportunities of working with builders, but the need to establish separate specialized marketing operations to fulfill the requirements of this clientele. A new home department functioning as a specialized operation within a larger brokerage company may make a great deal of economic sense, if a broker is working in a metropolitan market that has sufficient volume of new housing to justify investing in time, personnel, and management systems required to be effective and profitable.

Nevertheless, the number of real estate companies that either have specialized departments or devote themselves to new home sales as a major part of their activity is relatively small. The great majority of brokers operate companies that list and sell anything, without regard to acquiring separate specialized departments or functions. Those same brokerage companies frequently list and sell builders' homes much as they do resale properties. They often work on a slightly reduced commission (often 1 percent less than the normal resale commission) when working with builders, and they may provide some on-site staffing and management guidance, and open the doors to cooperation with other brokers through multiple listing systems or normal broker cooperation programs.

Advantages of Using Brokerage Companies

Brokerage companies that lack specialized departments to work with builders are seldom as effective as they could be or as the builders anticipate they should be. A high degree of dissatisfaction often exists in builder-broker relationships because of the client's expectations versus the actual operating procedures of the agency.

A brokerage company could provide a builder with many services that are unavailable to most construction and building companies operating on their own. These include the following:

1. *Market research.* Brokers who are active in the marketplace

have a great deal of information that they are constantly reviewing every day. This information provides valuable assistance to their builder/clients in understanding what is currently happening in all aspects of real estate marketing, particularly in the area of finance.

2. *Land acquisition and exploration of new properties.* A broker is often presented information about property suitable for development that is going to be for sale. A builder may discover such information only through brokerage contacts. The very nature of the brokerage business creates a constant stream of opportunities resulting from the salespeople's and brokers' efforts to uncover potential parcels for development that can be steered to the clientele with whom the broker is currently working.

3. *Design and development advice.* Although many brokers are not experts in design, some real estate companies have cultivated their knowledge of selling techniques to the point that they can translate into feasibility studies prospects' design criteria and specific recommendations for housing. In this way, brokers can help the builder create the right products for a specific market. That can be an invaluable service in preventing design failure.

4. *Solutions for the needs of the trade-up market or owners who have properties they must sell before they can purchase.* One of the big markets that a broker reaches (that is often difficult for a builder to handle) is the market of present owners. They are frequently the best buyers. The majority of families living in the United States own their own homes, and the best buyer for a new home is probably someone who has one to sell. This is especially true in the upper price range of housing. The majority of potential prospects have a property that has to be sold before they can complete the purchase of a new one. Brokers who sell resale properties and have trade programs or equity release plans to supplement their normal activity can provide a valuable service to builders who are not in the resale business or who cannot handle the trades on their own.

5. *Attraction of the transferee and relocation market.* The metropolitan markets of America and of many foreign countries heavily depend upon the immigration of new people attracted as a result of employment opportunities. In the last decade, at least 20 percent to 30 percent of residential sales have resulted from people relocating from one city to another, whether for business purposes or for personal objectives. The transferee is a highly motivated individual who must find a home within a relatively short time span and does not want to be tied to only one specific housing opportunity when first investigating an

area. Such buyers want complete orientation and they normally want to see everything that is available. The builder typically does not get this exposure in the beginning of orientation to the market, whereas brokers (particularly those who belong to real estate networks and franchises) do. They have the cooperation of colleagues in other cities referring buyers to them before they relocate.

6. *Provision of an adequate number of sales personnel to meet the staffing requirements and servicing needs of builder/clients.* Real estate organizations usually have a larger number of people working for them than any one builder will have, and the available human resources can make a major difference in the capacity of a builder to reach his or her market. Having more people in the marketplace talking about property, showing property, and even staffing open houses gives the builder/client a greater number of individuals who may be able to secure opportunities for specific projects.

There are pluses and minuses to having many people involved, as this section discusses later. The number of people associated with a brokerage company is usually a distinct advantage to a builder, however, in comparison to the limited number that any one company could justify on its own.

7. *Provisions for assisting salespeople in training, education, and motivation, so as to help them perform professionally.* Sales management takes time and expertise. Builders are usually busy with their own activities and usually have neither the time nor the desire to train and develop new home sales personnel. Supervising salespeople does not fit under the category of the things they would prefer to do, nor will they normally realize the highest yield from their own talents in that area. Thus, having a broker who has the time and talent plus the personnel to maintain this vital function of management over specialists in new housing gives builders the advantage of a staff working for them without the out-of-pocket costs for that organization. If salespeople are working on a percentage of gross sales price, they are paid only when the properties are sold and settled.

8. *Supervision of the packaging and processing of real estate transactions.* Assembling a mortgage package and presenting it to appropriate lenders requires expertise and time. Again, a lack of proper supervision of people who know how to structure those packages and where to secure the best financing for an individual buyer can cause lost sales or unnecessary complications in the processing of sales. Brokerage companies that have finance departments or escrow secretaries plus management that facilitates financial guidance of prospective

buyers can offer an invaluable service to builders who do not have the same skills within their own organizations.

9. *Marketing and advertising new homes.* This is the responsibility of the agent in most cases in which an outside agency is used. In such a situation, the builder need not bear the cost or the challenges of trying to develop advertising and marketing programs that will do the job. The broker frequently advertises a variety of properties to attract a sufficient number of buyers into the marketplace so as to cross-feed them to the properties they are qualified to see. A builder who advertises only one property draws fewer people, most of whom will not even qualify for that particular property. The more properties the broker represents, the more people will be exposed to the system, and the greater the odds that any property in that system will be exposed to the right buyer. This is one of the major advantages of a well-organized marketing entity with ongoing advertising and marketing programs that expose property effectively to the largest number of potential buyers.

Guidelines for Working with Brokers

Having considered some of the reasons why builders select brokers (or elect not to use their services), keep in mind that there are no set criteria in this business. Every case is different when trying to meet a specific opportunity of selling builders' homes or particular projects. Even the best real estate companies may be unable to meet the marketing requirements of an individual builder or project that is outside of their marketing area.

Some of the guidelines for working with brokers that a builder should follow are these:

1. Select a broker who has sales and listing power within the marketing area where the properties are to be represented.

2. Work with brokerage companies who understand new home marketing techniques and have salespeople who can effectively represent new housing opportunities.

3. Try to select brokers who have personnel who will commit themselves to working with the builder on a specialized basis and who have at least one or two individuals in that company who will devote the majority of their time to that enterprise.

4. Work with brokers who have the capacity to handle contingent sales and trades if the trade-up market is a logical part of the builder's target markets.

5. Select brokers who are involved in referral and transferee programs if the exposure to additional opportunities is greater as a result of their own capacity to attract buyers from other cities through relocation networks.

6. Select brokerage companies that are well managed and that have training, education, and expertise in motivating salespeople to achieve.

7. Appoint brokerage companies whose personnel match the profile of the particular types of buyers to whom the builder is trying to sell. As noted later, not all salespeople can sell the same kinds of clients, and there is a profile of success that relates to how well the buyer and the salesperson communicate.

8. Finally, consider the corollary services a broker can offer in such areas as research, market design, advertising, and land acquisition. These can enhance the value of one brokerage company over another in meeting the builder's requirements. Broker agents should look at their services in terms of what they can offer to builders, keeping in mind whatever items they perceive to be of value to their target builders.

Figure 10.1 is a checklist for establishing contractual relationships with builders and developers.

HOW TO EFFECTIVELY LIST BUILDERS' HOMES

Meet the Builder's Needs

Resale agents are exposed to opportunities to work with builders and are sometimes confused as to what roles they should play and how they should proceed in trying to obtain the favorable attention of their prospective clients. An agent who wants to win a builder's attention should think through in advance the builder's motivations, abilities, and needs and tailor the presentation specifically to that builder's situation. It does not pay to generalize when working with any client, particularly a builder. Every entity has its own opportunities and issues, which it faces on a day-to-day basis. The more research you do in reference to that builder, in knowing the properties they own, how salable they are, the nature of the builder's organization, the financial relationships that company already has, the marketing systems they are using, and the markets they are trying to reach, the greater your capacity to direct your message to the items of greatest interest to that potential client.

Figure 10.1. Checklist for establishing contractual relationships.

COMMISSIONS AND/OR RETAINER FEES:
1. Retainer fee _____
2. Sales commission _____
3. Other fees _____
4. Contract terms _____
5. Tract numbers and lots included _____
6. How fees are to be paid _____

PROMOTIONAL EXPENSES (Identify party responsible):
1. Advertising _____
2. Signs _____
3. Sign leases _____
4. Brochures _____
5. Publicity _____
6. Artwork _____
7. Model home expenses, including utilities _____
8. Sales after construction _____
9. Sales after furnishing _____
10. Telephone expense _____
11. Other _____

AGENTS' RESPONSIBILITY FOR:
1. Accepting contracts _____
2. Granting occupancy before C.O.E. _____
3. Collecting rents _____
4. Selling furniture _____
5. Supervising builder's associates _____
6. Coordinating decorating _____
7. Coordinating advertising _____
8. Coordinating move-ins _____
9. Processing loans _____

Figure 10.1. (continued)

10. Opening escrows _____
11. Handling change orders _____
12. Handling color and material selections _____
13. Accepting trade-in sales _____
14. Accepting contingencies _____
15. Title company _____
    Officer _____ Telephone _____
    Address _____
16. Mortgage company _____
    Officer _____ Telephone _____
    Address _____
17. Staffing hours _____ Days per week _____
18. Handling options _____
19. Drawing occupancy agreements _____

    Rent per day $ _____ with $ _____ security deposit
20. Releasing keys _____
21. Cleaning models _____
22. Care of landscaping _____
23. Checking furniture inventory _____
24. Other _____

Try to think like a builder when you are listing builders' homes. *A builder is a manufacturer, not an individual seller of real estate.* An example might best illustrate this point. When you list an individual residential home, you are working with someone who has lived in that property usually for a number of years and thus has equity and who can negotiate based upon that equity. In addition, the seller's motivations are tied to something other than just making a profit on the property. Such a seller is involved in a major transfer from one location to another for any number of reasons, of which value is only one. In contrast, builders are in business to make a profit, and their motivations are tied to the efficiency with which they operate their enterprises.

Typical builders work with a relatively small margin of profit, considering the heavy capital investments, carrying costs for unsold housing, and the fixed overhead that is involved in maintaining an organization that builds and sells homes. The target pretax profit for most builders is approximately 10 percent of gross sales price. Unfortunately, most builders never realize that much from their operations, at least from the buildings themselves. (There are land profits that are separate, and they can usually be realized whether or not a home is built on the land.) Think of a builder as a manufacturer who has to maintain a certain volume of business and realize a reasonable profit from that business in order to continue to function effectively. Just selling one home for a builder does not mean that that builder is going to economically survive.

Real estate salespeople tend to think in terms of an individual commission on a single property. They think of 5 percent, 6 percent, or 7 percent of the property's gross sales price as the commission for selling that home. The builder sees that as an expense, not as an item of profit, and further, selling one home and paying that fee may have no relationship at all to the firm's real economic position. If the builder requires a turnover of 20 homes a year to break even on expenses and to pay fixed overhead (including carrying costs of land and buildings), selling 20 homes (even though that pays a substantial commission to the brokerage company) does not meet the objectives of the builder. Until the builder has sold at least 21 homes, no profit is made. In a community of 50 homesites, the builder normally must sell up to 75 percent before making a profit on at least the land development aspects of the project. In fact, it is common for a builder/developer to have to sell 80 percent of the land before real profits are realized.

With that in mind, if a real estate agent thinks in terms only of selling a specific number of properties for a commission and fails to take into consideration the builder's and developer's objectives of moving the entire parcel within a given time frame, there may be very little compatibility in the relationship. For example, salespeople often take the course of least resistance. They concentrate on selling that which is easiest to sell before they work on the more difficult things. Yet, in a new community all the profit is in the last 15 percent to 25 percent of the community. If those are not the most desirable sites, then the amount of profit to be realized and the increased price-value relationships will be adversely affected.

Take a Management Role

The point is that listing agents should think of themselves in a management role rather than as merely listing property when working with builders. They should think of themselves as assistant builders working alongside that enterprise to try to maximize builders' profits. Their objectives should be to increase builders' efficiency and improve the rate of turnover of the homes and sites assigned to the brokerage company for marketing. This means creating a total marketing plan, not just listing individual homes.

The listing presentation should be different for a builder than it is for a resale owner. The presentation should be modified to fit the needs of builders, based on their motivations and requirements. It should incorporate the following items:

1. A complete checklist of all the services your company provides to a builder, highlighting those that are unique or different from those that most real estate companies might propose. Identify your professionalism through the checklist of services you are prepared to offer, and identify each in a logical order.

2. A summary of the builder's marketing needs, based upon your research and understanding of the company's situation. This should be based on pre-inspection of its properties and investigation of its present operations. The more you know about the building company, its history, marketing success (or lack thereof), and the structure, the better your chances of securing the favorable attention of the prospective client.

3. Identification of the marketing strategies (at least in outline form) that you would employ if you were to represent that builder's homes. This should include the target markets you would attempt to attract, the methods of advertising and promoting the property, the responsibilities you would accept for staffing and supervising the homes, the competitive research and evaluation you would provide, and the management of the builder's marketing systems based on the criteria

already identified. This important part of your presentation sets forth the things you will do for builders that they may be unable to do for themselves.

4. Testimonials or recommendations from former clients, if you have worked for other builders or have the reputation of being successful in your area. Particularly helpful are testimonials from banking institutions and major employers in that region who have found your company or yourself able to handle new home sales professionally.

5. If you have a trade-in program or an equity release plan, place a great deal of emphasis on this particular aspect of your services. Explain how you handle the contingent sales and the trade-up buyers whose equities must be unlocked in order for them to purchase new housing.

6. Identification of your method of handling transferees and the relocation market as it applies to this builder's properties.

7. The forms, control systems, and checklists you will use to monitor and manage the new home projects. Explain in detail how you will report and communicate with the builder's team and how you will coordinate work with production and scheduling to maintain a solid working relationship.

8. A full explanation of your capacity to provide mortgage financing and to organize the mortgage application packages for the individual new home sales that you do achieve.

9. A presentation summary, in which you identify for the builder what it is you specifically propose to do, in what time frames, and how you will be compensated. Use incentives for yourself that indicate willingness to live by mutually established quotas and objectives. Suggest performance standards by which your services can be monitored. Include in the agreement a statement of willingness that if you do not meet sales requirements, the builder may terminate the agreement with advance (perhaps 30 days') written notice.

Before you make the presentation to the builder, this information should have been prepared. It usually takes more than one interview to reach this point. There is the investigative stage, the research and evaluation of projects and programs, and then the development of the presentation. This should be delivered in a professional manner to the builder or the builder's management team, in concert with others in your organization when their support seems advisable.

Admittedly, you can list builders' homes without going to this much professional effort, but if you really want a builder's attention and would like to secure more opportunities in this specialized area, you should acknowledge that the builder is not going to readily look to you for all of these services unless you demonstrate that you have the capacity to perform them. The concept of perceived value applies as much to brokerage services as it does to the homes for sale.

COMMISSION ARRANGEMENTS IN NEW HOME SALES PROGRAMS

Because of the very nature of the builder/manufacturer role versus that of an individual seller, real estate brokers have historically accepted variable commission rates from their builder/clients based upon the specific objectives and relationships of each operation. The builder has the capacity in most cases to produce a substantial number of homes in any given time period. One who is building ten homes a year is certainly worth ten times the attention that you would invest as a real estate agent in one specific listing for one seller. In many cases, the builder also is responsible for providing marketing programs. These may include an on-site model home, show home, or speculative house that can be used as a real estate office during the time of marketing. The builder might furnish, landscape, and promote that model office to attract business to the new homes. The brokerage company realizes the advantages of this marketing and usually is prepared to accept some adjustments in commission schedules in lieu of the costs it would otherwise incur for undertaking the same marketing expenses itself.

Consider the Services Provided

When working with any building company, clearly identify services that are going to be provided by the real estate company, as well as the services that the builder will perform as related to sales and marketing objectives. Once this has been done, the commissions and/or fees to be paid to the real estate entity handling sales can be established with consideration for the investment in time, money, and talent that each is contributing. The volume of activity will be a major factor in the economics for both parties.

If a brokerage company's full line of services is used, and the agency will experience all of the costs of advertising, marketing, staffing, managing, and coordinating the activities involved in marketing new homes for a builder, then the commission rate should be at its maximum. In the marketplace, that is often 5 percent to 7 percent or more of the gross sales price of the new home. If the builder is going to pay for advertising, model homes, on-site sales office, brochures, direct mail literature, special events and promotion, and other aspects of the marketing plan, then the sales commissions should certainly be adjusted to reflect that investment. In such cases, it is not uncommon for the commission to range from 2 percent for a volume operation to 4 percent or 5 percent for a more modest building program.

It is not the purpose of this book to provide guidelines for establishing commission rates and fees for the agents or builders who might use this text as a training device. The subject is covered here only to alert those who may be unfamiliar with the customs and practices of the industry as to what is considered normal and logical in these working relationships. The objective is to provide some direction for approaching the opportunities of marketing new homes in a method that will assure a reasonable return for all parties concerned.

Involving Outside Brokers

Another issue in establishing commission structures is the involvement of outside brokers through multiple listing systems or other cooperative ventures. The listing agent has one function, whereas the selling or the cooperative broker has another. If property is to be listed on multiple exchange programs, then it should meet the standards accepted in that particular region for commissions on new homes, in order to secure the full cooperation of sales agents in the area. It is not uncommon to have two levels of commissions, one commission set for an in-house sale and another for a sale made by a broker on the outside. The latter might involve an additional percentage amount so as to protect the listing agent while providing an adequate incentive to cooperative brokers. The same practice is often used with reference to new home salespeople who are staffing a community on-site and who need to be protected, so that they do not lose a commission because of an outside broker, but also need the assistance of cooperative brokers and agents to produce a maximum number of sales. The on-site person might receive a basic minimum fee, commission, or draw (or even a salary), while the outside broker is paid the normal sales commission (usually half of the gross commission customary for that area).

Consider the True Responsibilities

A related matter in terms of the commission structure is the subject of what listing agents really should consider as their responsibilities when they accept the opportunity and obligations involved in new housing projects. When you represent a builder, you must be more than just a resale agent who is listing property that someone else might have the chance of selling. It requires thoroughly understanding the builder's needs and objectives, willingly coordinating advertising and marketing programs, supervising on-site open house programs, co-operating with other brokers (when applicable), and playing the role of an account executive or a client supervisor, whose duties are to be an assistant marketing expert to the builder and the builder's team.

This involves a great deal of time. Many agents do not have that much time to devote to a builder/client, in which case they should consider having someone else in the company accept part of that responsibility and thus reduce the percentage of commission they might have otherwise received, so as to share the listing commission or management commission with those who have both the time and expertise to serve the builder/client's needs efficiently. In larger operations, a broker may have a new home division. This system allows the agent to better meet the standards of professionalism that should be applied to selling new homes than is possible when just working as individual agents without the synergy of a specialized team. Many companies in the new home sales business prohibit their salespeople from listing new home communities or working with builders other than as a referral agent. The responsibilities are then turned over to those who are in charge of that department. Thereafter, the procuring agents concentrate on other functions of listing and selling property and leave the management of the new home community to those who have the time and talent to devote to it.

Whatever the system, a commission in a new home operation is not merely divided into listing, selling, and company dollars. The commission is payment for a combination of services that a broker might perform. The methods for achieving the objectives of the builder should be thoroughly evaluated before finalizing working relationships.

Referral Commissions for On-Site Salespeople

When on-site sales personnel are functioning as specialists whose primary responsibility is to service the traffic and maintain control over the sales environment in a new housing community, and the brokerage is cooperating with outside agents who bring their customers to the community, there is a need for definitive understanding as to commissionable rights, interests, and responsibilities of all who are involved.

A formula should be applied to this situation as a method of relieving the tension that is caused by misunderstandings.

One way is to define the functions as follows:

1. Procuring the buyer.
2. Writing the agreement to purchase.
3. Servicing the buyer after the sale is made.

These three activities always exist in a new home sales program. Someone procures the buyer, whether through direct advertising, personal introduction, referral, or some other means. Someone writes the contract and someone services after the sale. If the same person does all of these, then, logically, the entire sales commission belongs to that individual. If, however, different people are involved, then the commission can be divided according to each person's contribution. Figure 10.2 is an example of records of commissions paid.

Division of the commission might be arbitrarily set as a value of one-third of the commission being assigned to each function. For example, if Agent A procured the buyers and brought them to the project (registering them with a protection period usually of 30 days), and Agent B on-site later closed the same purchasers, who came back to the project without the original salesperson, then Agent A is entitled to a portion of the commission for procuring, and Agent B is entitled to a portion for writing the agreement.

That leaves the responsibility of who will service the buyer after the sale. The person most likely to service the buyer efficiently is the on-site sales specialist. Buyers tend to return not to the agent who sold them the property (unless that agent is located at the community where the new home is marketed), but to the property they bought. Therefore, if there is an on-site agent, that agent will most likely be the person involved in communicating construction details, arranging for colors, choices and selections, handling the coordination between construction and sales, and supervising the ultimate walk-through and move-in.

Managers should recognize that servicing a customer after a new home sale is so critical that a fee should be paid to someone whose prime responsibility is to handle those details, even if it means paying an additional cost beyond the commission assigned to the sales function.

Figure 10.2. Sample sales commission form.

```
SALES ASSOCIATE_____  DATE_____
SUBDIVISION_____  LOT NO._____
BUYER'S NAME_____  SALES PRICE____
```

Commission computation

                                        Amount

    Base_____%

    Other

          Gross commission

Referral commission paid to:_____
Net commission remaining to:_____

Payment schedule

                Amount   Payment dates

    Approval   _____
                             (Approval date)
    Closing   _____
                             (Closing date)
    Other (specify)_____

Approvals

_____   _____
(Sales manager's acceptance)   (Date)

Multiple listing: ___Yes ___No
Broker involved_____
Remarks_____

Cancellation

_____ Recovered against_____
   (Date cancelled)   Date_____

Accounting use only: Date of closing_____
                        Date of commission paid__
                        Amount:_____

ON-SITE VERSUS OFF-SITE REPRESENTATIONS

From the builder's viewpoint, the most desirable situation for controlling sales is to have permanent new home sales associates on-site during prescribed staffing hours each day to work with prospective customers who are attracted to the homes or community by advertising, referrals, and other means.

However, it is not always profitable for the salespeople to engage in such staffing functions if the volume of sales and activity does not justify their full commitment to the enterprise. A general brokerage company is also preferable in terms of maintaining an adequate sales effort for activities outside of the project. The brokerage company can draw upon sources of business such as the transferee, the prospect who calls on one property but is willing to look at others, and respondents to a general promotion. Also, many projects are difficult to find and do not draw traffic readily because of location, limited advertising, or other factors. The inability to draw people to these locations can seriously affect the volume of sales that the builder/developer may require for a profitable investment.

The question of whether to have on-site or off-site representatives for new housing must be carefully evaluated against all of the criteria for a particular new housing situation.

The decision to staff with full-time on-site personnel should be based upon the following elements:

1. The amount of business that can be reasonably generated from prospects who are drawn to the project.

2. The quality and number of salespeople available for staffing the new home community.

3. The commission levels that can be justified by the builder/developer for compensating sales agents.

4. The relative value of the sources of prospective buyers that are not directly related to on-site marketing programs.

Even if full-time on-site personnel cannot be justified and occasional staffing is necessary, particularly during weekends and high-traffic periods, then the objective should be to avoid rotating sales personnel if at all possible. The same individual should be assigned to service the traffic on a regular basis, even if the hours of staffing are limited. Rotating people in and out of the system decreases the effectiveness of the sales representations made, increases confusion with reference to product knowledge and resident relationships, and lessens the effectiveness of the salespeople with be-backs, who see different people each time they return.

It is common to provide on-site and off-site representation concurrently when the project justifies double exposure. For example, the builder might have one or more full-time salespeople staffing the community on regular hours whose total activities are devoted to servicing the traffic and the business generated by the community's own marketing programs, while working with cooperative real estate brokers and outside agents who bring their prospects to the community on some referral or divided commission basis. In these cases, the on-site agent plays the key role in providing adequate, up-to-date information for the benefit of other supporting salespeople who are less familiar with the day-to-day operation of the community. The outside agent has control of the prospects and is able to prepare them for the community they are inspecting and to follow through after they have departed. A registration system of some type is needed to protect the interests of all concerned when groups of salespeople are working on one new home operation.

Another method of achieving staffing objectives without tying up valuable sales agents is to supplement the personal time and energy of salespeople with hosts or hostesses who do not function as real estate agents. Such people often effectively give continuity to a community's representation hours and they are less expensive than commissioned salespeople. If at all possible, secure the services of a host or hostess from local residents, because they will know more about the community and can give information without violating the licensing or professional role of the assigned salespeople. The guidelines for their involvement should be clearly determined by sales management so as not to conflict with the functions of the professional salespeople who are responsible for presentation and closing.

MODELS AND DEMONSTRATION HOMES

The Case for Models and Demonstration Homes

One of the primary reasons for using model homes and other demonstration properties is the simple fact that the imagination level of most people is extremely low. It is difficult for the majority of individuals to comprehend or picture what a home will be like before it is actually constructed and furnished. A model home is a sample environment, or a representation of what the community or project will look like when it is completed. It gives the prospective buyers an opportunity to touch and feel the real property rather than to merely look at floor plans and artists' concepts of anticipated housing construction.

The model home also gives the sales personnel property to demonstrate in their basic presentation sequence. It is far easier to show a home's benefits when you have one to actually use than it is to merely talk about it with graphics as your only support system. As already noted, the presentation and demonstration of perceived values is one of the primary functions of new home specialists.

Using model homes in this way is a competitive advantage. Competition often dictates that you must have some on-site product representation, or you will not secure the confidence of your prospective buyers who are shopping other communities. Differences among competitors should be dramatized. This same guideline is frequently a determination in how much decorating and landscaping must be included in the presentation.

Decorating is almost always a plus, but the lack of it is not necessarily a complete minus. The homes that need to be decorated are those that are difficult to visualize when they are not furnished, those that have unique features that would be fully appreciated only if they were dramatized with complete furnishings and proper decor, and where competition has established a marketing advantage in providing well-designed and effectively decorated homes.

It is almost always best to select models or speculative demonstration properties on the basis of the following criteria:

1. The number of models or demonstration homes should be limited to three to five if at all possible, so as not to confuse the buyers with too many alternatives. If more floor plans are available to the prospect, the properties selected should be representative of categories, and the variations should be handled by individual presentations after counseling by the sales personnel.

2. The models or show homes should be placed on average or typical sites rather than on the best locations in the community. When the choice sites are used for models and the inventory that is constructed for sale is *not* in a comparable environment, the sales agent is forced to down sell the location after having involved the customer with a superior setting. This is always difficult.

3. The first home or model seen by the customers is preferably one that is in the middle of the price range and housing types rather than being the most expensive or least expensive. The advantage is that it becomes a qualifier for the salesperson to be able to direct the cus-

tomer to either a more expensive or a less expensive property. It also avoids limiting the interests of either the marginal buyer or the prospects who can afford a much better property.

4. Models should not be placed in locations that will adversely affect future values. For example, if the community is going to represent a wide variety of housing types in the future and the location chosen for the models is one that will permanently affect all other properties as the customer approaches the area, the consideration must be what influences these properties will have on future values. In many situations, builders have made the mistake of putting the first homes in the lower price range on the main street or access area and later wanted to upgrade the community as the project matured, but were unable to do so effectively because the stage had been set for less expensive housing at the beginning.

Selling New Homes Without Models or Demonstration Properties

On many occasions, it is either undesirable or impractical to have demonstration homes. This is particularly true in the early phases of selling a new community, when construction may not have even commenced. This presale period requires a different marketing approach than would be used if models and a complete sales center were available.

During this phase of construction and marketing, it is important to have effective graphics and displays that will overcome the difficulties of being unable to show these specific properties to the potential buyers. In this sales phase, it is best to have enlarged floor plans or even three-dimensional models, which can be used to help buyers translate the product design into the desired future housing picture. Interpretation of two-dimensional floor plans can be difficult. The more effectively graphics overcome this resistance to understanding housing designs, the easier it is to involve a prospect, even without the actual homes to demonstrate. The actual floor plans in three-dimensional scale are frequently among the best sales tools at this stage.

The decision as to whether or not to use models or demonstration properties is critical in developing the sales strategy. If this phase is not effective and everything has depended upon it, then the ultimate success of the building enterprise may be seriously jeopardized. Whenever possible, it is prudent to have the insurance of planned future models and show homes, even if presales without them have commenced in the early phase of marketing. If they are never needed, then they can be withdrawn from the plan at some predetermined time. Not to reserve those locations and have them for models, when and if needed, is to imply that presales and marketing will be totally successful. Often, that is not the case, and failure can result from the lack of flexibility to perceive what is needed in the future.

SELECTION AND RECRUITMENT OF PERSONNEL

How to Select New Home Sales Personnel

As already noted, not everyone is qualified to become a new home sales specialist, for the same reason that not everyone is suited to be a real estate salesperson. There are specific differences in the profile of effective new home real estate personnel that separate them from the typical resale or general brokerage agent. Some of these qualities include the following:

1. The ability to adjust to a controlled environment and be effective each day in a limited area of operations. Many salespeople find it too confining to their personalities and the nature of operations to be limited to one specific sales environment such as a model home or an individual subdivision. If they are forced to work within those controls, they may become less communicative and frustrated, which adversely affects their ability to communicate with prospective buyers. The best salespeople in this regard are those who like the involvement with one particular program and who maintain a fairly stable emotional balance each day without having to be constantly moving from one situation to another to keep themselves motivated.

2. Ability and willingness to work with details and to follow through. New home salespeople have a greater amount of detail work and procedural activities due to the very nature of selling new properties. Product knowledge, forms and systems, and constant follow-through are essential elements of their day-to-day activities.

3. Identification with the community. Since a high percentage of new home sales are the result of referrals and satisfied residents who live within the community once they have been sold, the salesperson should have a strong identification with the people who are living there and with the prospective buyers who are attracted to the community. This means profiling the salesperson to match those who will be residents. For example, a salesperson who is going to sell condominium housing must be able to appreciate the lifestyles of individuals who buy condominiums. Not all salespeople are comfortable with that housing concept. If you are selling to the luxury market, the sales-

person must be able to identify with those high achievers and maintain the social standards that characterize such people's lives.

4. Ability to move from low gear to high gear rather quickly. The nature of on-site staffing in most new home communities is one of fluctuations between high activity and low activity. The salesperson may not have seen a prospect for several hours when one suddenly arrives.

Certainly, every sales agent in real estate must have a high social sensitivity and a fair degree of assertiveness to be effective in a commissioned enterprise. Communication skills and other talents are common to all real estate people but less important in some other professions. When looking for new home salespeople, determine the qualities you want for your specific project, and carefully profile the salespeople to fit the profile of prospective buyers.

In determining the kinds of sales consultants that you want associated with new homes communities, some of your criteria include reviewing the sales price range of the housing product and the types of buyers who will be most likely attracted to it, the dollars that are available for compensation of sales associates versus what the professionals are used to earning, and the number of salespeople needed to efficiently handle the traffic that will be developed for that community.

Recruiting New Home Sales Personnel

Sources of Personnel. If new home sales specialists are not readily available in the market area for a new project, then the recruiter must take steps to seek prospects from a variety of sources. Experienced personnel are more difficult to find because they are usually already associated with a company where they have built their referral business and are probably making a reasonably good living. There is nothing wrong with exposing your opportunities to others, but be sure to keep an ethical posture within the real estate community by maintaining reasonably sound working relationships with other professional real estate organizations.

Sometimes a resale agent can make an effective new home sales specialist, has an affinity to new housing, and would prefer the controlled opportunities in working for a builder's new projects, rather than merely handling all types of properties in day-to-day real estate business. If the manager desires to seek salespeople outside of the profession itself, then the following sources are most likely to be successful:

1. Use your own sales staff as a resource to find other salespeople.

2. Involve your business associates and those with whom you carry on daily activities who have a reason to see you succeed.

3. Advertise for new agents not only in the personnel section but also in other portions of the newspaper, such as sports and financial sections, where potential candidates may be attracted who would not read the personnel columns.

4. Recruit from your customers and people who have known the organization who might have an interest in selling real estate.

5. Develop a reservoir of hosts and hostesses who can become potential full-time salespeople, once they have learned the basics and have gained some understanding of what the professional is all about. about.

There are a variety of other sources and methods of attracting salespeople. While this book is not a complete management guide, it is important to suggest that if additional people are needed, they should be located on a planned basis, not by accident.

The interviewing, screening, and selection process must be conducted carefully. It is usually best to have two interviews with any potential sales applicant, to use a position application for a screening interview, and to have two separate people conduct the interviews, or at least have a two-stage interview system, so that a complete evaluation can be given from more than one viewpoint. Figures 10.3, 10.4, and 10.5 illustrate a three-stage evaluation procedure.

It is also wise to check references and background experience, by either telephone, face-to-face interviewing, or asking key questions of people who have known the candidate.

Experience has taught that it is unwise to hire in one's own image and to project one's own likes and dislikes with reference to a salesperson. Each salesperson is an individual, and it is much more important to think in terms of how he or she will work with prospective buyers.

It is also true that what a person has been in the past is what he or she will tend to be in the future. Do not try to remake people. Accept them for what they are and build upon their strengths rather than their weaknesses.

Figure 10.3. The first stage of a three-stage evaluation.

SCREENING INTERVIEW FORM

	1	2	3	4	5	6	7	8	9	10
PERSONAL APPEARANCE	Poor appearance, careless, unkempt		Lack of attention to dress and personal grooming		Generally neat and of good appearance		Very careful of appearance		Immaculate in dress and person	
PHYSICAL CHARACTERISTICS	Pale, sickly, too fat, slouchy		Poor appearance, not clean cut		Good normal physical condition		Energetic, clear skin, alert eyes		Excellent condition, especially attractive	
VOICE	Unpleasant, irritating, squeaky		Indistinct, hard to hear		Pleasant, clear, well-modulated tone		Very clear, easy to understand		Unusually pleasing in quality, strength, and clarity	
POISE	Shows some lack of self-control		Ill at ease, embarrassed		Normal amount of poise		Entirely at ease		Unusually self-possessed	
ABILITY TO COMMUNICATE	Confused, illogical		Somewhat vague or foggy		Gets ideas across well		Logical, clear, and convincing		Superior ability to communicate	
ALERTNESS	Slow, thick-witted		Somewhat slow, asks poor questions		Grasps things easily, a good listener		Alert, asks intelligent questions		Exceptionally keen, alert, and understanding	
PERSONALITY	Poor personality, harmful to him or her		Personality questionable for the job		Pleasant personality, satisfactory for the job		Very desirable personality		Outstanding personality for the job	
TOTAL RATING	UNACCEPTABLE		DISMISSED		GAVE APPLICATION		MADE APPOINTMENT FOR____		TIME: _____ PLACE: _____	

Figure 10.4. The second stage of a three-stage evaluation.

FIRST INTERVIEW FORM

	1	2	3	4	5	6	7	8	9	10
DOMESTIC SITUATION	Poor situation, harmful to him or her		Definite weakness is evident		Normal home life, no negatives		All indications are positive		Should be helpful to him or her	
FINANCIAL CONDITION	In debt, very likely a problem		Weak financially, potential problem		Average financial condition		Above average, indicates stability		Outstanding, stable financially	
EDUCATION	High school with no evidence of self-education		High school plus some self-education		Two years of college		Three years of college		Four years of college, earned degree	
PART-TIME WORK RECORD	No part-time work experience		Spasmodic record of work		Average amount of work		Good record, helpful to him or her		Consistent, mainly in sales	
EXPERIENCE IN SALES WORK	No experience in sales		Small amount of experience in sales		Average amount of experience in sales		Better than average experience in sales		All past experience in sales	
STABILITY	Too many jobs, long periods of unemployment		Changed jobs frequently, periods of unemployment too long		Reasonably average time on each job		Average of two years on each job, short periods of unemployment		Long time on each job. No time of unemployment	
PROGRESS	No apparent progress		Slight evidence of some progress		Average progress made to date		Above average progress		An outstanding progress for a person of this age	

284 New Home Sales

Figure 10.4. (continued)

	1	2	3	4	5	6	7	8	9	10
MILITARY RECORD, INCLUDING INCREASE IN RANK	No increase in rank, no explanation		No increase in rank. Good explanation		Small increase in rank		Increase in non-commissioned officer rank		Increase in commissioned officer rank	
	1	2	3	4	5	6	7	8	9	10
FUTURE GROWTH AND DEVELOPMENT	No change of growth or development		Slight chance of growth or development		Average possibility for growth and development		Better than average growth possibilities		Can picture developing into management position	
	1	2	3	4	5	6	7	8	9	10
REMARKS:										

Note: After the distribution of a formal job application and review of same, the interviewer should fill out this form, scaling it on a basis of 1-10 for each item.

Figure 10.5. The third stage of a three-stage evaluation.

SECOND INTERVIEW FORM

NATURAL ENTHUSIASM	Listless, tired, bored		Calm, possibly indifferent		Normal interest, some enthusiasm		Lively expression, both facial and oral		Sparkling and effervescent, full of life	
	1	2	3	4	5	6	7	8	9	10

What clubs or organizations did you belong to during school? _____

Do you like to play cards? _____

Do you enjoy parties with lots of people? _____

Do you ever introduce yourself to strangers? _____

ABILITY TO MAKE PEOPLE LIKE AND RESPECT HIM OR HER	Cold, aloof, tendency to alienate people		Slow to warm up, somewhat lacking in friendliness		Friendly and adaptable, normal sociability		Warm and friendly, easy to like		Outstanding sociability, makes friends quickly	
	1	2	3	4	5	6	7	8	9	10

What was your ambition when you graduated from high school? _____

When did this ambition change? Why? _____

What position would you like to hold ten years from now? _____

What do you plan to do to obtain such a position at that time? _____

AMBITION	No apparent idea of desires and future		Uncertain ideas about future		Normal desire to succeed		Clear idea as to future desires		Strong, healthy ambition	
	1	2	3	4	5	6	7	8	9	10

Figure 10.5. (continued)

How did you get to this (or that) job? _____
How do you handle objections when selling? _____
Why do you want to work for our company? _____
Why do you feel that we should hire you? _____

SALES DRIVE	Submissive, easily influenced	Lacking in drive and desire to persuade	Normal desire to persuade	Strong drive, tendency to dominate	Vigorous drive to persuade people
	1 2	3 4	5 6	7 8	9 10

Did you ever hold positions of leadership during school? _____
Do you ever feel that you must guard against being overly aggressive? _____
Have you ever felt that you should try to develop your forcefulness? _____

AGGRESSIVE-NESS	Weak, submissive, withdrawing	Lacks force and purpose	Normal forcefulness and self-confidence	Above average force and aggressiveness	Very aggressive and forceful, tenacious
	1 2	3 4	5 6	7 8	9 10

How did your previous employers treat you? Explain. _____

Who is the boss in your family? _____
Have you ever worked on a committee? Explain. _____

What do you do when you need someone's cooperation? _____

Managing and Marketing New Homes for Builders

Figure 10.5. (continued)

CO-OPERATION	Lacks the ability to co-operate	Below average in co-operativeness, possibly a problem	Normal co-operativeness	Easy to get along with	Highly co-operative, a pleasure to work with
	1 2	3 4	5 6	7 8	9 10

What is the one greatest requirement of any man or woman for a successful career in selling? _____
_____
_____

Employee versus Independent Contractor. Another issue in the United States is whether to have independent contractors or employees for sales associates. This affects the Internal Revenue Service's requirements for withholding and tax exemptions. It also has an impact on commission schedules and other matters.

In new housing communities, it is common for the builder/developer to seek an employee relationship because of the increased control. In the general brokerage business, independent sales contractors are more common than employees, primarily due to commission relationships and the desire of sales associates to be independent contractors. It is not this book's objective to make specific recommendations on this subject, but to point out that there are distinct and unique differences between the two situations and that the decision should be made in advance of any recruiting effort.

EDUCATING NEW HOME SALES AGENTS

The development of salespeople is a continuous process in any sales organization. Professionals want to grow and improve regardless of how effective they may be. This book is one of many resources available to those who desire to add to their knowledge and skills in the real estate sales profession. Managers or real estate brokers who are interested in adding to the effectiveness of their sales programs need some type of orientation system and ongoing educational program for all of the people involved in new housing operations.

Probably the most effective method of teaching people how to sell property is to give them the opportunity to experience firsthand the various approaches to working with prospects. On-the-job training has historically been more effective than most other methods of educating people in sales careers. The problem with this method is that it demands experience. Experience may be the best teacher, but the tuition is relatively high. Without some controlled systems and indoctrination checklists, the salesperson may make costly errors and fail to achieve the kind of results that are vital to the survival of both the salesperson and the builder.

To supplement the practical experience gained in face-to-face selling, the broker or manager should have some type of training schedule or checklist training system to augment whatever is available in the salesperson's own arsenal of information. For example, when a new community is first introduced to the market, there should be complete, logical checklists of all of the important factors concerning that community.

The more sophisticated development organizations usually hold a complete indoctrination session when each new product line or project is ready for sales activity. In these orientation meetings, all of the salespeople work together with management in a total review of the research, land development programs, site plans, floor plans, materials, specifications, and sales procedures to be used in marketing the property. Such systems are an excellent way to avoid costly errors. They shorten the learning cycle so that people are ready for the opportunity to help prospective buyers when first exposed to the new property.

Education is also provided in the form of sales meetings or staff conferences held on a regular basis, preferably once each week. These are most effective when they are well-organized and stimulating events. It is the manager's responsibility to see that salespeople are given all of the information they need for filling their roles effectively. It is equally the responsibility of salespeople to inform management about the activity they are experiencing, and to make recommendations in areas that need additional input.

One of the best approaches for helping salespeople to improve themselves is to have available a library of books, tapes, films (when appropriate), and other learning aids that can be used at the salesperson's convenience or under management's scheduled orientation system. To lack a method of guiding salespeople, particularly in reference to the introduction of a new project, is to risk misrepresentations and lost sales from inexperience and lack of knowledge.

MOTIVATING SALESPEOPLE TO ACHIEVE OPTIMUM RESULTS

No single way of motivating salespeople works effectively with everyone. One formula that sales management often uses is based on the MORE concept. Each of these four letters stands for a primary motivation.

The MORE Concept

M = Money. Money is certainly a prime motivator with all salespeople. Profit incentives are an essential part of the free enterprise system, and the only way to get the most out of salespeople is to give them a chance to earn at a very high level when they perform at optimum standards. That is why the commission approach is usually so successful. The salesperson is paid for what he or she achieves. When individuals are on draw accounts, advances, or salaries, there may be a tendency for them to put forth less effort than they would if they were to receive commissions only when the transactions have closed.

The value of having some economic stability in a new home sales program with underlying compensation systems, such as draws and advances, is that it reduces the financial insecurity of salespeople during the long period of time that it takes to build and deliver housing. In any case, the amount of the commission and the incentives provided should be adequate to attract the real pros in the business and give salespeople something that is worth their extra effort to achieve. Bonuses and quota incentives can add to the earning power of a salesperson while stimulating specific production objectives.

O = Opportunity. Every person likes to have a future potential beyond merely what is available today. Offering opportunities for growth and advancement to those who deserve them often leads to far more effort than the immediate compensation justifies. Sometimes a salesperson has to go through the learning process on a fairly low-income project while looking forward to better opportunities in the future. Those who perform and continue to demonstrate increased capacity to do the job should be given preferential treatment on any new openings for additional properties that may be represented, or advances to the management level of a real estate company.

R = Recognition. There is no substitute for recognition as a motivator. A personal recognition can be in the form of simply acknowledging an individual's efforts by complimenting him or her for hard work and dedication. Sending personal notes when satisfied with salespeople's results, or seeing that their mates and others in the family are included in the recognition, can add immeasurably to their feelings of self-esteem and accomplishment.

In this area, there are many types of awards, such as million dollar clubs, membership in the Sales and Marketing Council of the National Association of Homebuilders, and contests. These and others, such as the ones shown in Figure 10.6, may add to personal recognition for sales success. You always get more out of individuals when you show that you appreciate what they have done.

E = Ego Drive. Probably the most important motivating factor in any salesperson's career is his or her own personal ego drive. That is the fuel in the motor that keeps the engine running! It is the personal desire to be the very best one can be and to be self-motivated for personal growth and satisfaction. Management can and should provide a

Figure 10.6. 26 motivation ideas you can use . . . tomorrow.

1. Salesperson of the year award
2. Salesperson of the month award
3. Salesperson of the week award
4. Company newsletter
5. Letter from president or builder principal
6. Letter from sales and/or marketing manager
7. Dinner with spouse and sales representative
8. Membership in an industry sales and marketing council
9. Salesperson of the week picture in sales/information center
10. Stamp or award programs (such as Green Stamps)
11. Inclusion of spouse in promotions and contests
12. Ongoing program of contests and incentives
13. Spiffs, or special incentives, on problem homes, slow movers
14. Earn a blazer
15. Trips to conventions, seminars at company's expense
16. Christmas club for sales representatives
17. Motivation cassettes with a prize program
18. Real estate book-of-the-month club
19. Host a party at your home
20. Take a helicopter flight over the subdivision
21. Identify the company with a sport during that season
22. Promote from within when an opening occurs
23. Enter the top sales consultants in industry award programs
24. Use the warm, human approach
25. Quizzes and homework assignments
26. Sales meetings with agendas

climate in which people want to accomplish, and thus encourage the salespeople's natural ego drives to rise to their full potential each day.

Personal counseling sessions on a regular basis (preferably at least once every three months, and a major one once a year) are important aspects of sales management. Only through personal counseling can a manager learn what is important to a salesperson and give him or her the necessary direction, guidance, and recognition.

Involvement

In addition to the normal sales management concepts any alert manager would apply, there is another aspect of motivation for new home salespeople that should not be overlooked. That is the matter of involving them in the research and input stages of the development of any new program or product.

By asking salespeople to critique and give their own thoughts and ideas about a new home, land plan, option list, or any other aspect of a housing development system, the manager achieves a number of benefits. One of these is securing good ideas that may be applicable to improving the product line. Another is the benefit of having the salespeople feel involved and thus important. A third is that, no matter what changes or recommendations are made, if the salespeople had a part in helping to formulate them, they are more committed to seeing that the product is properly represented and sold. Their own egos are now on the line with those of management to translate their convictions into actual sales.

Communication

Most important of all in the aspect of sales management is the function of seeing that every day is a stimulating event, and that positive communication occurs among production, finance personnel, sales managers, and salespeople. There is sometimes an apparent void between construction-oriented people and sales personnel. Historically, the two philosophies of operation are diametrically opposed in their approaches to life and to business. Unless there is effective management between the two, and willingness on all sides to realize that sales is the ultimate objective in every building organization, the salespeople may feel less important and thus isolated from the total picture. It is true that nothing happens until something is sold, and the salespeople are literally writing the checks of the others in the organization who depend upon sales activities for the economic success of the enterprise.

That fact should be conveyed to and understood by all involved in the building and development organization.

THE RESPONSIBILITIES OF ON-SITE PERSONNEL OR LISTING SALESPEOPLE

When there is a new project with model homes, sales office, and an active sales environment requiring on-site staffing, there is a need for a checklist of basic responsibilities for those who will be assigned to that sales arena. Figure 10.7 is an example of such a checklist. Responsibilities include such incidental items as checking to see if the models and speculative inventory are ready for sale each day, and coordinating with maintenance and construction personnel items that have to be completed to keep the community in prime condition. Other tasks are organizing sales aids and seeing that the office has all of the supplies and materials that it requires. There are forms and procedures to be completed.

In the more effective companies, a policies and procedures manual or a guidelines operating manual is used to help managers and salespeople avoid making mistakes in the critical areas of day-to-day operations. Later on, this chapter provides information on how such a manual should be organized.

The on-site people should not feel as though it is beneath them to do routine maintenance housekeeping activity. If the beds need to be made, cigarettes and papers picked up, flowers watered, or anything else cared for, then the agents should step in and see that it is done, whether by other personnel or by themselves. The staffing hours should be respected. If the models and sales office should be opened by noon each day and closed at 6:00, then those full hours should be maintained. The real pro will arrive early enough to check the models and have everything organized before the scheduled time for office hours begins, and be willing to stay as long as is necessary to interview prospects who have arrived late in the day.

COMMUNICATING AND REPORTING TO BUILDERS AND MANAGERS

One of the responsibilities of sales management and, in turn, of salespeople assigned to specific new home communities is to provide regular reports on a variety of matters that are important to developing and supervising successful marketing strategies. These reports include:

Figure 10.7. Sample checklist for on-site sales personnel.

MODEL HOME CHECKLIST

☐ Check all directional signs en route to models and replace as necessary.

☐ Set in place all Open and Open for Inspection signs.

☐ Unlock all model homes as scheduled and check for any unfavorable showing conditions.

☐ Turn on lights in all rooms and replace any burned-out bulbs.

☐ Adjust heat or air conditioning to assure comfortable temperature level.

☐ Use air sprays to eliminate unpleasant odors.

☐ Adjust bedspreads, lamps, ornaments, pictures, and any other items out of place or in disarray.

☐ See that display signs, directionals, and cigarette containers are in proper location and condition.

☐ Note any items needing repair or touch-up and report them for immediate attention. Model homes should always be in showcase condition for inspection.

☐ Note condition of the yards, walks, signs, and all other exterior factors and report any needed improvements.

☐ During watering season, turn on all sprinklers, moving regularly to water all grassed and shrubbed areas thoroughly and evenly.

☐ In winter, remove snow from paths and sidewalks between models and model parking areas, steps, and model stoops.

☐ Assist janitors in keeping models and sales centers in top condition. Observe efficiency of the janitorial service and report observations.

☐ At night when locking up the models, carefully inspect them to be sure that no one remains inside. Lock all windows and doors to prevent entry; report or correct any unusual conditions.

☐ Inspect the physical status of model signs and For Sale and Sold signs.

☐ Take down all Open and Open for Inspection signs at the close of each day's model hours. If the models are closed and locked, Open and Open for Inspection signs must not be falsely displayed.

- Traffic control reporting sheets;
- Copies of prospect cards and prospect analysis forms;
- Inventory status reports;
- Model home condition reports; and
- Sales status reports.

CREATING COOPERATIVE BROKER PROGRAMS

Establishing the Program

Whether or not new home sales responsibilities involve an outside brokerage company, it is frequently valuable to establish a cooperative working relationship with real estate brokers in the area surrounding the community. Such companies can give additional sales value to the new home marketing operation. This is particularly true if the price range of the properties involves a trade-up market potential, or would appeal to transferee buyers or those who would usually be seeking general brokers' advice before making a housing decision.

Potential cooperating brokers should be selected carefully before establishing working relationships. In some market areas, it is appropriate to work through a multiple listing system or other real estate information exchange groups.

There are some disadvantages of this type of marketing when opening it up to everyone only creates confusion and lessens the exclusiveness of the properties being promoted. If everyone can show the properties, they may not receive the maximum amount of attention you need from those brokers whose clients and customers are the most likely candidates.

One of the more effective systems for avoiding this is known as the *preferred broker* or *designated broker* method. Under this arrangement, only those brokers who have profiles of customers and clientele that specifically meet the needs of the new community and of the builder with whom they will be working are selected. Selected brokers should have salespeople who are able to represent new housing effectively, and relationships with them should be able to produce some long-term benefits to both entities.

By identifying the sales patterns of various real estate companies, evaluating their personnel, and studying their facilities and operational techniques, a builder or sales manager can make reasonable determinations as to which offices and specifically which salespeople are most likely to be of additional value in the marketing efforts for the building operation. These people can then be contacted one by one or in groups and given an opportunity to work under a preferred or designated plan. Once they are involved in this system, they should be given orientation sessions, detailed literature and information with which to work, and a person with whom to communicate on a regular basis who represents the new home community or the builder. The cooperation level will be enhanced if there is excellent communication between the brokers and the builder.

Motivating Brokers and Their Agents

Brokers and their agents can be one of the greatest sources of new home sales. If, however, brokers are not motivated, you will get absolutely nothing for your effort. Special incentives or recognition programs are a valuable way to get outside salespeople to work with building projects. The following paragraphs describe some ideas to help stimulate that brokerage sales base.

Contests. Brokers and their agents respond to contests. Handle this by creating a contest (usually built around a trip) and writing this up in an attractive bulletin. The bulletins are mimeographed and *taken* (not sent) to the respective brokers' offices by your sales personnel. If bulletins are sent, they may not be distributed properly. The salesperson contacts the broker, informs him or her of the contest, and then makes certain that the bulletin is posted.

These contests are structured to attract the agents, not just the broker alone. They may be a trip for two for selling a specific house, or they may be given for an office hitting a specific volume in a 30-day period. As a rule, most broker contests have best resuts when kept within a 30-day time frame.

Personal Selling. It is paramount to assign the key brokers to your new home salespersons for one-on-one solicitation. Just calling a broker on the phone or sending a letter urging an agent to visit your property will not do the job. Motivate your salespersons to spend the one or two morning hours prior to opening a subdivision visiting brokers' offices. Encourage the salespeople to hold sales meetings for the brokers. A saying in the business is that if one of your new home salespersons is not in a broker's office every two weeks, you can write off that broker's participation.

Quickie Promotions. From time to time, spotlight concentration homes and offer mini-vacations or football tickets to those who account for a sale. These are action stimulators that help keep your name up front.

Agents vs. Brokers. In most cases, individual agents account for new home sales, while brokers are, particularly in the larger operations, primarily administrators. Therefore, everything you do should be targeted to attract the agent's attention. The key here is to have the broker's permission before you directly solicit agents. Going over the brokers' heads will make most of them nervous. Whenever an agent makes a sale, write a letter of congratulations to that person through the employing broker.

Broker Breakfast. From time to time, sponsor broker breakfasts held at your community or a nearby eating facility. At this breakfast, make a short (no longer than 30 minutes) presentation on your inventory, financing, and product availabilities; then suggest that the agents and their brokers caravan your project starting at a specific time. Usually one salesperson leads the caravan through specific houses within the community.

Information Worksheet. If you are not a member of a multiple listing service, you may do a quasi-MLS promotion by printing your own product worksheets, complete with a photograph of every house that is for sale. Distribute these product sheets to the brokers and their agents on a continuing basis. Since the sheets are similar to MLS forms, the brokers and their salespersons can readily understand them.

Broker Recreation Days. Where you manage a large community with recreation facilities, sponsor a spring or fall broker recreation day. This day is billed as a period of relaxation for brokers, their agents, and spouses. Have a mini-golf tournament and a complimentary lunch in addition to tennis and swimming. Naturally, attempt to promote personal inspections of the houses for sale. This type of activity should normally lead to an increase in broker participation.

Information Manuals. Where broker participation is weak, send out a complete information manual on the project complete with a copy of your contract, the project's restrictions, inventory sheets, complete pricing breakdown, and the benefits of the community. These manuals are sent to the brokers for distribution to their sales teams. In most cases, opt to have your salespersons attend a sales meeting and distribute these manuals personally. While this program is expensive, it can be effective, especially if you encourage the addition of future inventory sheets to this manual.

Broker Recognition in Advertising. Where broker participation is heavy, take a portion of your advertisement—usually a 1½" strip at the bottom—and list all of the participating brokers who have made a sale for you in recent months. List their company names and addresses. This type of co-op advertising builds goodwill, and you will find that you do not lose prospects who might otherwise call the broker directly instead of coming to your property.

Courtesy to Brokers. Put a slug in every advertisement that says, "Courtesy to Brokers." After a given period of time, brokers know that they can earn a split commission at your projects (not a lessened commission, but a full 50-50 split), and that they are fully protected. This is one of the greatest reasons why brokers will participate with you: *a fair pay plan*.

Communication. Keep the lines of communication open between you and your brokers at all times. This is why one-on-one visits by salespersons are so important. When a dispute arises, settle the dispute on the spot, even if you have to give in or resort to a weighted compromise. In everything you do, be clear, concise, and complete.

Protection. It is absolutely imperative that brokers know that their prospects are protected when they visit your community. To alleviate skepticism, have each broker and/or the agent register on a preprinted registration card, putting the names and address of the prospects on the registration card. The agent is given a copy of the card, and the salesperson assures the off-site representative that, should the prospects come back by themselves to buy, the broker and, in turn, the agent will receive a commission.

Publish the Rules. In the sales office, have the rules of working your community published and posted on a bulletin board or on a handout piece. This eliminates many misunderstandings, since this is the same set of rules that has been delivered to the broker and promulgated to the agent. Putting rules in writing will avoid many problems.

Referrals. The biggest *unspoken* problem in builder-broker relations is *who gets the referral after the sale is made*. Publish on your rules memorandum that brokers and their agents will have the right to work your homeowners for referrals. You are not giving them anything an aggressive agent would not do anyway, but you are instilling the confidence that you will not lock out leads and cut off possible future earnings.

Pay Promptly. Nothing stimulates and motivates a broker more than receiving a paycheck the same day or, at the latest, the day after a sale. Pay as fast as you can, with the full details of the sale noted on the check and in an accompanying letter.

RESPONSIBILITIES OF LISTING AGENTS OR BUILDER'S SALES MANAGERS

Whether on-site or off-site, the management of a new home community or a builder/developer's marketing programs entails a variety of activities that should be efficiently supervised for the ultimate benefit of all concerned. This is not an area that one can afford to leave to mere chance. Too many risks are involved in the building business to afford the luxury of having less than dedicated, systematized managers in charge of the ultimate responsibility of seeing that the properties are sold and closed expeditiously. To assist those who are formulating or managing new home sales programs, the following paragraphs describe project sales management responsibilities.

Sales Forecasting and Sales Expensing

Sales forecasting and sales expensing are the sales manager's bottom-line objectives.

Forecasting. Basically, the manager begins sales forecasting by setting realistic goals by month for six-month increments. The manager should then adjust these goals monthly. The next step is to record all promotional events and the resulting projections on a calendar for easy reference.

The manager should increase sales forecasts for months that are known to be good and decrease sales forecasts for less successful selling months.

Expensing. The manager expenses according to a predetermined percentage. Check dollar figures to be sure that these correspond to the correct percentages.

The manager should budget to pay for the desired caliber of sales personnel. Co-broker arrangements should be budgeted at the going selling commission.

Some expenses that should be included in budgeting are the costs of producing ads and signs, establishing and maintaining model homes and sales offices, and special events. Some often overlooked items are salespersons' tools; photography; artwork; contests, incentives, and other motivation techniques; special product displays; referral incentives; and a project newsletter.

Sales management should participate in budgeting and be held responsible for expense controls.

Coordinating Communications

An important responsibility of the sales manager is to keep him- or herself, the sales force, customers, and other departments and agencies informed. Some ways of doing so are to listen to the sales force; listen to and interpret what customers are saying; develop total awareness of the competition's strategies; and monitor the sales operation for consistent direction.

Communicating through and to the Sales Staff. The sales staff has three critical paths of communication to follow. These are: sales to project manager, sales to construction superintendent, and sales to escrow lender.

The sales manager can help the salespeople do their job by establishing sound sales objectives and monitoring their progress. Some ways of doing so are scheduling weekly sales or training meetings, holding monthly or quarterly review sessions, dovetailing goals and incentives, and ensuring that sales goals and cash flow projections realistically coincide.

The sales manager is responsible for the recruiting, selection, training, and motivation of the sales force—the people who make it happen. Time and effort from the sales manager can transform a mediocre sales team into an excellent, successful one. Therefore, sales managers should constantly upgrade their personnel.

Knowing what salespersons like best in a sales manager might help direct these efforts. Research has shown that salespeople prefer a manager who: knows the job; exhibits self-confidence without arrogance; does not blame others for personal mistakes; does not hog the credit for accomplishments; has an even temper; stands up for salespeople's rights; can reach a firm decision; is predictable; believes in the salespeople's importance and respects them; protects salespeople from their own weaknesses.

Communication with Customers. The sales manager is the customer's contact with the firm's top management. Thus, he or she should protect the customer's best interests with an eye to *quality control.*

Specifically, the sales manager should keep buyers informed on progress prior to their move-in. Managers should accept their share of the responsibility for problems and keep cool with irate clients. Managers, as well as the sales force, should treat all customers with courtesy and respect.

Communication about the Community. The sales manager should also be an information source about the community. He or she should keep track of what the competition is doing at all times. This includes analyzing the competition's pricing and financing policies. The manager should also keep up-to-date on changes with the community structure, involving matters such as ordinances, zoning changes, new businesses. The manager should determine the community's sensitivity to the company.

The manager should refer this information upward to top management. Where this information would help the sales force, the manager should also communicate it to them.

Assisting with Management Decision Making

The primary way in which the sales manager can assist in management decision making is to maintain the necessary flow of data. Some of these data include information about customer behavior, market conditions, and plans and product needs. Information gathering should be part of a project reporting system that includes monitoring the sales operation, building a sales tracking system, and organizing an effective follow-up system.

Monitoring the Sales Operation. The sales operation can be monitored through weekly reports, prospect cards (more informative than a registration book), an advertising scrapbrook, and sales-in-progress spread sheets.

Building a Sales Tracking System. A sales tracking system can be built through records. A wall map is one technique. Others are a post-sale data sheet to be filled out immediately after the sale, and post-sale buyer research undertaken four months after the sale. Cancellation reports are a valuable source of information, as is a report of the cost of each lead or sale.

Organizing an Effective Follow-up System. Sales managers can organize an effective follow-up system in several stages. The first stage would be a prospect review between the salesperson and the manager. Then, sales meetings would supplement these efforts. Third, the sales manager should encourage salesperson and company mail-outs. The telephone is another relatively inexpensive way to make contacts.

Other techniques the sales manager should consider using are a spot-check follow-up procedure and customer incentives for referrals.

Putting Management into Sales

The key to all these efforts is to put *management* into sales. In other words, management skills are important to direct the efforts of the sales staff. This is detail-oriented work that involves defining the problems and needs, setting priorities, selecting solutions, and continually following up. The ultimate objective is to maximize profits, by increasing sales, reducing expenses, or both.

This work can be divided into six management functions:

Plan. The manager begins with a plan. This entails setting goals and collecting market data.

Organize. The manager must organize information and plans. There should be a total marketing analysis program. The manager should consider whether the salespeople's goals are consistent with the company's.

Direct. The manager must continuously direct the sales force. For example, he or she should see to it that salespeople know how to fill out the necessary forms.

The manager must coordinate the work of the sales staff with that of the construction people, to see that move-ins are smooth.

If a problem exists within a sales organization, it starts with management. Either the manager hired the wrong person, or the manager did not train properly.

Motivate. The manager must motivate salespersons to realize the company's goals, and thereby to reach their own. This means that the sales manager must have empathy for the salespeople. Other sections of this chapter have discussed specific motivation techniques.

Communicate. The sales manager must communicate up, down, and horizontally. Communications should be clear and in writing whenever possible. This avoids misunderstandings.

Control. The sales manager must maintain control over the work being done by the sales force. This involves knowing that traffic is being processed properly. If a good system is in place, the manager can feel confident that salespeople will follow up.

Continual monitoring is necessary. One method is a weekly lead review. Control manuals are also important.

Beware of assumptions. Do not assume the sales staff is taking care of business. Do not assume they know what to do. Do not assume they are keeping you and others informed. Do not assume other departments are on schedule. Instead, ask questions, review performance, and monitor control sheets.

Areas that require control are leads, follow-up, prospecting, merchandising, personnel, fact gathering and analysis, meetings, move-in dates, loan applications, reporting, construction, closings, color selection schedules, service, and quality control.

The Sales Manager's Authority

The sales manager represents the company to the customer, and therefore is provided broad authority within the guidelines of policy and procedures.

This authority is *earned* through consistent performance. To earn authority, the sales manager must keep all levels of management informed with facts, alternatives to situations, and solutions. The sales manager also must initiate positive, commonsense action that consistently achieves results. He or she must lead by example: thinking, communicating, doing, and developing people skills. Remember, authority is backbone, not wishbone!

The Sales Manager's Objectives

Ultimately, the responsibilities of the sales manager achieve certain important objectives. The sales manager should develop the salespersons into the best-trained and most professional sales force in the marketplace. He or she should anticipate potential problems and create solutions, with an eye for detail and positive action. He or she should set high standards for performance, to maintain a challenging work environment.

Other objectives of sales management are: to contribute to corporate objectives with positive results; to exercise judgment and establish controls; to attain customer satisfaction and a good reputation; and to achieve favorable results by ethical means.

POLICIES AND PROCEDURES MANUALS FOR NEW HOME SALES

The best way to avoid the pitfalls of management in any enterprise is to have documentation of all of the procedures and systems that salespeople, staff personnel, managers, and others should use to implement management's objectives. The assumption underlying such a manual is that one should not have to resolve personally every issue that comes up because it was not dealt with in a routine fashion from prior experiences. The standards, steps, and procedures for opening a new project, staffing it, organizing the sales office, handling traffic, maintaining models, supervising move-ins, and so forth should all be in a manual of some type. Surprisingly, a large percentage of small builders and brokers lack procedures and methods for handling these details. Although this book is not the appropriate place in which to thoroughly evaluate various procedural systems, it is appropriate to at least provide the basic elements of a policies and procedures manual for those who do not yet have such a system.

The best policy manuals have the following characteristics:

1. They are loose-leaf and identified by category and sections so that they are easy to refer to and update.

2. They are numbered by some control system such as decimals, so that material can be added or deleted as needed without having to change the entire manual or page numbering system.

3. An individual within the company is appointed to supervise all manuals and to make additions or corrections as needed.

4. A limited number of manuals should be produced, so that supervision does not become complex and the manuals can be readily controlled. Usually this means that one manual is available for each on-site project, one for each manager who is involved in the operational procedures, and a control copy for the secretary or staff person responsible for keeping the manual up-to-date.

Figure 10.8 is an example of a policy manual outline. It includes standard operational procedures for new home sales.

Figure 10.8. Sample outline for a new home policies and procedures manual.

```
SECTION 1.0:   ORGANIZATION AND HISTORY OF THE COMPANY
        1.1    History
        1.2    Benefits
        1.3    Organizational chart
        1.4    Administration of marketing and sales activities
        1.5    Position description for sales representatives
        1.6    Goals and objectives

SECTION 2.0:   EMPLOYMENT AND COMPENSATION
        2.1    Employment policies
        2.2    Basic compensation plan for the sales department
        2.3    Accounting procedures
        2.4    Reimbursable expenses
        2.5    Contingent sales
        2.6    Intra-division/inter-division sales
        2.7    Forfeitures and cancelled transactions
        2.8    Bonus arbitrations
        2.9    Limitations on recommendations and referrals for subcontractors, suppliers, etc.
        2.10   Termination and compensation agreements

SECTION 3.0:   STAFFING ASSIGNMENTS AND RESPONSIBILITIES
        3.1    Staffing assignment procedure
        3.2    Community and product indoctrination
        3.3    Competitive analysis and the competition report form
        3.4    Staffing hours and days off
        3.5    Use of telephones
        3.6    Brochures, sales literature, and office supplies
        3.7    Standard on-site sales office operating procedures
        3.8    Weekly traffic and sales reporting system
        3.9    Model home control
        3.10   Inventory control
        3.11   Advertising and promotion
        3.12   Vehicles and customer presentation

SECTION 4.0:   ORIGINATING AND PROCESSING SALES CONTRACTS
        4.1    Prospect registration systems
        4.2    Prospect control and follow-up procedures
        4.3    Product presentations
        4.4    Cost estimate worksheet
        4.5    Standard sales contract
        4.6    Deposit monies and receipts
        4.7    Purchaser information sheet
        4.8    Processing and acceptance procedures
```

Figure 10.8. (continued)

```
         4.9    Mortgage processing
         4.10   Change orders, options, and extras
         4.11   Color and decorator procedures
         4.12   Production scheduling dates
         4.13   Cancellations and noncompletions
         4.14   Contingent sale of purchaser's existing property

SECTION 5.0:    CONSTRUCTION COORDINATION, MOVE-IN
                PROCEDURES, AND CUSTOMER SERVICE
         5.1    Coordination between marketing and production
         5.2    Pre-move-in inspection procedures
         5.3    Key release procedures
         5.4    Move-in and utility connection procedures
         5.5    Rental agreements
         5.6    The homeowner's warranty package
         5.7    Customer service procedure
         5.8    New resident activities

SECTION 6.0:    PERSONNEL POLICIES AND PROCEDURES
         6.1    Policies and procedures
         6.2    Attitude and conduct
         6.3    Dress code
         6.4    Personal habits
         6.5    Buying and selling real estate
         6.6    Involvement with referrals and outside real estate activities
         6.7    Vacations, time off, sick leave, etc.
         6.8    Automobiles and insurance
         6.9    Recognized holidays
         6.10   Sales meetings
         6.11   Legal matters
         6.12   Company fringe benefits

SECTION 7.0:    COMMUNITY CONTROL MANUAL
```

SUMMARY

The challenges and responsibilities of managing builders' sales and marketing programs should not be taken lightly by those who are privileged to have this assignment. If it is worth the invested time to market and sell the new homes, condominiums, or individual sites, it is certainly worth the time to do it professionally and in an organized manner. That is why the opening comments of this chapter were directed to listing agents and managers, challenging them to accept the responsibilities of doing more than merely placing a piece of property on the market and hoping it sells.

A builder is a manufacturer who has a limited profit margin and works under a high degree of risk. A tremendous amount of capital is required to put together any new housing community. The success or failure of that venture rests on the effectiveness of the marketing strategies, the sales personnel, and the management programs that must guide and coordinate the various activities that combine to make an effective campaign. One of the reasons there are so many unsuccessful ventures is that too little time and attention has been devoted to sales management and the development of professional sales personnel.

11: Improving Communication Skills

High on the list of talents needed by the professional in real estate sales is the ability to communicate in ways that motivate other people. Human communication is effective only if it is a two-way channel. Each person has a transmitter and a receiver, and for a meaningful conversation to occur there must be transmission and reception by all participants. As an analogy, if a local radio station were blaring away at three o'clock in the morning, and all the receivers in the city were turned off, no matter how good the announcer was, he or she would be unable to communicate. Likewise, until you have turned on your listener's receiver, it does little good to try to convey your message.

The skilled communicator learns how to turn the other person on, and measures the degree of reception as he or she progresses. The communicator measures reception by answering questions such as:

"Do we have a channel on which we can communicate?"
"Are we on the same wavelength?"

If the answer is "no," the parties must take whatever action is necessary to correct the situation before they can proceed.

Since timing is so important in the sales business, the skill with which you communicate can make a substantial difference in your earnings. By qualifying better, targeting presentations well, and leading prospects to early decisions, you can close one sale and move on to another while an amateur is still playing around with the first customer. From beginning to end, the sales process is a communicative process.

THE IMPORTANCE OF LISTENING

Unfortunately, too many real estate salespeople think that communicating means talking. They act as though they had been vaccinated with a phonograph needle. More important than talking, however, is the ability to discover how others feel and to learn what they already know about a particular subject.

True, your presentation must maintain your prospects' interest and generate some excitement for what you have to offer. But if you do all the talking, you will not learn a single thing about your prospects' thoughts, experiences, and motivations. Successful teachers know that it does not matter what they know until they know what their students know. The same thing is true for educating others to the advantages of your products and leading them to a sale.

MAJOR RULES FOR COMMUNICATING

This chapter does not attempt to provide a complete discussion to how to communicate with others. However, it is important to review some of the major rules for communication as they apply to new home sales. This chapter uses a formula based on:

$$4 \times A = L U C K$$

This represents eight rules or fundamental principles of effective communication that might be called the art of defensive persuasion. This chapter examines each of these points, defines them, and then shows how you can apply them to your daily activities.

The First A = Acceptance

To successfully communicate with anyone requires a climate of acceptance in which to establish lines of communication. If two people are going to attempt a meaningful exchange of ideas and objectives, each must first accept the other. In sales, this is called getting on common ground, or breaking the ice.

Salespeople often fail to create a climate of acceptance because they are so involved with themselves that they can never really become involved with anyone else. The pros in this business understand that they must keep themselves in perspective and learn to find others as interesting and as important as they are to themselves.

Every person has the potential to feel important. If a person does not believe he or she is important, that person retreats and begins to have doubts. By making other people feel important, you make it easy for them to accept themselves and thus to accept you. When people are comfortable in your presence, communication becomes effortless and fruitful.

Are buyers comfortable when you talk with them? Do you give them a feeling of confidence that allows them to tell you how they really feel? Can they express their fears and doubts because of the climate of acceptance that you have created? Unless you can achieve these things, you will be unable to communicate well.

Do not take yourself so seriously that you cannot relax and become involved with your prospects. Many real estate pros have a natural sense of humor. Perhaps that is what helps them survive, for it is also a great tool for communicating with people. A little natural humor can ease the tension of trying to generate a sale when numerous doubts remain in the buyer's mind.

The Second A = Attention

To communicate effectively with anyone, obviously you need his or her attention. One of the easiest ways to gain attention from a person is to call him or her by name, for this momentarily short-circuits the person's brain and triggers an automatic response.

Attention has been defined as the most vivid experience of the moment. There are four tools you can use to achieve it:

- Sound and its mate, silence;
- Physical expression;
- Visual aids or props;
- Action or cooperative response from the other person.

All of these will be discussed in detail later in this chapter.

The Third A = Agreement

The objective of all communication in sales is to obtain understanding and, eventually, agreement. Doing so is like building a bridge. You start on the prospect's side, with the foundation established by careful qualifying. Then, plank by plank, little agreement by little agreement, you build a bridge until the gap between the prospect and a specific property is closed:

> "This is a good location for you in terms of your personal needs, isn't it, Mr. Greene?"
>
> "Based on your requirements, this home does seem to have most of the things you want, doesn't it, Mrs. King?"

By constantly confirming your position and allowing buyers to react, you can stay alongside them and react as they do. When they hesitate, stop and give them a chance to express their fears or ask the questions that must be answered before they can proceed.

Whenever you can agree with a customer, do so. Like most people, the customer admires the wisdom of those who agree with him or her. If there is something with which you disagree, avoid saying, "I disagree with you." This is a negative approach that tends to switch off mental receivers. Handle the disagreement more gently by staying on the prospect's side and leading him or her to new thoughts without violating his or her self-importance. For example, say:

> "Mr. Johnson, I understand how you feel, and if I were in your shoes I would probably feel the same way. Have you thought about this possibility . . . ?"

Remember that people screen everything they hear or see against the backgrounds of their personal experiences. Since it is impossible to know exactly how another person feels, you must watch what you say to keep open the lines of communication and the paths to agreement. The magic words of empathy and understanding are: "I understand how you feel." They can also be the prelude to an objective third-party or first-party story:

> "I understand how you feel. Mr. Jones felt the same way, and he found . . .," or,
>
> "I understand how you feel. I felt the same way, and I found. . . ."

Again, it is always easier for prospects to see and understand someone else's problems than their own.

The Fourth A = Asking the Right Questions

It must be obvious by now that asking the right questions is one of the principal rules for effective communication. From qualifying to closing, the kinds of questions you ask are what finally lead the buyer to make a decision in your favor. The question is the key to communication. Properly worded and asked with interest, it can be used to unlock the other person's response and thus obtain a clue to your next step in building the bridge to agreement.

Five good things happen to you when you ask the right questions. First, you reinforce the climate of acceptance because your questions indicate that you are interested in the other person's opinion, and that makes him or her feel important. Second, you gain the other person's attention. Third, that person starts talking and giving away clues to his or her interests, emotions, motivations, and status in the decision-making process. These clues allow you to target the next portion of your planned presentation. Fourth, you buy a little time to think. This gives you an advantage, for, without having to open your mouth and risk saying the wrong thing, you can listen and evaluate what you hear, see, and feel. Fifth, you are psychologically in control at the moment, because the person asking the question is always in control if the other person responds without asking a question in return. That, in a nutshell, is what is meant by the art of defensive persuasion.

With all this to gain, why not practice asking more questions than you hear? The control you will achieve as a result will immeasurably improve your ability to communicate and negotiate with your customers.

L = Listen

Learn to listen so you can really hear and absorb what others are trying to tell you. After all, God did make people with two ears but only one mouth. He was trying to tell us something. Twice as much listening as talking is a good rule in life. For anyone in sales, it is vital.

Listening is an art in itself. When you listen well, you use your eyes as well as your ears. Look at the speaker after asking the questions and tune your eyeballs to VHF—very high frequency. If you show that degree of interest, the odds are that prospects will tell you more than they had originally planned. You will thus have made it easier for them to reveal the things you must know to achieve your sales objectives.

As already indicated, body language can provide many clues. Thus, not only listen to what prospects say, but equally important, watch what they reveal by what they do not say. Do not be a passive listener waiting for the next chance to speak. Rather, participate in the two-way exchange that is taking place.

U = Understand What You Hear

Do people always say what they mean? Of course not. Words are a poor vehicle for human communication and thought. They can easily prevent you from understanding what is meant unless you learn to question and explore them. Remember, words produce mental images that vary according to personal experience, education, and knowledge. So, do not jump to conclusions.

C = Confirm What You Understand

When in doubt about what your customer really means, take a moment to verify it:

> *"Is this what you mean, Mr. Greene? Did I understand you correctly? You plan to ...?"*
> *"Permit me to clarify my understanding of what you just said. You would like to ...?"*

Reflective questioning allows you to confirm what you hear and remain in control at the same time.

K = Keep Control at All Times

Keeping control does not mean doing most of the talking. To the contrary, it means asking questions and directing the conversation in ways that are helpful to those you want to understand. People are responsive to people. It is your job to help customers to respond to you in positive rather than negative ways. A good way to achieve this is to follow the eight rules to better communication:

1. Create and maintain a climate of *acceptance* at all times.
2. Command and hold the other person's *attention*.
3. Build bridges to *agreement* and understanding.
4. *Ask* the right questions.
5. *Listen* with active interest and full attention.
6. *Understand* what you hear.
7. *Confirm* what you understand.
8. *Keep control* by knowing the roles you play.

NATURAL COMMUNICATION TOOLS

The five basic senses are hearing, seeing, touching, smelling, and tasting. These are the sensors that feed information to the brain by means of an intricate network of nerve cells, muscles, and organs. They are like doors that can be unlocked with the right keys or tools.

In new home sales, customers' senses of smell or taste are seldom appealed to for primary communication. In most daily encounters, salespeople are concerned with the first three: sound, sight, and touch. Touch might better be broadened to the term *action,* namely, that which involves physical or cooperative response from someone who is affected by the salesperson.

Understanding how to use your natural tools to command maximum attention in these areas will improve your ability to communicate with others. This chapter takes each of the three major senses and shows ways to use them to influence and control others.

Sound: The Most Important Tool

From prehistoric times, when people first uttered sounds that others recognized as expressions of pain, joy, sorrow, or other emotions, people have relied heavily upon their voices to convey their thoughts, feelings, and needs. And, as with early man, the human voice is still the most important tool of communication.

What a marvelous instrument, the human voice! It is capable of conveying almost every thought or emotion a person can generate. With a wide range of sounds and capacity for self-expression, people can move others to action, evoke sympathy, provoke anger, and unleash the unlimited power of human understanding. Not to use to maximum advantage the instrument you have been given is to be as careless as a violinist who is content to play on a Stradivarius with broken bow and untuned strings.

Training the Voice. It is surprising how many people take the voice for granted. People do not really hear themselves as others hear them, or reflect on the impression they make. If you had a crippled leg that could be cured with proper treatment, would you willingly go through life without doing something about it? Of course not. How much more important, then, are the sounds you produce with your voice. Nearly everything you want in life depends upon securing the cooperation of other people and certainly upon your ability to relay your desires to them in ways that will make them react favorably.

Trying to communicate with a mechanism that is crippled because it has not been properly trained or exercised limits your own growth.

Have you ever heard yourself on a tape recorder? Did you sound the way you thought you would? Chances are that you were surprised, because people never really hear themselves as they sound to other people.

If you have not heard your voice, take the time to practice with a tape recorder and try to listen objectively to the quality of the sounds you produce. If you are dissatisfied with what you hear, then it might be wise to develop a personal program for self-improvement.

There are many elements to effective speaking, which can be classified broadly into four areas:

- Pitch;
- Pace;
- Power;
- Pause.

Applied with balance and contrast, these four *P*'s can be keys to better speaking.

Pitch. Your voice has a natural range of sounds of an octave or more within which you can comfortably express yourself. The best speaking voices are lower pitched and resonant. Higher-pitched tones are usually irritating, while lower ones tend to be soothing and pleasant. Within your normal range, you have great flexibility, and you can learn to emphasize the more resonant, low-pitched sounds, rather than the strident higher notes. This takes practice, but with singing, humming, and correct breathing, you can adjust your pitch.

Modulation is varying the pitch to produce interesting contrasts and provide dramatic emphasis to the words you speak. With conscious effort, anyone can improve his or her ability to modulate the voice and give it more resonance.

Pace. The speed—or pace—with which you speak is another key element in your effectiveness as a communicator. Most salespeople tend to speak too fast. They race from word to word, machine-gun fashion, forcing their listeners to either keep pace or miss the message.

Numerous studies have demonstrated that most people are poor listeners, retaining less than 25 percent of what they hear. Thus, the onus is on the speaker to compensate for this deficiency. Controlling the pace of the spoken word is one way to do so.

It is also important to keep in mind that contrast is a vital element of communication. When any single technique is used to the exclusion of the others, it becomes self-defeating. Thus, while the listener hears and retains more when you use words deliberately and at a measured pace, you must change the pace from time to time to create interesting variations.

Power. This is achieved through a combination of volume, enunciation, and projection. It is normal to think first in terms of volume as the obvious way to get more attention with your voice; speak louder, and maybe the other person will listen. Once in a while, this is the only approach. Yet in most conversations, soft tones, well enunciated and projected, are more commanding than loudness. Even more important is the response received from one technique versus the other. Loud sounds seem unfriendly and abrasive to the listener, while quieter tones are usually soothing and more easily absorbed.

Whether loud or soft, the ability to enunciate clearly and distinctly is vital to all speech. Coupled with it is the need to project the voice. Bottling up the sounds inside the body does little to help listeners understand what you are saying. Effective projection is achieved by proper breathing and by controlling the flow of air with efficient enunciation. A well-trained speaker can whisper and still be heard in most situations.

Pause. Coca-Cola has used the slogan, "The pause that refreshes." To paraphrase this, any pause refreshes the ear of the listener. A pause offers contrast to sound. Sound is totally ineffective without silence to accent it. The pause is a form of oral punctuation, and it serves both speaker and listener well. It allows the listeners to absorb what has been said, while preparing their ears for what is to come. It also gives the speaker time to reflect on the fluency of his or her presentation and to set the stage for the words that follow.

There is a sense of timing to speech just as there is to most things in life. The pause provides a rhythm that can hold the listener's attention. Just as sound itself is a tool to help command attention, so is silence when it is timed effectively. Speakers who have lost their audiences through unexpected interruptions have immediately regained full attention by silence alone. The sheer concentration of the audience was immediately riveted on the speaker's moment of silence.

In a conversation, a pause can also evoke response from people who cannot stand the pressure of the unspoken words surrounding them. Salespeople can learn to use this technique to advantage. When working with a prospect who seems hesitant to open up, try letting the silence following a question persuade the prospect to respond. Do not rush to fill the void yourself.

The Voice in Action. You can learn how to gain attention and influence people with your voice. It is only a question of knowing what to do and having the courage to do it. When you say "hello" or "good afternoon," does it really sound like "I'm glad to see you" or "My day is better because we've met"? Or, does it betray an attitude of indifference and self-involvement? When you tell someone about the things that happen to you, do they sound as interesting, exciting, dangerous, pleasant, or eventful as they really were? Does your voice give color and meaning to your thoughts?

Getting down to the basics, regardless of how well you use your voice, it is the enthusiasm, warmth, and interest you project that others respond to. If you want more attention, let your inflections, tones, and words really convey your thoughts and feelings. When you increase the power of the transmission, you can worry less about the quality of the reception.

Paint Pictures with Words. Words are to a communicator what paints are to an artist: the ingredients the artist has assembled in his or her own creative way to convey meanings to others. Like colors, words have value ranges. They can be warm or cold, exciting or dull, dramatic or moody, depending on how they are selected and brushed onto the conversational canvas.

To have more power to hold attention and create an environment in which your ideas are transmitted with greater impact, try using powerful words—those that carry strong meanings and produce vivid mental images. When words have been overworked and overused, they lose their meaning. Figure 11.1 gives examples of powerful words you can substitute for overworked ones. Try to think of your own to add to this list.

Sight: Visual Tools of Attention

The eyes are pathways to the mind and nearly as important as the voice in their power to command attention. Thus, you can gain attention with visual stimuli; first, by gestures and facial expressions, and second, by introducing props or visual aids to control the eyes of the listener.

Figure 11.1. Use power words to convey your message.

Here is a list of words common to home sales presentations, with suggested alternatives. Add your own improvements regularly.		
Subject	**Common expressions**	**Improved expressions**
Purchasing a home	House Buy Cost Down payment Deal	Home Invest Investment Initial investment Transaction Opportunity
	Contract Offer Monthly payments Sign Lot	Purchase agreement Proposal Monthly investments Approve Homesite Acreage Location
	Lot hold Closing papers Closing costs Prorate Prorations Mortgage Second mortgage Reduce Reduction	Homesite reservation Ownership documents Transfer adjustments Adjust Adjustments Financing Additional financing Adjust Special value
Size	Small	Cozy Efficient Pleasant
	Large	Expansive Spacious
Sound	Noise level Sound barriers Sound transmissions	Sound level Acoustically engineered Decibel ratings
Homeowners' association	Homeowners' association	Community services association

Improving Communication Skills 319

Figure 11.1. (continued)

Subject	Common expressions	Improved expressions
Homeowners' association (continued)	Maintenance fees	Community improvement fees
	New lifestyle	Improved lifestyle
Rooms in a home	Living room	Formal living area Entertainment center
	Family room	Family activity center Informal living area
	Convertible room	Library Retreat Multi-purpose room Attitude adjustment room
	Kitchen	Food preparation center Garden kitchen Country kitchen
	Bedroom(s)	Master suite Owners' suite Sleeping wing Quiet zone
	Basement	Lower level Future amusement room Service and bonus storage area
	Patio or deck	Outdoor living room Garden terrace Sunshine room
Building design elements	Floor plan	Room arrangement Interior design
	Space	Dimension Openness Flow of space relationships Definition of space

Figure 11.1. (continued)

Subject	Common expressions	Improved expressions
Building design elements (continued)	Architecture	Design concepts Harmony with environment
Land plans	Subdivision	Community neighborhood village(s)
	Planned unit development	Environmental community Balanced environmental plan Open-space community
	Streets	Automobile circulation patterns Streetscapes Curvilinear planning
	Sidewalks	Pedestrian circulation area Paths Walkways
	Landscaping	Parks Open space Natural gardens Manicured lawns
Sales words	No, it's not included.	That's an optional Decorator's concept. Custom option Design alternative Personalized feature Available if desired Something you can do after taking possession.
	Find	Discover Appreciate Experience Enjoy

Although props such as those discussed later in this chapter are valuable tools for holding the interest of others, your own expressions and actions are the best tools. People are capable of producing positive, negative, or neutral reactions just by how they react to what others say. Keep this in mind when reading the following discussion of how to use visual tools to greatest advantage.

The Eyes Have It. Have you ever noticed how your eyes can act as a magnet to attract attention? Just looking at someone can compel him or her to look at you. Next to your voice, your eyes are your most effective attention-getting tool.

Like most of your physical attributes, you cannot remake your eyes. But you can learn to turn up the intensity with which they transmit your inner thoughts. Enthusiasm, zest for living, and excitement are conveyed by sparkling eyes. Lifeless, dull, and colorless eyes betray a feeling of indifference to the world and the people in it.

When speaking, focus your eyes on your listener. That does not mean you should make him or her uncomfortable by staring, but rather that you should use your eyes to maintain visual contact at all times. Your eyes can convey part of the meaning behind your words, while simultaneously monitoring your listener's reactions so that you can adjust your presentation.

Similarly, when listening to other people, watch how they use their eyes, expressions, gestures, and body to convey what they really feel and mean. More important, when you turn your visual attention on people, they are likely to try hard to make themselves understood because of your obvious interest.

The process is like the spark that starts an engine: Unless there is enough power to unleash a chain reaction, the motor coughs, sputters, and stops. Conversation is started by the sparks of attention shown by the participants and fed by the interest each develops in the other. Without such attention, the conversation, like the car with a weak battery, will not get started. Admittedly, there are times when you do not want to keep a conversation going, and the surest way to end it is to shut off your attention.

Your Face Reflects What You Feel. If your eyes play the leading role in conveying nonverbal messages, your facial expressions are the supporting cast. How expressive are you? Do you show interest in people by projecting your emotions? You can learn to be more expressive primarily by allowing your muscles to act in concert with your feelings.

Observe little children, and you will see natural expression at its best. They tend to reflect their every emotion without embarrassment or hesitation. As people grow up, they learn to restrain these basic impulses and gradually lose much of their ability to communicate in this nonverbal manner. If you want people to be responsive to you, do not bottle up your interest and enthusiasm for life. Relax—and others will relax with you. Help others to express their feelings more fully by using your own as a catalyst for communication.

Allowing others to see your friendship and understanding increases their interest in you. A friend once described a smile as "the light in the window that says your heart is at home." Smiling at someone creates a feeling of goodwill and friendship. The smile says:

"I like you."
"I'm glad you came."
"I am friendly."

The person at whom you smile invariably smiles back, thus triggering a favorable response that can be the prelude to conversation. In one sense the person is returning your expression, but in a deeper sense his or her smile reflects the pleasant feeling of well-being you have given.

If you have trouble smiling quickly and naturally, you can improve this valuable asset by conscious practice. Stand in front of a mirror and smile at yourself in different ways. The smile that counts is the one that comes from deep inside and shows sincere interest in others—but you have to let it out if it is to work for you.

Gestures: Actions that Reinforce Words

You have undoubtedly heard someone say about another person, "If you tied his hands behind his back, he couldn't say a word." Perhaps you are this way too. Most people use gestures to give visual emphasis to what they say, and they feel constrained if they cannot use their hands and bodies to accent their words.

Gestures help bring one's thoughts to life in ways that the voice alone cannot fully accomplish. To be really effective, gestures should be natural, not studied or contrived.

In a class for training public speakers, one young student was particularly reticent about using his hands. When I asked him why, he replied, "I just don't know how to gesture," and as he said these words, he automatically raised his hands in an outward motion of helplessness. After we both enjoyed a hearty laugh, he returned to the stage and began to let his hands reinforce his speech in a relaxed, natural way.

Everyone gestures hundreds of times each day. People nod their heads, shrug their shoulders, move their bodies, and use their hands in a variety of ways that tell others how they feel. If you sense that you are inadequately using your natural powers to gesture, then force yourself for a period of time. Ultimately, if you work at it, your muscles and emotions will act in unison with the rhythm of your words.

PROPS AND VISUAL AIDS

Props and visual aids range from such simple things as pens, pointers, or papers to the graphics and displays in sales offices. In a more sophisticated form, they may be overhead projectors, color slides, or complicated teaching machines. Such props and visual aids can augment your natural tools.

Educators know the value of visual aids in teaching, and sales managers know the impact of sales presentations that incorporate visual materials. The benefits that make props so valuable include the following:

- They control the eyes of the viewer, thus concentrating his or her attention on a specific subject.
- They transmit information in visual form and help to reinforce what is said.
- They supply information in a logical order; each visual frame becomes a foundation on which the next one can be structured.
- They allow the speaker to use showmanship to increase the audience's interest.

In simple conversations, people employ props to control attention and stimulate interest. When they gesture with a pencil, a sheet of paper, or a pair of eyeglasses, they add emphasis to their words. In selling, brochures, charts, pictures, and forms are used to involve the buyer while the salesperson leads the buyer's thoughts and emotions toward a targeted conclusion. Research has shown that information transmitted in both visual and oral forms, rather than by either alone, is normally 87 percent more effective in the areas of understanding, credibility, and retention.

Finally, showmanship is another reason for using visual aids during communication. Magicians, comedians, clowns, and artists use colorful or unusual props to distract the audience from their sleight of hand. Visual aids can serve the salesperson in a similar way. Introducing attention-getting visual tools at the right time creates a sense of drama that heightens your listeners' interest. Showmanship can convert the commonplace into a stimulating event. While some people seem to possess more natural showmanship than others, every individual can learn to inject drama and suspense into his or her conversation.

COOPERATIVE RESPONSE

Getting the other person to do something with you—engage in a physical activity or respond in a way that encourages him or her to move from a passive to an active state—automatically improves your chances of retaining the person's interest. If you ask him or her to do something that also involves other senses, the resulting impact is even greater:

"Feel this velvet wallpaper, Mrs. Smith."
"Try putting these together."
"Please, take my pen and write these figures down."

If the customer follows your suggestions, you have gained a measure of psychological control, while creating mental and emotional involvement in the events you have staged.

CONCLUSION

With practice, you should be able to control the amount of qualifying time you spend with any potential buyer by using your tools of attention. Your voice should reflect interest, enthusiasm, and warmth. Your eyes, facial expressions, and bodily gestures should emphasize what you say and reinforce your prospect's interest in you. When introducing visual aids or props, use them in ways that will generate further interest and attention. Mixed with all of these actions, also obtain prospects' cooperative response by asking them questions and getting them to do things with you that will increase their involvement.

On high-traffic days, you may want to change your approach, to give yourself more freedom to separate the real prospects from the suspects. On low-traffic days, you can invest more time in customers, to increase their interest while qualifying them in greater depth. In any case, your tools will always be the tools of communication discussed in this chapter.

12: Creativity in Selling and Financing

THE NEED TO UNDERSTAND CREATIVE FINANCING IN TODAY'S HOUSING MARKETS

The world of real estate financing has dramatically changed in the 1980s. The normal concepts that previously existed have undergone a revolution, due to rapidly fluctuating interest rates, shortages of mortgage funds, and attempts by institutions to adjust to the uncertainties of long-term financing. A prime example of this revolution was the introduction of the variable rate mortgage in the mid-1970s —followed by graduated mortgage payment plans and renegotiable mortgages with limited time periods. The types of mortgage financing are now so complex and the variety so great that it is difficult to keep pace with the changes.

It is not the purpose of this book to educate you about all the various aspects of home financing. This information is best obtained from your local mortgage lenders and your company, since your current local needs are not necessarily applicable to salespeople in other areas of the nation. Instead, the focus of this chapter is on checklists of creative ideas for arranging financing for new home prospects. Understanding the basics of primary financing plans is no longer sufficient. It is also vital to know how to help potential homebuyers arrange their personal assets so as to qualify for available mortgage programs. Other questions arise when the customer is trying to sell an existing home in order to buy a new one, or when the salesperson needs to overcome the customer's fears of accepting financing plans that will be less desirable in the future.

The first part of this chapter lists proven concepts to meet specific situations. Refer to these guides whenever you need ideas to help you resolve a financing challenge.

CREATIVE FINANCING CHECKLISTS

Terminology

Some of the terms and phrases used in this chapter may be unfamiliar. Refer to the glossary that follows this chapter for any term or phrase you do not completely understand.

One phrase needs special explanation: the term *key seller*. As used in this chapter, a key seller is any seller whose property is being sold subject to the sale of another home. This can be a builder whose new home sale is contingent upon unlocking the equity in the buyer's present residence. It also can be a resale seller whose sale is subject to the sale of yet another property. Related phrases, such as *equity guarantee, equity loan,* and *bridge loan,* are defined in the glossary.

Key Seller Assistance Plans

This section of the creative financing checklist identifies ideas that can be used to assist homebuyers finance and purchase a home. The key seller normally makes some concessions or agrees to special approaches in order to achieve the desired sale. Your builder may be unable to employ these techniques. Sometimes they are applied only to individual "spec" homes that must be sold during a clean-up phase. In any case, these concepts can help buyers who have homes to sell and whose prospective purchasers must, in turn, sell their older homes to complete the transactions.

Installment sale agreements:

- Contract for deed.
- Land contract of sale.
- Wraparound mortgage or deed of trust.
- Purchase-money mortgage.

Equity option plans:

- Lease with option-to-purchase agreement.
- Equity savings plan (with or without occupancy).
- Option to purchase with forfeitable deposit or liquidated damages.
- Reservation agreements with release clauses.

Primary financing assistance plans:

- Buy-down mortgage agreements to reduce interest rates. Paying discount points to secure financing commitment.
- Prepaid interest for a specified period of time, such as the first year.
- Use of compensating balances with lender to secure financing for buyer.
- Key seller pledges to lending institution (with or without security deposits) the necessary guarantee to obtain loan for buyer. Conditions for pledges are often tied to specific mortgages.
- Agreement to pay for costs of refinancing within specified time period, such as one year.

Secondary financing assistance plans:

- Key seller accepts second mortgage or deed of trust on key home to finance part of equity.
- Key seller accepts second mortgage or deed of trust on buyer's equity in present home.
- Key seller accepts blanket mortgage or blanket deed of trust on both key and buyer's homes.
- Key seller makes equity loan to buyer from proceeds of key home sale and financing proceeds.

Programs used by builders and Realtors® to reduce costs, risks, and financing fears of buyers:

- Commission loans (Realtors®).
- Sweat equity programs to build down payment or establish qualifying amounts (builders).
- Guaranteed buy-back agreements. These normally have time limits and exclusions. They often cover only the return of the initial cash investments and require that property must be in new condition as received.
- Guarantee to refinance property within specified time period, or to pay for the costs of refinancing, with limitations.
- Rate-watcher's guarantee. A commitment to keep the buyer posted on financing opportunities after the sale is made. There are no obligations to incur any costs for this service.
- Agreement to pay certain prescribed costs of refinancing (without liability for securing).

- Acceptance of escrow assignment against sale in progress on buyer's home.
- Acceptance of assignment of rents as security against investment property owned by buyer.

Sources of Capital or Credit Available to Homebuyers

This section identifies various resources often available that homebuyers can use to secure funds for a housing down payment or for improving their capacity to qualify for new financing. Although many of these sources are effective only with marginal, low-cost housing situations, others apply even to luxury housing. Some represent duplication of ideas contained in other sections but are indexed here because they specifically refer to ways buyers can improve their own opportunities to purchase housing.

Basic sources of personal financing:

- Cash-valued life insurance, which can normally be borrowed by the beneficiary at low rates of interest.
- Credit unions—often excellent sources of short-term loans and occasionally of long-term financing.
- Unsecured bank loans based on financial statement and credit history.
- Passbook loans against savings, money certificates, treasury bills, bonds, etc., that owner does not want to sell or disturb.
- Consumer finance companies for originating or consolidating loans.
- Close relatives, associates, or friends.
- Company loans or employer guarantees.
- Stock options that might be sold or pledged.

Basic sources of income (credit or cash) from productive efforts:

- Advances on wages.
- Personal savings.
- Assignment of future income from bonuses, commissions, dividends, annuities, interest, or profit-sharing agreements.
- Income tax refunds.
- Trusts, pension funds, or inheritances.
- Notes, securities, bonds, stocks.
- Additional employment for one or more members of the family.

Chattel that can be sold, hypothecated, or pledged as collateral for cash or credit:

- Automobiles or other vehicles.
- Jewelry, valuable coins, stamp collections.
- Art collections.
- Hobbies and hobby equipment such as cameras.
- Household furnishings (not very practical except for low-income housing).

Real estate assets that can be used to secure financing or capital:

- Originate a second mortgage and use proceeds to purchase or finance a home.
- Originate a new first loan on property and use proceeds to purchase or finance a home.
- Secure an equity loan from any one of a number of sources, including banks, Realtors®, key seller, builder.
- Convert property into investment rental and pledge security, if needed, of either rental income or property itself.
- Sell the property with terms, and assign interest in contract for deed or second mortgage to the key seller.

Creative concepts of personal financing arrangements:

- Have corporation purchase the property and sell it back under long-term agreement.
- Establish life estates with or without trusts where family relationships dictate this approach.
- Enter into a shared appreciation mortgage financing plan with someone interested in receiving a portion of the equity gain when sold plus a normal return on the loan. This is often done with a close relative, such as parents or children.

Third-Party Homebuyer Assistance Plans

This section lists ideas that may apply where there are third parties interested in the purchasers' homebuying needs. These are usually most appropriate with close relatives, such as parents or children. However, they may also apply to employers, business associates, or others who have a motivation to be of assistance.

Gifts and endowments:

- Gift letters (made with or without actual contributions).
- Letters of commitment to make a contribution if it is needed in the future.
- Trust endowments, such as parents might provide for their children.

Underwriting guarantees and warranties:

- Co-signatures on notes and mortgages to provide sufficient qualifying credit.
- Continuing guarantee agreements—normally executed to the lender to extend the liability beyond the real estate to those signing the guarantee.
- Letters of credit—most often used by corporations on behalf of employees or by banks, particularly for transferees whose properties are not yet sold in the cities of origin.

Pledges and secured collateral from third parties:

- Pledging part or all of the equity or net proceeds from the sale of the key home as security in a savings account against the buyer's new loan. Term and amount are negotiable with the lending institution.
- Assigning assets in personal or real property as security for performance of qualifying buyer.
- Maintaining a compensating balance at a bank or savings institution as an incentive to the lender to make the necessary loan to the buyer.

Ventureships and participating real estate interests:

- Shared ownership with equal interests either as tenants in common or in joint tenancy.
- Purchase by one party (or corporation) and lease to purchasers under option to buy or equity accumulation plan.
- Ventureship purchase agreement that specifies one party to receive the equity gain and the other the tax shelter.
- Shared appreciation agreements in exchange for lending the money needed to complete the purchase. This is now being done by some primary lenders, but it also can apply to third

parties who make loans or provide guarantees needed to qualify the buyer.

Plans for Helping Equity Buyers to Unlock Their Equities

This section deals with the various programs that have been successfully used by Realtors® and builders to handle equity buyers' situations. Since this is merely a checklist and not an instructional manual, the details for each procedure must be obtained from a more comprehensive source, such as The Creative Financing Skill Development Series (published by the Real Estate Education Company) or Dave Stone's books *Creative Financing* (The Stone Institute, Inc.) and *The Guaranteed Sales Plan* (National Association of Realtors®).

Guarantee agreements:

- Guaranteed equity purchase agreements, otherwise known as the guaranteed sales plan.
- Direct purchases or cash-out purchase agreements.
- Guarantee-to-finance agreements.
- Reverse guarantees made to the key seller by the trader or Realtor®.
- Sell-back agreements giving equity buyer an opportunity to repurchase without cost if he or she desires to cancel the guaranteed equity agreement and providing he or she waives any contingency on the key home.

Equity loans or advances:

- Equity loans made to bridge the sale of the older home to the new property. Such loans may be secured or unsecured.
- Commission loans (made by real estate agents).
- Bank guarantees to back up the buyer's equity loan from another source.
- Pledges of compensating balances or other equities to secure interim financing for the homebuyer.
- Stand-by commitments made by lending institutions or third parties to provide equity loans if needed.
- Letters of credit from corporations interested in completing the sale.
- Overage loans made by primary lender against secured balances.

Equity participation plans:

- Builder and Realtor® agree to share loss or gain on the acquisition and resale of the equity property.
- Builder agrees to provide the funds for acquisition and Realtor® trader agrees to take all risks of loss or gain.
- Equity buyer purchases property with agreement to split all proceeds in excess of an agreed-upon net with the trader, Realtor® or builder in exchange for the guarantee and/or an equity advance.
- Equity participation agreements with primary lenders on the acquisition and resale of equity property.

Time-limit purchase agreements:

- Reservations or hold agreements with time limits while trade or appraisal is being made.
- Release clauses in purchase agreement on key home where contingencies are involved. Normally 48 to 72 hours are given to the buyer to release the contingency or be canceled from further rights in the property.
- Agreement to hold prices for equity buyer if actions are pursued to complete sale of equity home as specified.

Factors to Consider When Qualifying a Buyer for Financing

This section lists items that a lender usually considers when qualifying a buyer for financing. Some general guidelines are shown in Figure 12.1. To back up the necessary information, buyers should submit the items shown in Figure 12.2.

Employment:

- How long has the buyer been on the job?
- Has the buyer switched jobs frequently?
- Are past and present jobs related?
- Normally, if the buyer has been on the job for a short period of time, lenders may consider the buyer premature (buying too early).
- If the buyer has had several jobs over a relatively short time, there must be a very good reason or reasons, such as a truck driver changing companies or a mechanic changing shops.
- Past jobs and present job should be related.

Figure 12.1. Conventional qualification sheet.

Credit guidelines

Stability of income	Income for past two years must be verified.
Secondary income	Overtime, bonuses, part-time jobs, etc., will not be considered unless established for three years. Need three years' W-2 forms to establish.
Spouse's income	Generally 100 percent will be considered if proven for two years.
Self-employed	Will not be considered unless records for three years are available and they show stability.
Age of borrower	Maturity not to go beyond age 80. Retirement income must be established.
Past credit	Record must be nearly spotless.

Income test

1. Borrower's monthly gross income and spouse's income $_____

2. Monthly mortgage payment including taxes and insur-taxes and insurance (this answer should not exceed line #1) $_____
   Multiply by 4 $_____

3. Monthly mortgage payment including taxes and insurance $_____
   Other debts with over 10 months to run
   (monthly payments).................... $_____
   $_____
   $_____
   $_____

   Total of mortgage payments and other debts $_____

   Multiply by 3 (this answer should not exceed line #1) $_____

If neither the answer to line #2 nor to line #3 exceeds line #1, the borrower should qualify. It is important that the amount put on line #1 be computed only after considering the credit guidelines.

Figure 12.2 Items needed at time of application.

- ☐ Name, age, and social security number of borrower and co-borrower.
- ☐ All household and/or family income that is to be counted toward the loan:
  - ☐ Name and address of *all* employers for the past two years.
  - ☐ Position and length of time on job(s).
  - ☐ Income: base earnings, average overtime, commissions, bonuses.
  - ☐ Documentation on any child support payments if they are to be used as income.
  - ☐ Verification of social security benefits, VA benefits, other benefits.
  - ☐ If self-employed, copies of past two years' federal income tax returns, including Schedule C.

  Information as to all sources of money to be used for down payment and closing costs.

- ☐ Bank accounts (checking and savings): name and address of bank(s), current balances, account numbers, name accounts are in.
- ☐ Stocks and savings bonds: type and current value.
- ☐ Life insurance: amount of coverage and approximate cash value.
- ☐ Year, make, and current market value of automobile(s).
- ☐ Approximate value of furniture now owned.
- ☐ Current balance, account numbers, and monthly payments on all open credit accounts and loans.
- ☐ Name and address to whom payments are made.
- ☐ Same information on any paid accounts as on open accounts, going back at least two years.
- ☐ Typed letter explaining any adverse credit, including bankruptcy. Explanation of circumstances of bankruptcy, including copy of schedule of bankruptcy and reinstatement of debts.

Figure 12.2. (continued)

- ☐ Monthly house or rent payment and average monthly utilities.
- ☐ Copy of purchase agreement and listing sheet.
- ☐ Landlord information: names and addresses of all landlords for the last two years.
- ☐ Certificate of eligibility or copy of Form DD214, if VA loan.
- ☐ Nearest living relative: name and address (for VA only).
- ☐ Divorce decree and verification of child support, if applicable.
- ☐ Rental income (leases permit better evaluation of income derived from rentals); profit and loss statement showing rent collected monthly, mortgage payment, utilities, net profit.
- ☐ Former homes: if sold within past two years, any available papers for verification.
- ☐ Checks for appraisal and credit report, if applicable.

- If there has been more than one job, there should be a letter explaining the change and relationship of the jobs, income, etc.

Income:

- Use pay stubs to verify income.
- Due to the economy, is the buyer working a full 40 hours or less?
- Has the buyer been off work due to layoff, illness, or accident?
- If the buyer has lost income due to layoff, illness, or accident, there should be a letter explaining this.
- FHA probably will not count all of the buyer's overtime as income unless it can be well documented.
- *Support income*—if applicant desires the income to be counted, it may be taken into consideration for underwriting purposes.
- *Co-applicant's income*—will be considered on an equal basis as that of the applicant if it is needed to qualify for the loan.
- The same requirements must be met as those of the applicant.
- *Rental income*—FHA normally will consider only 2/3 of this income. Have copies of leases, if possible.

- *Welfare, AFDC income*—FHA will consider all if the children are 13 years old or younger. The income of children who are over 13 years of age will not be counted.
- *Social security and pension income*—same as for welfare income.
- *Self-employed*—Use federal income tax returns for the last two years, financial statement, and a year-to-date profit and loss statement completed by accountant.

Present housing expense:

- The proposed mortgage payment should be compared to the previous mortgage or rent payment.
- A reasonable increase creates no problem.
- In the event of a major increase (approximately 5 percent of gross monthly income), closer scrutiny is required. For example, if the buyer's present housing expense is low, but the applicant is unable to save money and has incurred much debt for which he or she is having trouble paying, it would be difficult to justify a major increase in housing expense.

Assets:

- Does the buyer have sufficient assets for the down payment and/or closing costs?
- If the buyer has sufficient assets, where will they come from?
- Down payment and/or closing costs *cannot* be borrowed.
- If all or a substantial portion of the down payment and/or closing costs were put up in earnest money, then the source of these funds must be verified.
- If the verification of deposit is going to show a large deposit made recently, the source of these funds also will have to be verified.
- If the down payment and/or closing costs, in part or whole, are to be derived from the sale of other real estate, a copy of the offer to purchase and closing statement must be obtained. If this is the case, FHA will normally make the approval of the loan subject to the sale of the property.
- *Gift letter*—if the down payment and/or closing costs are derived from a gift, a handwritten letter from the donor is required. It must include:
  1. Relationship to applicant;
  2. Complete address;

Creativity in Selling and Financing   339

    3. Telephone number; and
    4. Statement that no repayment is intended.

- The funds from the gift must be either deposited in the buyer's bank account and verified or verified in the donor's account.
- *Bonds or stocks*—should be verified with copies of each or with a letter from a bank official stating that he or she has witnessed the bonds for ownership and worth.

Liabilities (credit):

- How is the buyer's credit?
- All accounts must be rated; this is done through the credit bureau. *Exception:* Some creditors do not cooperate with the credit bureaus; therefore, attempt to have the buyer obtain a letter from these creditors to rate the account. If this cannot be done, use a copy of the buyer's last billing statement. Accounts are rated I-1 (excellent) to I-9 (normally a collection).
- A buyer should have good credit, without a series of slow accounts, collections, or bankruptcy.
- Normally, a buyer who has credit problems confined to a short period of time, for which there is a good explanation of the cause, may be accepted.
- Every bankruptcy situation is different, and there is no guarantee that the loan will be approved.
- Normally, the reason for a time period from the bankruptcy to applying for a loan is to see how the buyer has handled his or her credit from that point. In other words, has the buyer gone back to the creditor (reaffirmed) and re-established his or her credit, and are all the accounts up-to-date and in good standing?
- The reason for filing bankruptcy plays a big part in whether or not the buyer will be accepted. Did the buyer get so far into debt by foolish spending, or was there a specific reason such as one account, for example, a car that was a lemon and for which the buyer could get no satisfaction and had no other choice?
- A good, detailed explanation letter must be written to explain bankruptcy.
- Any past due accounts must be brought up-to-date.
- Any accounts rated less than I-1 will need a letter of explanation.
- *Suits, unpaid collections, judgments, or repossessions* are handled much like bankruptcies. They must all be paid (with very few exceptions) before a buyer can apply for a loan. Pay-

ing them at the time of applying for a mortgage is also frowned upon and viewed as being paid only to obtain a mortgage.
- Again, letters of explanation are necessary.

Owning other real estate:

- You should know the following:
    1. Address;
    2. Is it to be sold?;
    3. How is it presently financed?;
    4. Sales price;
    5. Original mortgage amount;
    6. Lender and account number;
    7. Unpaid mortgage balance.
- If the present home was purchased with an FHA-insured loan, and the buyer wishes to buy another home through FHA without selling the first, find out the following:
    1. Is the present mortgage amount paid down 15 percent or more from the original mortgage maount?
    2. If not, but you think the present market value has increased, an appraisal can be ordered. If the mortgage has been paid down 15 percent or more from the present maximum mortgage amount, the buyer can usually qualify for another FHA loan.

Before the salesperson or management submits the package to the lender, the salesperson or manager should review the checklist shown in Figure 12.3, to be sure that all items usually needed have been covered.

AN APPLICATION OF CREATIVE FINANCING TECHNIQUES

The Case of Mary and John Jones

Mary and John Jones have been thinking about buying a new home for some time now, but they have hesitated doing so because they have limited reserve funds for the down payment. They do, however, have a fairly adequate monthly income to meet the mortgage requirements for the loan they will need. They are under 30 years old and have two young children. John is a junior executive with a major corporation in the area and has a secure and promising future.

Figure 12.3. Mortgage loan closing checklist.

Note provisions:
- ☐ Cosigners, if any
- ☐ Type of prepayment clause
   Closed?
- ☐ Participation clauses
   Basis
- ☐ Note rate versus state usury rate (corporate or individual)
- ☐ Balloon balances, if any
- ☐ Seal affixed, if corporate

Mortgage (or deed of trust):
- ☐ Even date with note
- ☐ Contains maturity date
- ☐ Identified with note, as required
- ☐ Additional signatures to subordinate other interests such as leasehold or life estate
- ☐ Properly recorded in county records
- ☐ Are escrows required?
- ☐ Closed or open-ended?

Title insurance policy:
- ☐ Amount of policy
   Who insured?
- ☐ Legal description versus mortgage description
- ☐ Unquestionable identification of mortgage lien insured
   First?
- ☐ Exceptions allowed, such as easements and other rights
   Detrimental to your position?
- ☐ Nondrilling agreement, where applicable
- ☐ American Land Title Association (ALTA) endorsement
- ☐ Mechanic's lien coverage
- ☐ Encroachment survey insured
- ☐ Protection under reversion clauses
- ☐ Deed restrictions, if any

Closing statement:
- ☐ Executed by borrower
- ☐ Status of taxes and insurance
- ☐ Prepayments on assumptions, if any
- ☐ Regulation Z, if required

Survey:
- ☐ Current as to improvements?
- ☐ Covers all property mortgaged?

Figure 12.3. (continued)

Survey: (continued)
- ☐ Stake survey or loan survey?
- ☐ Insured by title policy?

Insurance coverage:
- ☐ Mortgage clauses
- ☐ Amount of coverage
- ☐ Types of coverage applicable to this type of property
- ☐ Notification to mortgagee in case of nonpayment or cancellation

Financing statement, if any:
- ☐ Filed with secretary of state
- ☐ Covers furniture, fixtures, furnishings, equipment, and replacements thereof
- ☐ Covers products of collateral, if any
- ☐ Set records to refile at proper intervals

Conditional assignment of leases, if any:
- ☐ General assignment of all leases, or just specific ones?
- ☐ Rights in event of condemnation or destruction of property
- ☐ Leases superior or inferior to mortgage?
- ☐ Require subordination agreement, if needed

Appraisal report:
- ☐ Note purpose of appraisal and date
- ☐ Appraiser's qualification concerning type of property
- ☐ Final completion report in respect to plans and specifications

Application, miscellaneous:
- ☐ Special-application requests, if any
- ☐ Credit reports
- ☐ Photographs of security
- ☐ Compliance with applicable zoning laws

Last Sunday, John and Mary Jones visited your new community and showed interest in a model that seems to meet their needs and motivations. However, they resisted when you tried to close them because their savings came to only about half the total down payment that your financing would require. Time and circumstances did not permit you to explore this matter further on Sunday, so you made an appointment for a convenient time in the middle of the week.

During the interim, you prepare yourself to solve the financing situation so that you can try to close the sale. How many ideas can you come up with?

Possible Financing Techniques

The following paragraphs suggest ideas that you might develop to solve Mary and John Jones's need for additional equity capital or financial assistance in buying their new home. Obviously not all will apply to any given situation, but by reviewing this list you should find more than one approach that will work in any individual case.

Add your own ideas to this checklist and then keep it handy. It will be of value to you in many selling situations.

Borrowing against Life Insurance. Borrowing against life insurance is a good way to secure the necessary cash for the down payment if buyers have cash values in life insurance. Cash-valued life insurance policies usually have interest rates built into their policy agreement that are much lower than mortgage or bank rates. Because these loans are made against assets the buyers already have, they may not even have to be repaid and seldom affect buyers' credit ratings for qualifying for a mortgage.

Negotiable Securities. Stocks and bonds are examples of negotiable securities that can be used as collateral to borrow money from a bank. Most banks will lend up to 50 percent of the value of such negotiable securities.

A Margin Account. Negotiable securities can often be placed in a margin account that provides the buyer with funds at terms that are frequently better than what a bank would offer. The stockbroker has a continuing interest in the portfolio, and he or she is likely to make these arrangements if they are in the client's interest.

An Advance on Future Wages. An advance on future wages may be a practical approach, especially if the buyer's employer has reason to want the employee to buy a new home, as would be the case with a transferee. The employer may have more motivation than anyone else to assist the buyer and is in a position to arrange to have the funds paid back easily through nominal deductions from future paychecks.

A Credit Union. If the buyer works for a company that has a credit union, it is often an ideal source of equity capital. Credit unions are designed to help employees buy homes, cars, and other necessities. Many of their loans do not require reporting in the same fashion as bank loans because they are connected with the employee's relationship to his or her company. Thus, the employee's relationship with the credit union is confidential.

Loans or Gifts from Relatives. Loans or gifts from relatives usually involve parents who are willing to help their children buy a home. A gift letter is normally necessary as a rider to the mortgage papers to validate that source of funds.

Sometimes outsiders, such as employers or friends, will make such loans. This, however, is less common.

Future Bonuses. Unclosed commissions or anticipated income above salaries can be pledged with the lending institution as security for an interim loan. For example, a real estate salesperson can borrow against unclosed transactions, or a farmer can borrow against crops that are not yet harvested. The percentage of loan to total assets is often 50 percent or less, as the bank will insist on having a margin of security to protect its interests.

A Secondary Loan. If a buyer owns other real estate, such as an unsold home, a secondary loan can be arranged and secured with this real property. For example, the builder could accept as a down payment against the new home a second mortgage against the old one until it is sold or the second note paid off in some other way.

This is perfectly legal, even in the case of FHA loans. It is essential that it be disclosed, however, as it affects the buyer's ability to qualify for a new mortgage.

Refinancing Real Estate. If the buyer owns real estate that he or she plans to retain, refinancing the mortgage may be a practical way to raise capital. Property appreciates in value, and if the existing loans are less than the maximum loan-to-value ratios permitted, new financing is usually possible.

A Blanket Mortgage. A blanket mortgage is another way to switch equity between two properties when there is a need to secure additional capital to close one of them. The existing property and the new property can be blanketed with one loan, either a first or a second, covering the equity in both properties. If either home is sold, the blanket mortgage, of course, would have to be paid off. In the event that the properties are in two different counties or states, the record of interest on the part of the one holding the blanket mortgage would have to be recorded in both places.

A Personal, Unsecured Loan. If the buyer has reasonably good credit, a personal loan from his or her own bank is a possibility. In fact, it is usually wise to explore this source first. Also, if your buyer owns a local business, and the bank has an interest in the growth of that business, there is strong reason why it would want to help your buyer.

A Pension Trust Fund. If a pension trust fund has accrued assets for future distribution, it can sometimes be used as collateral for borrowing purposes.

Valuable Personal Assets. Personal assets such as jewelry, many types of equipment, hobby collections, and cameras can be used as collateral for loans from some institutions. The rates for this kind of loan are often higher than for regular bank loans, but may be preferable in many cases to alternatives that would require faster repayment, etc.

An Assignment of Future Rents. If your buyer owns rental property that he or she does not want to refinance or encumber with second loans, an assignment of future rents can be used to secure additional funds from either private or public institutions. The builder may, in some cases, be willing to take such security for part of the down payment. Under such an assignment, future rent monies, or portions thereof, are paid directly to the person having the assignment. The assignment also could be used as security for the loan in the event the buyer fails to meet his or her obligation on time.

Passbook Loans. These can easily be obtained against savings accounts the owners may not want to disturb. People can borrow against their own savings, or against the savings of others who are willing to allow those savings to be used as security for the additional funds. Of course, such savings are frozen from withdrawal until the loans have been repaid, but they also continue to earn normal interest as long as the passbook loan is current.

Parents may be willing to allow their savings to be used as security for their children's loans from a mortgage company because it is easier to pay back the savings institution rather than the parents, and it removes part of the mental obligation of a payment to father, mother, or other relative. This is commonly done to secure high loan-to-value ratio loans, such as 95-percent or even 100-percent loans. The difference between that amount and the normal 80-percent or 90-percent loan-to-value ratio is frozen and cannot be withdrawn until the loan is repaid. However, the money continues to earn the normal rates of interest so long as the borrower makes the mortgage payments.

A Business Loan. If your buyer is a local business executive, business equipment, inventories, accounts receivable, etc., are all valid collateral for business loans. Banks are the prime sources of such loans, and if the buyer has a good relationship with his or her banker, it may be easier for him or her to obtain a business loan than other types.

Automobiles. High-valued items can be individually refinanced if the equities are substantial enough. It is not uncommon to take a note against a car and, along with it, the registration for protection until the loan is repaid. People tend to trade in cars more frequently than they do homes; therefore the note is likely to be paid off sooner than if it were pledged against real property.

Outright Sale of Assets. Sometimes people have assets they have not considered selling but that are not as important as their desire to buy a home. Valuable items that could be sold to generate the capital might be preferable to securing a loan. This would be especially true if the buyer's earnings were barely high enough for the required mortgage and if additional payments for special financing might keep him or her from qualifying.

A Purchase-Money Mortgage. If your building company is willing to carry it, a purchase-money mortgage for all or part of the purchase price is a possibility. In this case the builder becomes his or her own lender. He or she will—and should—normally require a higher interest rate than an outside lender would. The builder may want to break the loan into two parts, so that the second could be paid off or be sold or discounted if the builder needs the capital. The first, which is much more secure and has a different discount rate, would be retained. One total mortgage with a nominal down payment has a higher discount than a loan protected by a second mortgage that has been treated separately.

Savings. The buyer may be able to save enough money between the date of the original purchase agreement and the final closing to cover the down payment. For example, if the home is not yet started and it will take several months to build, the time may allow the buyer to save the necessary money.

Sweat Equity. The buyer may agree to perform some part of the work that must be done to the new home. This is known as *sweat equity*. If the buyer already has construction expertise, this is far more practical than if he or she is a novice. Also, such things as painting, finishing of a recreation room, and landscaping can be done by most people. Admittedly, there are many complications in the administration of sweat-equity programs, which is why they are usually limited to low-income, low-cost housing. However, exceptions can be found in all price ranges.

The Co-Mortgagor or Co-Guarantor. Those who will most likely be willing to lend their credit as co-mortgagors or co-guarantors are close relatives with a personal interest in the buyer, such as parents, grandparents, or aunts and uncles. Such a co-mortgagor can also be an employer who is willing to play this financial role owing to confidence in the employee and in his or her future. This is a common method of reinforcing the marginal homebuyer's ability to qualify for the maximum mortgage.

A Pledge or Assignment of Security. A pledge or assignment of security from the seller can be used as a method of securing a maximum loan—or even one that exceeds normal loan-to-value limits. For example, if the normal down payment is 10 percent of the sales price of the new home, and the buyers have only 5 percent to put down, the builder might pledge the extra 5 percent to the lending institution as security until the loan was reduced to the legal limits. This could be in the form of an actual savings deposit made to the savings and loan association, which would earn interest, or it could be an assignment against other assets of the builder. It becomes a pledge in which the builder stands responsible for the loan until it is reduced, and the builder is not out of pocket unless the buyer fails to make the payments.

In return, the builder usually insists on some form of secured protection from the buyer until the mortgage is fully qualified and the funds released. This is usually in the form of a trust deed or some other collateral.

Compensating Balances. A person may deposit substantial funds in a bank or savings and loan association with an unwritten understanding that the lender will make certain loans in return. This is known as a *compensating balance.* For example, if a relative of the buyer has large deposits or checking balances with a particular bank, that bank has a good reason to give particular consideration to any loan requested by that individual. If the employer wants a mortgage approved for a key employee, the bank with whom the company deals has a valid reason for trying to grant the loan. The same thing applies on a smaller scale to any buyer who has good relationships and a healthy compensating balance with his or her bank. That may be the first place to consider trying for the mortgage you need or for additional equity capital.

The Real Estate Salesperson or Broker. This is certainly not one of the favored approaches, but a real estate salesperson or broker sometimes is willing to loan all or part of the commission he or she would earn from making a new home sale to salvage a sale that might not otherwise be completed. Whether or not there is any security against real property depends on the nature of the transaction and the arrangements the salesperson or broker thinks are adequate to protect his or her interests.

A Contract of Sale or Contract for Deed. This has long been used as a substitute for deeding property to buyers with mortgage security when the initial equity payments are lower than desired. Under this method of selling real estate, title does not pass to the buyers until they have made sufficient payments against the contract to equal equity accumulation that will qualify for normal mortgage financing.

The laws concerning contracts for deed, land contracts, or contracts of sale vary among states, and thus the validity of this approach should be reviewed with legal counsel.

A Lease with Option to Buy. Arrangements can normally be made to apply a portion of the rent each month towards the down payment until the prearranged sum has been received by the builder/seller or whoever may be holding the assets at that time. At that point, normal financing is completed, and the home is closed.

One of the disadvantages of the lease-option is that it provides no real assurance the buyer will ultimately close the sale, and the house remains on the builder's books as inventory. It is usually wise to get a substantial forfeitable option at the time the lease-option is executed so that the builder receives at least some money if the buyer should fail to complete the sale.

The Buyer's Spouse. If not currently employed, the buyer's spouse may be willing to take a temporary job until the down payment has been raised. You may even be able to suggest where to find such employment. This solution puts no strain on the family income and allows the buyer to accumulate the capital in time for the closing.

Personal Property Items. Rugs and draperies, furniture, special fixtures, various types of equipment, or other personal property items can be separated from the real property and treated independently. Separate financial arrangements can then be made for those items, such as a note to the seller or financing from other sources.

A Deed of Trust. If these are legal in your state, a deed of trust, or a contract for deed, or a wraparound or all-inclusive deed of trust can be used to achieve the objective of both deeding the property to the buyer and providing the seller with the protection that a deed of trust permits. Under a deed of trust, the borrower conveys title to a trustee who holds title for the benefit of the borrower and lender. Its main advantage is that in the event of default, the trustee has the power to foreclose by a sale of the property at public auction rather than by taking formal court action.

An Open-End Mortgage. An open-end mortgage or an open-end deed of trust can be used to help meet special situations that will call for later refinancing. With the open-end provision in the first mortgage, the buyer can borrow an additional amount up to the limit at a lower cost than through refinancing with a new loan. Any balances that are due others (such as the builder/seller) can then be repaid easily from the proceeds of such an open-end loan, which has been secured after several years of equity accumulation or from prepayments made by the buyer on agreed-upon amounts.

Not all conventional lenders will allow this type of mortgage, but you may be able to find some who do. One point to remember, however, is that the term of the pay-off period usually stays the same. Thus, the monthly payments will be higher for the remaining term of the loan if it is increased to its original amount.

Private Insurance Plans. Private insurance plans insure the excess amounts above the standard loan-to-value ratios that are authorized by conventional lending institutions or by government regulatory agencies. Thus, a 95-percent loan-to-value ratio might be obtained instead of the maximum 90 percent, with the extra five percent being insured through one of these companies.

Check with your local savings and loan associations to see if they have such loans available. There will be a premium of several discount points or processing points to either the buyer or the seller for placing this insurance, but that may be far more worthwhile to the buyer than some of the other arrangements for securing the down payment.

Add Nonrecurring Closing Costs to the Basic Loan. Recently many lending institutions have permitted the inclusion of nonrecurring buyer's closing costs in the amount of the loan, thus decreasing the money necessary for closing. The FHA also allows this procedure if the home qualifies on its basic evaluation.

Nonrecurring closing costs are those costs that are experienced on a one-time basis at closing and would normally be paid by the buyer. Some examples: the mortgage origination fee (not the seller's discount points on an FHA mortgage, as they must be paid by the seller) and the title and settlement costs directly related to processing the sale. Excluded are recurring items such as the prorations of taxes, insurance, and interest.

Decreasing the closing costs decreases the amount of cash a buyer must have on hand when buying a home. Explore with your lender whether or not this concept will work on a specific loan.

Income Tax Refunds. During the early part of the year, ask buyers who are short of cash if they will be receiving income tax refunds, and whether such refunds may be adequate to make up the deficit in the down payment requirement.

Christmas Club Funds. Many people today use Christmas Clubs to accumulate money to spend at Christmas. During the latter part of the year, it is sometimes practical to suggest that buyers use their Christmas Club funds to buy themselves a home rather than spend the money on presents.

Special Corporate Financing. Where transferees are involved, many companies make special financing arrangements to facilitate the acquisition of a home. This is usually explained to the transferee at the time he or she makes a move, but in some cases the transferee may not know about it. Inquire whether or not there are a corporate relocation plan and special company financing that might assist buyers who lack adequate capital.

Stock Options. If the company's stock has increased in value, these options can often be exercised and then the stock sold or transferred to others and the profit from the transaction used to purchase a home.

Annuities or Dividends. People who anticipate annuities or dividends at specific times of the year can pledge them, or use them when they arrive to increase their down payment. You might inquire whether or not your buyer expects any annuities or dividends from stocks or other securities.

Letters of Credit. Letters of credit can be used in special cases, usually for more expensive properties or sizable transactions. A letter of credit from the bank of an individual who has substantial credit but whose funds are momentarily tied up can often suffice in closing a transaction with a builder/seller. Such a letter of credit becomes, in essence, a pledge from one bank to another. It is the security that the individual does have adequate funds, and that a date merely needs to be set for the transfer with a note to back it up. A letter of credit is a supplemental instrument to prove that there are adequate banking arrangements to meet future obligations.

Escrow Assignments. When a transaction has not been closed but is in escrow, an escrow assignment is frequently used to provide an irrevocable transfer of funds from the sale of one piece of property to another. The escrow assignment itself can be used as a security tool once it has been documented. Sales have been known to close with the escrow assignment becoming the security of the down payment necessary to complete another transaction. There must be careful verification that it is a complete escrow and that the document providing irrevocable assignment can be depended upon to fulfill the monetary requirements of the transaction.

SOME CREATIVE MORTGAGE ALTERNATIVES

This checklist indexes some of the mortgage alternatives that may or may not be available in your market. As the real estate industry and the banking communities strive to improve financing methods to contend with the ever-changing economy, more and more of these vehicles will be used.

Contract for Deed or Land Contract. Contracts for deed are discussed in a separate section, beginning on page 353.

Deferred Interest Mortgage. The borrower would be given a lower-than-standard initial interest rate, which would be repaid, with an additional fee, upon the sale of the home.

Dual Rate/Variable Interest Rate Mortgage. Borrowers pay two interest rates—a short-term rate for the interest on the outstanding balance and a long-term rate for the monthly payments.

Flexible Loan Insurance Program (FLIP) Mortgage. Part of the borrower's initial investment (down payment) is deposited in a pledged savings account, from which money is drawn each month for five years to supplement initially reduced monthly mortgage payments.

Flexible Payment Mortgage. Payments cover only the interest on the mortgage for the first term (five or ten years). Payments are then escalated to begin amortization.

Reverse Annuity Mortgage. The lender makes regular payments to the retired homeowner on a fixed income, then collects the debt upon the sale of the property or death of the owner.

Step-Rate Mortgages. Interest rates are scheduled to increase at a predetermined rate and at predetermined intervals.

Alternative Mortgage Instruments

Equity Participation. (Equity participation mortgages are also known as shared appreciation mortgages, or SAMs.) For such a mortgage, a lender or third party offers the borrower a below-market interest rate or offers to participate in the down payment or monthly payments, in exchange for a share in property appreciation upon resale at a specified future date.

Graduated Payment. A graduated payment mortgage is arranged so that monthly payments start out low and increase gradually to a predetermined limit that is higher than for level payment mortgages. This type of loan anticipates that buyers' future incomes will increase, so they qualify for larger loans than their present incomes would permit with a conventional loan.

Renegotiable. A renegotiable mortgage is a short-term loan (usually for five years or less) secured by a long-term mortgage with interest rate adjustments made at predetermined intervals. The rate can go up or down. Renewal is automatic according to previously agreed-upon terms.

Rollover. A rollover mortgage is a short-term loan (usually for five years or less) with payments based on a long-term amortization schedule and the outstanding balance due at the end of the short-term loan. An offer to renew or refinance is guaranteed at the lender's terms. The borrower has the option to accept terms or pay the loan in full.

Rollover Variation. A rollover variation mortgage is a blend of the rollover and wraparound. It permits a buyer to purchase an existing home with a mortgage that pays off the existing one and finances the remainder of money the buyer needs to purchase the house. The rate on the new loan can go up or down every three years, depending upon current costs of money.

Variable Rate. A variable rate mortgage is a single long-term loan that features periodic interest rate changes based on the movement of a predetermined index. Changes are reflected in the monthly payments, term of loan, or both.

Wraparound. Wraparound mortgages are a blend of two or more mortgages. The buyer obtains a mortgage to pay off the seller's mortgage and to obtain additional funds needed to buy a house. The lender, in essence, lets the buyer assume the seller's mortgage by writing a new one that is a combination of two interest rates and much less than the prevailing rate for a conventional loan. For instance, if the seller's mortgage is a 9-percent loan, and the prevailing rate is 15 percent, the rate on the wraparound would be somewhere in between.

CONTRACTS FOR DEED OR LAND CONTRACTS

Types of Contracts for Deed or Land Contracts

Differential. A differential contract means, as the words indicate, *the difference between.* It is used when the subject home has an assumable (assignable) encumbrance against it, and a prospective buyer has only a portion of the remaining balance between the existing financing and the market price in the form of cash down payment. Thus, the remainder must be in the form of a secondary contract that may be either held by the seller or sold on the open market to a disinterested third party. Example:

Sale price	$100,000
Mortgage (first)	(60,000)
Down payment	(20,000)
Differential contract	$ 20,000

Overall or Wraparound. An overall or wraparound contract differs from the differential contract in that any underlying encumbrance on the subject property remains the full liability of the seller. The seller pays for underlying mortgages, and the purchaser pays the seller for the *overall* contract (the entire sum between the down payment and sale price) that "wraps around" any encumbrance of record at time of closing. To illustrate:

Sale price	$100,000
Down payment	(20,000)
Wraparound contract (of which $60,000 covers the amount of the first mortgage)	$ 80,000

Items that Must Be Clarified under a Contract Sale

In a contract sale, the contract must clarify, on its face or in a supplement, that the fee owner (contract holder) must be named as an interested party on the homeowner's insurance policy. This ensures that the fee owner is made aware if the insurance lapses.

The contract also must specify who is liable for the real estate taxes on an annual basis. The fee owner should be notified by the municipality if the buyer is in arrears.

Other items that should be specified include:

- The term (years) or balloon date of the contract;
- The monthly investment (payment) for which the buyer will be responsible;
- The annual interest rate of the contract (which must adhere to usury laws);
- The date interest begins to accrue;
- A statement that title is deeded out or offered on a contract-for-deed basis;
- All other essentials of a legal binding agreement to purchase (see page 341).

A contract for deed (or land contract) may be named differently. Whatever it is called, it is available throughout most markets, and it is one of the most effective methods of financing.

Benefits of Contracts for Deed

Benefits of contract-for-deed financing include:

- The buyer can normally meet less stringent requirements to qualify.
- The seller is not faced with any mortgage placement fee (points).
- Closing costs are kept to a minimum.
- There is no mortgage or government inspection (work orders or other requirements) to contend with.
- Normally, the buyer receives a favorable interest rate.
- The time that elapses between sale and closing (escrow) is shortened.
- The purchaser can work in or borrow the down payment.
- Assessments can normally be assumed by the purchaser.
- Owners (buyers) who are forced into a redemption situation need only pay the amount of interest in arrears, to make the contract current.

Drawbacks of Contracts for Deed

Some possible drawbacks arise under a contract for deed. These include:

- The subject property is normally purchased as-is.
- A purchaser who uses this method of financing could purchase property with a minimal initial investment (down payment), do extensive damage to the property, and then decide to vacate the property and abandon his or her responsibilities.
- If the seller holds the contract and is forced to sell it in the local market, he or she may be forced to accept an undesirable discount. Thus, this arrangement is advantageous to the seller only if he or she does not need cash.
- Normally, the cancellation (foreclosure or redemption) period is shorter than for a first mortgage. This may pose a concern for the purchaser of the home.
- Because the cancellation period is normally only 30 days, the seller (or owner of the contract) may be forced into a legal action more frequently than under another arrangement.

Elements of a Sound Contract Investment

For a contract investment to be a good one, it should contain the following key ingredients:

- The locale of the subject property must be sound.
- The shorter the term (years to maturity), the stronger the contract.
- The structure must be sound. (If the holder of the contract forecloses, the property probably will be sold.)
- The larger the initial investment (down payment), the sounder the contract. The down payment should be in the range of 10 percent to 30 percent.
- The larger the monthly principal and interest payment, the better the contract looks to the investor.

WRAPAROUND MORTGAGES

A wraparound mortgage is a mortgage that literally engulfs any existing encumbrances and is subordinate to them. All current encumbrances remain on the property as unsatisfied obligations, with the total or wraparound becoming a second, third, or fourth interest in the subject property.

When to Consider the Wraparound Mortgage

A wraparound mortgage is a viable financing option under the following conditions:

- When there is resistance to a second mortgage;
- When prepayment is either prohibited or subject to exorbitant penalties;
- When a lender cannot refinance a particular borrower, due to lending restrictions;
- When a single payment is desired (rather than each underlying encumbrance being paid separately);
- When terms different from those in the existing mortgage are required;
- When the desired debt service (monthly cost) is lower than a first and second mortgage together might have;
- When the existing mortgage has favorable terms and/or rates that are not obtainable at the present time;

- When the need is for a simple financing package that affords a great deal of flexibility;
- When the need is for a financing vehicle that produces a high yield while remaining within the guidelines set forth in state usury law;
- When flexibility is required but existing encumbrances cannot be disturbed;
- When the need is for better long-term encumbrances than can be obtained through a conventional lending institution.

Types of Wraparound Mortgages

There are three types of wraparound mortgage. These are:

1. The additional funds wraparound mortgage.

2. The extended term wraparound mortgage.

3. The simultaneous wraparound mortgage.

CONCLUSION

It takes special effort to keep current in a rapidly changing subject such as real estate financing. This effort is necessary, however, if you are to serve your customers adequately. Homebuyers often feel overwhelmed by the information involved in planning to finance a new home, and they will naturally turn to you for help. If you can provide customers with up-to-date information and guidance, they are more likely to be satisfied and to tell others of their satisfaction. Thus, the financing ideas in this chapter are intended to make you a more knowledgeable, more successful seller of new homes.

The information in this chapter is only a beginning, of course. You must couple it with your own time and effort. Read further in areas in which you need further background. Practice the techniques suggested throughout this book. Motivate yourself to work hard and use your time wisely. Only with your effort can this book accomplish its purpose of making you the best new home salesperson you can be.

Glossary

Abandonment of homestead. *See* Notice of abandonment.

Abeyance. A temporary suspension of action; an undetermined condition awaiting action.

Abstract of judgment. Record of a court's judgment which creates a general lien upon all real estate and chattel property when recorded.

Abstract of title. A digest or summary of documents or records affecting title to property.

Abutting owners. Owners of real property whose lands touch or border highways or public-owned lands.

Acceleration clause. A clause inserted in a note, mortgage, or deed of trust which requires immediate payment of the entire debt if certain conditions are violated during the normal term of the loan. Alienation of title is the standard violation involved, although failure to maintain the property, pay taxes, etc., are other factors generally included in this clause.

Acceptance. Consent to an offer or contract.

Accessibility. Ease of access or approach to a property.

Accession. A property owner's acquisition of title to improvements that were made on his or her land without his or her approval.

Accommodation. An obligation assumed without consideration.

Accretion. The gradual addition of land by action of natural forces such as shoreline movement caused by streams or rivers.

Accrued depreciation. The actual depreciation of property at any given date, as contrasted to *book depreciation.*

Acknowledgment. A formal declaration before a duly authorized officer, by a person who has executed an instrument, that such was his or her act and deed.

Acquisition. The process of acquiring or purchasing a piece of property.

Acre. An area of land measurement containing 43,560 square feet.

Act of God. Any disaster that is the result of natural causes, such as wind storms, lightning, floods, or earthquakes.

Addendum. A special addition to any form or contract that affects the total form or contract.

Adjudication. The act or process of reaching a judicial decision. Adjudication in bankruptcy brings the entire estate of the bankrupt owner under the jurisdiction of the court at the date of filing the petition.

Administrator. A person appointed by a probate court to settle the estate of one who has died without leaving a will.

Administrator's deed. A deed given by one who is acting as the administrator of an estate.

Adult. One who has reached legal age, when privileges such as voting and contracting are attained.

Ad valorem. Based upon or according to value. Property taxes are determined ad valorem.

Adverse possession. Open and notorious possession and occupation of real property under an evident claim to title, which may, if uncontested for a prescribed period of time, result in actual title transfer to the offending parties.

Affiant. One who makes a sworn statement, such as an affidavit.

Affidavit. A written statement sworn to or affirmed before an officer authorized to administer oaths.

Affirmation. A solemn declaration, usually made by one who, on religious grounds, is opposed to making oaths.

Agency. The act of serving as agent for a principal in the negotiations of business.

Agent. Someone who is authorized to represent another individual.

Agreement of sale. Any contract that establishes the terms of sale between a buyer and a seller. Deposit receipts and earnest money receipts are two forms used by real estate salespeople.

Air rights. The rights involved in real estate ownership that control the use of air space within the vertical planes above the ground owned or leased by the holder of the estate.

Alias. A name assumed by an individual in place of his or her legal name.

Alien. A person living in one country who is a citizen of another.

Alienation. The process of transferring title to property from one person to another.

Alienation clause. A clause in a mortgage, note, or deed of trust which accelerates the loan balance in the event title is transferred to a third party without the approval of the beneficiary.

Allegation. The act of making a formal assertion or statement of fact in a pleading.

All-inclusive deed of trust. A deed of trust that encompasses prior mortgage obligations known to trustor and beneficiary. It is similar to a contract of sale but with the advantages of a deed of trust concerning foreclosure rights.

Allotment. A plot of land that has been divided into small sections with or without improvements.

Alluvion. The land added to property by the process of accretion. Alluvion becomes the property of the owner of the land to which it is added.

Amenities. Items that are marked by such qualities as pleasantness, comfortableness, and agreeableness. In appraising, the amenities of property are those qualities that increase the pleasure of ownership and are not necessarily related to monetary values.

Amortization. The process of paying off a debt by installments, normally by equal installments over a fixed period of time. A fully amortized loan has no *balloon payment*.

Amortization table. A printed schedule of the monthly payments required to amortize a loan for specific interest rates and time periods. A book of amortization tables is standard equipment for real estate salespeople.

Anchor bolt. A metal bolt imbedded in the foundation of a building to anchor the construction to the foundation.

Ancillary. A subordinate document or instrument normally attached to a prior document in a subservient position, designed to aid the principal one. An ancillary bill, suit, or attachment indicates the existence of another instrument with precedence.

Annexation. The act or process of adding land to a basic unit, such as bringing land within the limits of a city or municipality.

Annuity. The return from an investment of capital, with interest, in a series of yearly payments or other regular periods.

Annulment. In marriage, the decree that cancels or nullifies the marriage contract and returns the parties to their prior state or relationship. Property is not ordinarily affected by a decree annulling a marriage unless the parties involved submit it as an issue.

Antecedent. That which has gone before in the history of a person or thing. Antecedent events have preceded the current happenings.

Antecedent drainage. *See* Inconsequent drainage.

Application for discharge. The formal application of one who files bankruptcy papers seeking the *discharge,* or release, of all allowable and provable debts. If approved by the court, his or her debts will be discharged.

Appraisal. A formal opinion or estimate of value by one who is qualified to evaluate factors of value. In real property appraisals, the purpose of the opinion may affect the type of report issued.

Appraisal inventory. A list of all the individual items of property that were considered by the appraiser when preparing the appraisal report.

Appraisal surplus. The difference between *book value* and actual value when the latter is in excess of the former as established by an appraisal.

Appreciation. The added value of property resulting from various market influences, whether of a temporary or permanent nature. The opposite of *depreciation.*

Appreciation rate. The percentage figure used to compute the increase in value of real property based on future dates and various other conditions.

Approach to value. The appraisal technique used to compute value. The three commonly accepted approaches are comparison, reproduction cost, and capitalization.

Appurtenance. That which is attached to land so as to become a part thereof. Buildings and improvements are typical appurtenances; a property right may also be one.

Assemblage. The process of estimating the cost of bringing two or more parcels of land under a single ownership, as compared to the costs or values of the parcels when owned individually.

Assessed value. The value of real or personal property as established by an assessor for the purpose of levying taxes.

Assessment. A special charge placed against a particular property for some specific purpose, such as installation of sewers, sidewalks, or other improvements.

Assessor. One who determines the value of property for tax purposes.

Assets. Those things owned by an individual or company which constitute its tangible or intangible value.

Assignment. The transfer of an interest in some instrument, such as a mortgage, deed of trust, lease, or bond.

Assignor. One who assigns or transfers a property or a right to another.

Assigns; Assignees. Those to whom property or rights are transferred.

Assisted renegotiable mortgage (ARM). A renegotiable mortgage in which the interest rate for the first few years is bought down by the builder, seller, buyer, or third party to reduce the costs to the borrower. The loan converts to market rate or a predetermined amount at the end of the prescribed term.

Assume. To accept the obligations of another party.

Assumption of mortgage. The process of assuming personal liability for the payment of existing loans for which property is the security.

A.T.A. policy. A broad coverage policy of title insurance issued by title companies to protect lenders for many items not included in the standard policy. Usually paid for by the purchaser to secure his or her loan.

Atrium. The entrance hall or open court of a Roman-style home; a court.

Attachment. The legal seizure of the defendant's property as security for any judgment awarded by court to permit plaintiff to recover in the action. An attachment is a lien upon all real and personal property as a rule.

Attorney-in-fact. A person to whom a power of attorney has been given by another to act for either specific or general purposes on behalf of the one granting the authority.

Attorney's fee clause. A clause contained in many legal documents such as mortgages, leases, notes, requiring the maker to pay all costs incurred by the holder for attorney's fees, etc., in the event the maker defaults in performance of the contract or instrument.

Attraction principle. The pulling force of a commercial business center due to one or more of the various merchandising factors existing.

Auction. The public sale of property to the highest bidder.

Authentication. The certification of a document by the signature of an officer, whose seal is usually affixed to validate the procedure.

Authorization to sell. A *listing*.

Avulsion. The sudden removal of land from one property to that of another owner, usually by a change in the course of a river. By law, the owner of the part removed usually can reclaim it within a limited period of time.

Balance sheet. A financial statement setting forth the assets and liabilities of an individual or corporation to show current position of the parties involved.

Balloon payment. An amount due at maturity of a note or mortgage; an amount in excess of normal installment payments.

Balusters. The vertical members that support a handrail along a stairway.

Bankruptcy. A legal proceeding under federal statutes whereby an insolvent debtor may be ruled incapable of meeting his or her obligations. The debtor's properties may be sold or distributed to satisfy his or her creditors. A petition in bankruptcy may be filed by either the debtor or the creditors.

Base line. The survey lines established by U.S. Survey teams to divide the nation into townships. Base lines run east and west.

Bench marks. Permanent markers placed at strategic points by surveyors from which differences of elevation and topography are measured.

Beneficiary. One who receives income from a trust. Under a deed of trust, the beneficiary is the lender.

Bequeath. To transfer property by will.

Bequest. The property that is transferred by will.

Betterment. Substantial improvement made upon real property, as differentiated from mere repairs.

Bilateral contract. Any contract in which there is a mutual exchange of promises by two or more parties.

Bill of sale. The legal document used to transfer title to personal property.

Binder. Any agreement made preliminary to the actual contract to sell property, used as a temporary arrangement before entering into the formal deed or contract; usually requires a cash deposit of some kind.

Blanket mortgage. A mortgage instrument that names as security two or more parcels of land.

Blue sky laws. Statutes regulating investment companies, the conduct of their business, and the issuance and sale of their securities.

Board of equalization. The agency that determines the assessed value of public utility properties and controls county assessors and tax collectors to assure uniformity in tax assessment and collection practices.

Bona fide. In good faith; without fraud; qualified arrangements.

Bond. To encumber as with a mortgage; a certificate issued as security for the repayment of a loan out of future income or some designated fund.

Book depreciation. The amount set aside on the books of record to provide for the retirement or replacement of an asset.

Book value. The total cost of a property less the total depreciation taken to date.

Boom. An economic condition marked by rapid development of resources and population, when unusually good profits can be realized.

Boot. A profit gained in exchange of properties, not reflected by cash, upon which income tax is not deferred. Boot can be money or anything of monetary value used in an exchange to equalize equities.

Breach. To break a law or a contract by failure or refusal to perform some act specifically required in the agreement.

Broker. One who acts as an agent or negotiator for his or her principal when dealing with third parties.

Broker loan statement. A statement of charges and fees in connection with a real estate loan furnished to the buyer or mortgagor for his or her information.

Broker's demand statement. A statement or letter issued to an escrow holder by the broker setting forth instructions concerning the closing of escrow and disbursement of funds.

Btu. A measure of heat known as a British Thermal Unit commonly used in determining the output of heating equipment, such as furnaces.

Building and loan company. Same as savings and loan company; an institution organized to make real estate loans with the funds received from depositors, paying interest to the latter for use of their money.

Building code. The code or restrictions established by a government body—such as a city, county, or state—for regulating the construction of buildings of all types.

Building contract. An agreement entered into between a contractor and an owner for the construction of a building.

Building inspector. The authorized individual who reviews the various stages of building construction to verify conformance with the requirements of building codes.

Building restrictions. Same as *building code.* Also occasionally the restrictions contained within a deed or declaration of restrictions recorded to protect the usage of property by future owners.

Built-ins. The term applied to all appliances included in the construction of a property which become real property by nature of their installation.

Burdensome property. Under bankruptcy laws, the trustee is not required to take title to property that is unprofitable or subject to excessive liens and may obtain release from this property upon action by the court.

Business and professions code. That portion of state law which controls the activities of businesses and professions. Normally, all real estate law is included in this section.

Business opportunities. In real estate terminology, these are businesses in which real estate ownership factors are incidental to the businesses themselves and their leasehold rights. In California and some other states, special business opportunities licenses must be obtained from the Division of Real Estate before a broker or salesperson can represent properties involving the sale of businesses.

Butterfly roof. A type of roof characterized by two inverted wings, similar to those of a butterfly.

Buy and sell agreements. Contracts between owners of a business executed to protect the surviving partner(s) in the event of death of one or more parties to the agreement, in which the survivor(s) has the right to acquire, at predetermined amounts, the interests of the deceased party.

Buy-back agreement. A term used for a special trade-in housing contract which permits the one who accepted the trade-in to repurchase the property for a specified amount within a limited period of time at his or her option.

Capacity of parties. A term applied to the process of evaluating the qualifications of those who execute legal contracts. To have capacity to contract, these parties must be of age and mentally sound.

Capital. The financial reserves available for investment and the production of additional wealth; also the funds originally invested to begin an enterprise plus the additions made from time to time by the partners or shareholders of the business.

Capital charges. The amounts needed to amortize the capital investment in business, plus the interest such capital would normally earn.

Capital expenditures. The sums invested in a business or property which are considered a permanent contribution for the betterment of that asset. These are commonly such things as buildings, machinery, and necessary business equipment.

Capital gain. *See* Long-term capital gain.

Capital requirements. The sums of money needed to acquire or establish a business enterprise or investment, including working capital to maintain it.

Capital surplus. Sums of money or assets that are in excess of actual earned surplus normally resulting from increased evaluation of property, sale of stock, contribution of others, and other sources.

Capitalization. A method of appraising or determining value by using the net income and a reasonable rate of return.

Capitalization rate. The percentage rate of return or interest used to compute the appraised value by the capitalization method. The amount used normally is chosen as that which is reasonable for the risk involved.

Capitalizing the net income. The process of arriving at property value by the net income figures related to desired return. An apartment house earning $6,000 per year after all expenses would be worth $100,000 if a return of 6% per year is considered reasonable by the investor. To determine value under this method, multiply the actual net income by the figure 100 and then divide by the rate of interest desired.

Captive market. Business that is exclusively controlled by advantageous factors limited to the enterprises involved is said to have captive markets. Typical situations are those created by air terminals, hotel shops, and similar environmental factors.

Car port. A covered area, open in one or more sections, used to protect the car in place of a normal garage.

Carriage. A wood member on a staircase used to secure the treads and risers of the stairway.

Carrying charges. The various expenditures necessary to maintain a property from month to month, such as taxes and insurance.

Caveat emptor. A Latin expression used in law to designate the buyer's responsibility to investigate before purchasing. Literally: "Let the buyer beware."

CC & Rs. Abbreviation of "conditions, covenants and restrictions," as applied to real property titles.

Ceiling rate. The maximum rent or fee that may be charged as established by any governmental agency.

Certificate of conformity. A document that verifies that an acknowledgment made out of state meets the legal provisions of the state where executed and was acknowledged in accordance with the laws of the place where made.

Certificate of eligibility. The document that verifies the entitlement of an individual to the benefits of the Servicemen's Readjustment Act of 1944 by establishing his service record qualifications with the government agency.

Certificate of reasonable value. Commonly known as a CRV, this is the appraisal commitment of the Veterans Administration used to fix the value of a property being proposed for purchase by a veteran under the GI bill of rights. By law, the veteran cannot pay more for the property than the CRV appraisal.

Certificate of recordation. A document verifying that an instrument has been duly recorded by the county recorder's office.

Certificate of revivor. The certificate issued by the franchise tax commissioner to verify that the corporation formerly delinquent has made full payment of taxes due and which is generally recorded to lift a prior lien against property of that corporation.

Certificate of sale. Given by a sheriff at the foreclosure sale of a mortgaged property to the successful bidder. When the redemption period (one year) has expired, a sheriff's deed is issued in place of the certificate.

Certificate of title. A title examiner's opinion as to the condition of title for a particular parcel of real estate. Such certificate carries no guarantees and offers no protection to the purchaser against any hidden defects.

Certified copy. A true copy of an original document, certified by any officer or qualified person.

Certified Property Manager. Commonly known as CPM, this identification is bestowed upon any property manager who has met the requirements of the Institute of Property Management operated under the auspices of the National Association of Real Estate Boards.

Chain. A measurement of distance. An engineer's chain is a series of 100 wire links, each of which is one foot in length; a surveyor's chain is a series of wire links each of which is 7.92 inches long. The surveyor's chain has a total length equal to four rods, or 66 feet. Ten square chains of land equal one acre.

Chain of title. The history of a property as related to its various owners and encumbrances from the time of the original owner or patent or as far back as records are available for inspection.

Change-order form. A form used to communicate changes in construction to construction personnel and subcontractors.

Chattel mortgage. A mortgage or loan on personal property as contrasted to a mortgage on real property.

Chattel personal. Any personal property item that can be readily moved.

Chattel real. An estate related to real estate, such as a lease on real property or an interest in real property, such as the right of possession, use, or other personal privileges.

Circulation patterns. The flow of traffic through a property and the various effects design may have on such patterns.

Civil law. *See* Common law.

Clearance certificate. A certificate indicating that performance of a requirement has been completed, such as completion of termite work.

Clearance receipt. A receipt issued by the Board of Equalization showing that the owner or seller of a business has accounted for his or her sales taxes.

Client. The principal to a real estate transaction who employs the agent.

Closing costs. All of the settlement costs incurred by either buyer or seller in the transfer of title.

Closing statement. The settlement sheet, which contains a statement of debits and credits for the buyer or seller and which summarizes the costs involved when selling property.

Cloud on title. Any item affecting title transfer which prevents the buyer from receiving a clear title. These are usually nuisance items requiring quitclaim deeds or action to quiet title.

Cluster housing. A term used to describe houses that are grouped together to create more common areas between them and where normal setbacks and boundaries are sacrificed for the "open space" created by this arrangement.

Collateral. *See* Hypothecate. Any asset or property, both personal and real, pledged as security for money borrowed or for repayment of a debt, with right of ownership and use retained.

Collateral security. Items of value placed on record as additional security for the performance of any principal contract or note.

Collusion. An agreement between two or more people to defraud another of legal rights or to obtain some object forbidden by law.

Color of title. A title that appears to be good on the surface, but is in fact not good title.

Commercial acre. That which remains of an acre of land after deducting the area needed for streets, sidewalks, curbs. It is a loose term applied to usable acreage when other needs have been met to service the area involved.

Commercial paper. Notes or bills of exchange used in the normal course of business enterprise.

Commercial property. Any land suitable for use by business enterprise as zoned by city or county planning commissions or determined by normal usage. Commercial property is often valued by the front foot exposure to traffic.

Commingling. The mixing of one's own funds with those of a client. General confusion of accounts when there should be a fiduciary protection of another's interests.

Commission. Compensation for services rendered or duties performed such as selling or leasing a property.

Commitment. A promise to perform; in real estate, an agreement to loan a specified amount to a purchaser or seller in the event of title transfer or refinance arrangements.

Common law. A system of law resulting from past legal decisions or accepted traditions as begun in England and carried to most states of the United States.

Common property. Property owned and used by the public or a group of people who live in an area. Common property is open to equal use by all those owning it, or having public interest in it.

Community apartments. *See* Cooperative apartment house.

Community services association. *See* Homeowners' association.

Co-mortgagor. One who signs a mortgage or deed of trust as equally responsible for its repayment. The wife is usually co-mortgagor with the husband, although someone else might serve that purpose, such as a father.

Compaction. The process of compacting or tamping the ground to make it suitable for building purposes. Compaction tests often are required by building inspection authorities before authorizing construction.

Comparative analysis. The process of comparing the value of one lot or building with another to determine its reasonable evaluation. In appraising, this is one of the more important approaches to value.

Compensating balances. Controlled funds placed with a lending institution to influence lending activity.

Competent parties. Those who are qualified or mentally competent to enter into a contract.

Competitive properties. Properties that are competing for the same market at the same time. *See also* Comparative analysis.

Compound interest. Interest paid on both principal and periodic computations of accumulated interest amounts.

Condemnation. A ruling by a governmental body that a property must be altered or destroyed for reasons of public welfare. Also, the act of taking private property for public use by the right of eminent domain, such as for freeways.

Condemnation guarantee. A search made by a title company in lieu of a title policy when a property is undergoing a condemnation process.

Condemnation proceedings. The acts of government involved in the acquisition of land for public use by condemnation of private lands.

Condition. As used in real estate, a specific event or requirement that directly affects the instruments or documents involved in a transaction, and the performance or nonperformance of which may terminate or alter the obligations in the contracts involved.

Conditional sales contract. A contract to sell real estate to another upon completion of certain required acts, such as payment of specified sums, during the performance of which contract, the title to the property remains vested in the seller until completely fulfilled.

Condominium. A multifamily structure, subdivided to give fee title to individual occupants by a description of the air and ground space involved for each unit. Common property normally is owned by all participants in a condominium corporation or association.

Confession of judgment. An entry of judgment upon the admission or confession of the debtor without the formality, time, or expense involved in the usual proceedings.

Congressional grant. A grant of public-owned lands to an individual, or other entity, by an act of Congress.

Consent. Voluntary agreement; an essential element of a contract. Consent of the parties to a contract must be free, communicated by each to the other.

Consequential damage. A term used to define damage arising from the acts of public bodies or adjacent owners to a given parcel of land which impairs the value of that parcel without actually condemning its use in whole or part.

Conservator. One who is appointed by a court to conserve the estate of another, such as an elderly or sick person who is unable to do so alone. A conservator is different from a *guardian,* appointed for minors or incompetents, because no condition of minority or incompetency exists.

Conservator's deed. A deed to property given by a court-appointed conservator upon execution of his or her duties. The conservator's actions are subject to court confirmation, as in probate transactions.

Consideration. The sums of money, valuables, promises, or acts that are given in exchange for the performance of a contract. In most states there must be a valuable consideration in any contract that transfers an interest in real property from one party to another.

Constant payment. Any payment that recurs regularly and is a fixed amount that does not vary in any manner.

Construction rider. An addendum or addition to the construction contract to effect changes in the building agreement.

Constructive fraud. Any breach of duty that, without an actual fraudulent intent, gains an advantage for the person at fault; any act or omission that the law specifically declares to be fraudulent without respect to actual fraud.

Constructive notice. Notice given by public or recorded documents. The law presumes that everyone has the same knowledge of all instruments that are properly recorded and available for inspection.

Contiguous. Adjoining or bordering another parcel of land.

Contingency. Any requirement in a contract that must be completed before the contract can be considered ready for performance.

Contingent fees. Fees or commissions to be paid only if certain events or acts occur or specific results are obtained in the interim.

Contingent listing (or trade-in). A listing on real property that is tied to the sale or purchase of another property, one of which cannot be acquired without the sale of the other.

Contract. An agreement negotiated and entered into by two or more parties who exchange mutual promises to perform certain acts in accordance with the wishes of both.

Contract for deed. A purchase money instrument used to secure the remaining equity of the seller until the full purchase price has been received by the seller or substituted at some future date for another instrument, such as a mortgage or deed of trust. In law it usually is treated similarly to a mortgage, although fee title rests in the name of the original seller.

Conversion value. The value in real estate created by changing the use of property from one state to another, such as rezoning, or creating a higher and better use for the parcel.

Conveyance. In real estate, a document transferring title to property from one party to another.

Cooperative apartment house. A community apartment house where each occupant receives an undivided ownership interest in the apartment he or she uses and a common interest in all other facilities. This is usually effected by forming a corporation, with each owner receiving stock in the corporation equal to his or her investment. This is different from a condominium, where fee title is actually passed to individual owners of each unit.

Corner influence. The additional value attributed to a corner lot due to its various advantages for business uses.

Corporation sole. A corporation formed by the bishop, chief priest, presiding elder, or other presiding officer of any religious denomination, society, or church for the purpose of administering and managing the affairs and properties of that group. It has continuity of existence and may sell, convey, lease, mortgage, or otherwise deal in real and personal property in the same way as any natural person.

Corporeal. Having physical properties consisting of actual, tangible matter. In real estate, corporeal hereditament is property of such a nature as to be cognizable by the senses and is connected with the land.

Co-signer. One who accepts equal obligation for the performance of contract, note, or other act by affixing his or her name to the documents involved.

Cost basis. Usually the purchase price of property. As used in tax computations for capital gains purposes, it is the difference between the original cost basis and the adjusted cost basis on which the gain is determined and the tax paid.

Covenant. An agreement entered into by two or more parties; a promise by which to bind oneself to perform certain acts.

C.P.A. Abbreviation for Certified Public Accountant.

C.P.M. Abbreviation for Certified Property Manager.

Creditor's position. The part of real property market value that is represented by a first mortgage or that can be financed by a prime loan or mortgage.

Cubical content. The total space enclosed by the outside walls, roofs, and floors of a building, measured in terms of cubic feet or cubic yards.

Cul-de-sac. A street with access from one end only and closed at the other with a curved, bulb-like enclosure.

Cumulative attraction. A term used in describing the effect created in a shopping center site by the various influences each business has on the total attraction of business to the center.

Curtesy. The right which a husband has in a wife's estate at her death. States having community property laws have abolished the previous provisions of curtesy.

D.B.A. Abbreviation for "doing business as" under a fictitious name.

Dealer (in real estate). A licensed real estate person or company who buys and sells for his or her own account as a principal instead of an agent.

Debentures. Certificates issued to cover an obligation to pay certain amounts at a specified time under specified conditions bearing a fixed rate of interest.

Debtor's position. The excess amount above prime mortgages which evidences the equity of the borrower's position.

Decentralization. A term used to define the outward growth of business centers away from the downtown cores or central business districts and the location of industry in areas away from commonly accepted centers.

Decibel. A measure of sound transmission or noise, commonly used in housing or apartment units to indicate effective controls on sound waves between rooms or floors.

Declaration of restrictions. The document recorded by a subdivider or builder to establish deed restrictions concerning the use of land and improvements in the subdivision covered by them.

Decree. A legal decision issued by a court or other authorized authorities.

Dedication. In real estate, the term applied to the required or voluntary transfer of interest in real estate or improvements to city, county, or state agencies such as the dedication of streets, sidewalks, curbs, and gutters to the city in which the subdivision is located.

Deed. A written instrument which conveys title to real property.

Deed of trust. *See* Trust deed.

Default. Failure to perform the acts or promises made, such as the default on a mortgage note when payment is not made on time.

Defeasance. A provision in a deed or other instrument which, when violated, renders the document void.

Deferred maintenance. Repairs to a property which are required but not yet completed.

Deferred payments. Payments that are to be made at some future time.

Deficiency judgment. A judgment awarded by a court against a mortgagor or trustor when the security for the note was not sufficient to cover the obligation after it was sold to pay the balance of the loan.

Delineate. To outline, trace, or sketch pictorially for identification purposes.

Delivery. In real estate, the formal transmission of a deed to its new owner; once completed, there is no right to recall it.

Demise. In real estate, the conveyance or transfer of title to property for years, for life, or at will; to lease property; to bestow by will.

Deposit. An item of value or amount given in good faith to provide evidence of ability and willingness to complete the purchase or lease of real property.

Deposition. A sworn statement taken from a witness to an event or act for the purposes of providing evidence as to the actual circumstances.

Deposit receipt. A common name for the purchase agreement between buyer and seller used to contract for the transfer of real estate.

Depreciation. The gradual loss of value in property, personal or real, due to various factors, regardless of cause.

Depreciation rate. The annual percentage change in property values resulting from depreciation.

Depth table. A table used by real estate appraisers to determine the relative values in lots that have different depths from the fronting street.

Dereliction. The gaining of additional land by the receding of water from the banks of a river, stream, lake, or ocean.

Desist and refrain order. A directive by a government, state, or city official to cease activity when it appears to that party that some law is being violated.

Deterioration. One of the prime factors in depreciation evidenced by the loss in value due to wear and tear, destruction by the elements.

Devise. A gift of real property as the result of a bequest in a will.

Devisee. One who inherits property by will.

Devisor. One who bequeaths real property by will.

Direct trade. A trade-in transaction in which title is passed immediately to the trade-in company, without benefit of improving the seller's position.

Discharge. A discharge in bankruptcy releases a bankrupt from all of his or her provable debts, and a bankruptcy action is filed as an "application of discharge" to relieve debt obligations.

Dispossess. To take legal action to remove an occupant from the premises of real property.

Dissolution of corporation. The legal act of winding up a corporation for the purpose of dissolving its functions and assigning or selling its assets before final termination as a legal entity.

Dividend. A sum determined by the board of directors, paid to shareholders out of corporate earnings, as a return on their investment.

Documentary stamp. A revenue stamp attached to deeds, wills, and the like for payment of tax to the federal government due on such transactions.

Donee. The one receiving a gift.

Donor. The one giving a gift.

Dower. The right a wife has in her husband's estate upon his death, but which is negated by community property laws in those states having them.

Dry-rot. A term used to describe fungus growth on wood or other materials created from water absorption by such items. It is a major cause of deterioration in older buildings and is often caused by leaking stall showers and water pipes.

Duress. Unlawfully forcing one person to do an act he or she would not have performed otherwise.

Earnest money. A sum of money given to bind an agreement or an offer made to show good faith. *See also* Deposit.

Earnest money receipt. *See* Deposit receipt.

Easement. The right or interest of one party to another person's land or property for a specific or general use; may be qualified in many ways.

Economic life. The useful life of property improvements based on original intent and over which the structure is profitable to maintain.

Economic obsolescence. Loss in value created by factors outside the property, such as changes in neighborhood factors. This is one of the principal considerations in depreciation.

Economic rent. *See* Ground rent.

Effective gross revenue. Income received from the operation of a building before expenses but after vacancy and collection losses have been considered.

Egress. Means of leaving property without trespassing the property rights of surrounding owners.

Eminent domain. The right of government to take private property for public use when required for the general good. The government must make a just and proper compensation at the time it acquires the property.

Encroachment. Illegal and unauthorized use of another's property, usually by building something in part or whole on such property without permission.

Encumbrance. Anything that burdens the title to real property by limiting its totality. Mortgages, liens, easements, and restrictions are all types of encumbrances.

Endorsement. Signing the back of a note or other transferable document with a personal signature, which authorizes payment or transfer to another.

Endorsement in blank. Transferring by endorsement without qualification, which automatically makes the endorser equally responsible for the obligations involved.

Endorsement without recourse. A special endorsement which limits the responsibility of the endorser and does not guarantee future payment to holders of the instrument involved.

Equitable estoppel. A doctrine in law that prevents an owner from stopping sale of his or her property when he or she willingly permitted another to represent him or her as owner and knowingly permitted a sale to a purchaser through this representative.

Equitable owner. An owner of real property who has hypothecated his or her property while retaining the rights of use and occupancy.

Equitable remedy. In law, a remedy that is deemed by a court to be equitable and fair. Specific performance of a contract might be an equitable remedy in some cases.

Equity. The interest one has in real property as an owner above all existing indebtedness.

Equity guarantee. As used in trade-in housing programs, a guarantee to the owner of a certain specified sum within a specified time for all equities the owner might have above existing loan balances, in the event another buyer cannot be located in the interim willing to pay more than the guarantor.

Equity insurance. A *trade-in guarantee loan* or acquisition.

Equity loan. A loan made in connection with trade-in housing which is based on the equity of the owner and calls for repayment on terms usually related to the performance contract established by the trade-in company.

Equity of redemption. The right of an owner to redeem property after a lien-foreclosure sale. Under a mortgage foreclosure, this is usually a period of one year.

Errors and omissions insurance. An insurance policy available to real estate brokers and salespeople covering liability for errors and omissions in their contracts which might result in damages to clients or customers.

Escalator clause. A clause, contained in many leases, that requires the increase in taxes, insurance, and other items to be passed on to the tenant under certain conditions.

Escheat. The process by which the state acquires title to property when private ownership cannot be clearly established.

Escrow. A depository for papers, funds, and instructions with a third party who is then obligated to carry out all instructions, providing they are in complete agreement.

Escrow holder. One who takes on the obligation to carry out all instructions of an escrow from all participants thereto.

Estate. Any right that is vested in real property. Any interest, share, equity, or ownership in real property is considered to be an estate in real property. The same term may apply to personal property as well.

Estate at sufferance. The status of a lease or occupancy when there has been an unlawful retention of possession after expiration of a lease of different nature.

Estate for life. The right to use and occupy property during the life of the one but permission for occupancy remains on the same basic terms as original lease, or at the will of either party.

Estate for life. The right to use and occupy property during the life of the one owning the life estate, but after which it will revert to the original estate or others designated by recorded documents.

Estate for years. Another expression for a lease or leasehold estate.

Estate in reversion. The portion of an estate that remains when the other estates granted by the original owner have been terminated or fulfilled.

Estate of inheritance. An estate that may be inherited, but is not yet transferred.

Estoppel. A legal doctrine that prevents a person from asserting rights or facts that are inconsistent with previous positions or representations made by that person.

Estovers. Wood or other necessity that a lessee is permitted to use from the landlord's premises to provide necessary fuel, repairs, or tools.

Et al. A Latin expression used in legal documents meaning "and others."

Et ux. A Latin expression used in legal documents meaning "and spouse."

Exchange agreement. A contract that covers the understandings of two or more owners who agree to transfer their properties to each other with or without additional consideration.

Excise tax. A federal, state, or local tax that is imposed on purchases rather than on personal or real property.

Exclusive agency listing. A listing for the sale or lease of real property that permits the owner to rent or sell without paying a commission but does not allow any other agent, except the one named in the contract, to act on behalf of the owner.

Fannie Mae. The nickname given to the Federal National Mortgage Association operated by the government as a secondary market for federally insured loans.

Fee. When applied to real estate, an inheritable right in real property. Also a commission or remuneration for services performed.

Fee simple absolute. The maximum estate one can enjoy in real property.

Fee simple limited. An estate in fee granting fee rights to property as long as certain stipulated conditions are met, termination being governed by the occurrence of some event that is stated in the original establishment of the estate.

Fee tall. An estate of inheritance in real property which is restricted to some particular heirs or a class of person to whom granted.

Fictitious mortgage. A mortgage on personal crops, property, or future realization of profits from their sale. Such mortgages are created to buy the materials necessary to plant and operate a farm.

Fictitious name. An alias or name by which a person is known for business purposes and which is not necessarily the same as the person's real name. People often conduct business under *D.B.A.s,* or fictitious business names.

Fiduciary relationship. The position of trust assumed by an agent or confidant when acting on behalf of a principal.

Finance guarantee. In trade-in housing, an agreement to finance property at some future date in order to confirm a transaction at the time executed.

Finder's fee. A fee paid to a person who has furnished information that is beneficial to the agent in arranging the sale, without a participation, which requires a license.

Fixed charges. The continuing costs that are required in order to maintain a property for the reimbursement of capital invested in the property.

Flat note. *See* Straight note.

Flexible loan insurance program (FLIP) mortgage. A mortgage in which part of the initial investment (down payment) is deposited in a pledged savings account, which is used to supplement mortgage payments for the first few years of the mortgage term. This permits lower monthly payments in the initial years.

F.M.V. Abbreviation for "Fair Market Value" as established by recognized appraisers or by a government agency like FHA.

Foreclosure. The sale of property that has been pledged as security against the payment of a debt.

Forfeiture. The loss of earnest money for failure to perform under the terms of a purchase contract.

Fractional description. A description of real property that relates the parcel to the entire section of land involved.

Freddie Mac. The nickname for Federal Home Loan Mortgage Corporation, a government agency which guarantees mortgages for savings and loan associations only.

Freeholder. An owner of land in fee.

Front foot. The measure of a parcel of land, by feet, on the portion exposed to main traffic streets. This is used especially in commercial property pricing.

Front foot cost. The price of land expressed in terms of its footage on a main street. Business property might be priced at $1,000 per front foot on a highly desirable business street.

Functional obsolescence. A factor in depreciation of property caused by the inefficiency or decreased capacity of the property to serve the accepted needs of modern purchasers.

General index. The index of general liens and judgments maintained by the recorder's office which do not apply to specific properties but to all parcels owned by those involved.

Gift letter. A letter prepared for a mortgagee or government agency which verifies that the sums of money being used to acquire a parcel of property were a gift from a relative, made without obligation of repayment.

Gift tax. A state tax made on gifts received by an individual.

Ginnie Mae. The nickname for the Government National Mortgage Association, a corporation that buys mortgages from lenders (and sells them). Ginnie Mae was intended as an encouragement to lenders to buy mortgages and as a way to keep long-term investment money moving.

Good consideration. In real estate, a consideration for the transfer of real estate other than valuable property; commonly, love and affection.

Good will. The general reputation and business enjoyed by a company based on its name and past services. This is a purchasable commodity in the sale of business opportunities.

Graduated lease. A lease for real property which requires varying amounts of rents over the term of the lease.

Graduated payment mortgage (GPM). A mortgage that defers a portion of the normal amortization of principal and interest, so that monthly payments in the early years are easier to handle. Payments increase gradually over first few years to a predetermined limit that is ultimately higher than for normal fixed rate mortgages.

Grant deed. A deed to real property which carries implied warranties.

Grantee. One who acquires title to property by deed.

Grantor. One who conveys title to property by deed.

Gross earnings. Total revenue from all operating sources before deducting any expenses for collecting such revenue.

Gross income. Total revenue accrued before deduction of expenses.

Gross lease. A lease for real property in which the owner-lessor is responsible for all charges to the property which are normal, regular costs of ownership.

Gross multiplier. A number used to determine approximate selling price for income property by multiplying the gross income times this number: income x multiplier = selling price.

Gross profits. Profits accrued before the deduction of general expenses and taxes.

Gross revenue. *See* Gross income.

Gross sales. The total invoiced sales before adjusting returns, credits, etc.

Ground rent. The profit or net rent paid for the use of unimproved land, or the amount of the rent that should be properly credited to the land rather than to the buildings upon it.

Guardian. One appointed by a court to manage the affairs of minors or incompetents.

Guarantee of title. An opinion rendered regarding the condition of title based upon a review of the official records and backed by a fund to compensate those damaged by negligence.

Guaranteed mortgage. A mortgage acquired or negotiated by a mortgage company and sold to an investor with a written guarantee that all payments of principal and interest shall be made or the mortgage company will reimburse the investor from its own funds.

Guaranteed sales contract. A contract for a *guaranteed trade-in*.

Guaranteed trade-in. A contract to purchase real property executed by a trade-in company, builder, or dealer with the seller, in which a set time is allotted for the performance of the guarantee and during which the seller may sell to someone else for more money than the trade-in company guaranteed.

Habendum clause. The common name for the clause "to have and to hold," which is often inserted in deeds.

Head of family. One who is responsible for dependents. Does not have to be male or married in order to qualify.

Header. A house framing term for the structural member over doors, windows, and openings in walls.

Heirs. Those who obtain property from the estate of a deceased person.

Highest and best use. A term used in appraising real property to describe how a parcel of land can be used to generate the maximum return.

Holder in due course. One who receives in the course of business and in good faith a note for value without prior knowledge of any defects.

Holographic will. A handwritten will signed by the testator.

Homeowners' association. An organization structured to serve the interests of homeowners in matters of mutual interest. Normally, it is a corporation with voting stock owned by each individual owner, and management supervised by an elected board of directors.

Homeowner's policy. An insurance policy for real property which offers coverage for many things not insured under a standard fire policy.

Homestead. A home for which a Declaration of Homestead has been recorded and which thereby is given certain protection against future judgments.

Hundred percent location. The best location in a community for a commercial business enterprise.

Hypothecate. *See* Collateral. To pledge property as security for money borrowed or repayment of a debt but with the continued right of ownership and use.

Implied. Not expressly stated or written but understood to be included.

Implied warranty. A warranty assumed by law to exist in an instrument, although it may not be specifically stated.

Impound account. *See* Trust fund.

Improvement acts. Laws that authorize installation of street and other improvements, which may then be assessed directly to the properties involved.

Improvement bond. A bond issued by a district, city, or state for the installation of improvements such as highways and streets. Such bonds are sold to investors to finance the projects covered.

Incompetent. One who is unable to manage his or her own property and affairs, due to insanity, senility, or mental disability.

Inconsequent drainage. Drainage established prior to the deformation of the drained section and continuing after a change in the earth's surface.

Increment. An increase of some type. Used often to refer to the increase in the value of land resulting from population growth and additional growth.

Indemnity. Any guarantee against possible loss, such as an insurance policy.

Indenture. A deed or contract entered into by two or more persons, each of whom obligates him- or herself to perform certain things set forth in the indenture.

Independent contractor. One who operates a business separate from the other enterprises with which he or she may be associated. Real estate salespeople often work as independent contractors rather than as employees.

Industrial property. All the real and personal property, together with tangible and intangible assets, which comprise the total value of a manufacturing enterprise; also, the specific property on which such businesses can locate their operations.

Industrial bank. A lending company with broad lending powers, including the right to lend money on second mortgages.

Ingress. An entrance to property which does not trespass over the property rights of others.

Inherit. To obtain property as an heir.

Injunction. An order of court requiring the performance or nonperformance of some act.

Insolvent. The condition of having more liabilities than assets.

Institute of Real Estate Brokers. A division of the National Association of Real Estate Boards, which furnishes educational material to members.

Institutional lender. A recognized mortgage company or bank that is authorized to make real estate loans as well as purchase government insured loans. Banks, savings and loan institutions, insurance companies, and mutual savings banks are the principal ones involved.

Instrument. In law, any document by which the acts and agreements of the executors are made known to others.

Intangible property. Those things which do not have physical properties but represent values, such as good will and ownership rights.

Interim occupancy agreement. *See* Occupancy agreement.

Interlocutory decree. A decree issued by a court which is not final, but is binding upon the involved parties until finalized; commonly used in divorce proceedings.

Interstate. Between different states.

Intestate. Death without leaving a valid will.

Intrastate. Within a particular state.

Intrinsic value. True value, or actual value.

Inure. To serve to the use or benefit of someone.

Involuntary lien. A lien on real property which is imposed without the owner's authorization, such as taxes.

Irrevocable. Without the right to cancel or void the act involved.

Irrigation district. Special areas or districts created by law to furnish water to the lands involved. The members thereof are assessed if necessary.

Joinder. Acting jointly with one or more persons; joining.

Joint and several note. The same as a *joint note,* except makers may be sued together or individually in the event of a default.

Joint note. A note signed by more than one person, each with equal responsibility for payment, who must be sued together if action is necessary.

Joint tenancy. Equal ownership in property by two or more persons, with the four *unities* of joint tenancy—time, title, interest, and possession—assured to all, and the right of survivorship assured to the remaining tenants when one dies.

Judgment. A final determination or order of a court of law that sets forth the decision of the judge in a lawsuit.

Junior lien. Any lien which is subordinate to another lien that has prior claim on the security. Second mortgages and trust deeds are typical junior liens.

Key lot. A lot that is located in such a manner that one side adjoins the rear of another lot.

Laches. Inexcusable delay in asserting one's rights. Literally, "sleeping on one's rights."

Land contract. The sale of real estate by means of an installment agreement during which title remains vested in the original seller until the predetermined terms of sale are satisfied.

Land grant. *See* Congressional grant.

Lands, tenements, and hereditaments. A phrase used in early English law to mean all kinds of property of the immovable classifications. It is, in essence, real estate with all fixed improvements thereon.

Land trust certificate. A certificate that verifies a beneficial interest in real estate while title is held in trust by a trustee, who issues this proof of interest.

Latent. That which is concealed, hidden. A defect in property or title may be latent.

Lease. An agreement by which real estate is rented for a fixed period of time; an estate for years or leasehold estate.

Leaseback agreement. A device used to secure the right of occupancy under a lease as a condition of the sale terms on real property. Shopping center owners and other businesses often develop their own land and then free the cash investment by selling the property with a leaseback provision for themselves.

Leased fee. Land that is leased to others while the fee owner retains the rights to ground rentals and the further right of repossession when the allotted time has expired.

Leasehold estate. A less than freehold estate; a lease or estate for years.

Legal description. A property description that can be recognized by law and by which the property in question can be definitely located by reference to recorded maps.

Legal rate of interest. A fair rate of interest as recognized by courts where no rate is specified.

Legatee. One who receives personal property by will.

Lessee. One who contracts to rent property from the owner, or master tenant.

Lessor. One who rents property to another; a landlord.

Less than freehold. Another term for a leasehold estate.

Levy. To seize or attach property for payment of a debt.

Lien. An encumbrance against property, which becomes the security for the obligation. Typical liens are mortgages, trust deeds, taxes, assessments.

Lieu lands. Property which the state can substitute for lands granted it by the U.S. Government when such lands are of equal area to original grants.

Limited partnership. A business association in which the party so designated has only limited liability for the venture, while the general partner carries the major responsibilities under the law. This form of partnership is often used in syndicated ventures to acquire and develop real estate.

Line fence. The fence that separates the boundaries of two or more parcels of land.

Liquid assets. Any property or valuable securities that can be readily converted to cash. Real estate is seldom considered a liquid asset.

Liquidate. To sell property at its cash value in order to generate funds.

Liquidated damages. A specific sum of money to be paid under a contract in the event of a breach of the contract's terms.

Lis pendens. A notice recorded to advise all interested parties that a lawsuit is pending against certain defendants and their property.

Listing. A contract with a real estate broker authorizing the payment of a fee for the performance of specified services in connection with the property identified.

Littoral. Property that borders a large body of water, such as a lake, ocean, or sea is said to be littoral property.

Livery of seizin. The ancient English term for delivering possession of the land from one party to another, originally done by handing the new owner a handful of dirt from the land he is buying.

Loan broker law. A law covering the obligations and responsibilities of real estate brokers who negotiate the origination and sale of mortgages.

Loan correspondent. One who acts as the exclusive agent for a lending institution in a defined market area for the purpose of procuring loans.

Long-term capital gain. An increase in the value of an asset occurring over a period of at least six months' duration and on which the owner can claim special tax privileges when the property is ultimately sold.

M.A.I. Abbreviation for Member of Appraisers Institute, a highly skilled and elite group of appraisers who have met certain rigid standards.

Maintenance fees. Fees charged or assessed against property owners to pay for property maintenance, and related expenses of managing common property.

Maintenance reserve. An amount of money set aside during the operation of a building to meet expected repairs and maintenance expenses.

Majority. The age at which a youth becomes legally an adult able to vote and own property.

Marginal release. A notation on the margin of the recorder's books showing that a mortgage has been satisfied. This system is seldom used, having been replaced with the recording of *satisfaction of mortgage.*

Mark. The signature of one who does not know how to write. It must be witnessed by two or more persons to permit valid recordation.

Marketable title. Title to property which can be conveyed without inherent defects or clouds, which would impair its value to the new owner.

Market analysis. A report on the various factors and conditions that affect a given market and that will be influential in any decisions made regarding a business venture.

Market price. The price a property should bring, based on comparable sales of similar properties within recent months.

Market value. The price a property should bring from a fully informed buyer under no pressure to buy when the seller is under no pressure to sell.

Master plan. A guide to the use of property within a community, as established by a planning commission, to project the desired future growth and nature of the area covered.

Master's deed. *See* Sheriff's deed.

Material fact. Any information that, if revealed, might affect the decisions and judgments of those involved in a transaction.

Mechanic's lien. A lien that protects the interests of those performing work upon property when they have not been paid or when there is material furnished for which the builder or owner has not paid. The law provides specific remedies for such liens.

Menace. In law, the use of threats or violence to induce one to sign a contract.

Meridian line. The U.S. Government Survey lines running from north to south, used to establish township boundaries.

Mesne profits. Profits extracted from a property during the interim period when such property was illegally withheld from its rightful owner.

Metes and bounds. A method of describing real property by boundary markers and lines.

MGIC. The Mortgage Guarantee Insurance Corporation. One of the private companies that insure mortgages.

Minor. Any child who has not attained legal age.

Misdemeanor. A crime of lesser consequences, which is subject to minor jail terms, fines, or both.

Misplacement. Construction of a building on a property that is poorly chosen in terms of cost or the building's use.

Misrepresentation. Falsely representing to buyers property or facts about such property, or concealing from the participants important truths about the transaction.

MLS. Abbreviation for multiple listing service.

Modification agreement. A written change to a document which modifies the original terms by mutual agreement of all parties. This is commonly used to alter the terms of a mortgage.

Month-to-month tenancy. *See* Periodic tenancy.

Monument. An object placed at a fixed point by surveyors to establish their survey lines.

Moratorium. The suspension of liability for a debt during certain emergency periods when the government or lending institutions consider this step necessary for the public welfare.

Mortgage. A legal instrument used to make real property or personal property the security for payment of a loan. The mortgagor has one year for redemption after foreclosure and may maintain possession in the interim.

Mortgage banker. One who deals in mortgages, usually with his or her own capital or line of credit, selling such loans to other investors at more favorable prices and retaining the servicing responsibility for an additional fee.

Mortgage broker. One who negotiates the placing of loans but does not use his or her own capital for that purpose.

Mortgage certificate. An instrument used to signify partial ownership of a mortgage when there are many persons with a beneficial right to the mortgage, each with an undivided interest.

Mortgagee. The one who lends money secured by a mortgage. In its broader sense, any lender dealing in real property securities.

Mortgage insurance. Life insurance written to cover the amount of a mortgage on real property and paid in full in the event the mortgagor dies before the

Mortgage insurance. Life insurance written to cover the amount of a mortgage on real property and paid in full in the event the mortgagor dies before the balance on the loan has been fully retired.

Mortgage market. The general condition of the lending sources available at any given time to acquire and hold mortgages or trust deeds on property.

Mortgage participation. The assignment of a partial interest in a portfolio of loans to other lenders in order to recover capital and reinvest it for higher returns. This is a common practice among savings and loan associations, as well as some other lending institutions.

Mortgagor. The person borrowing the money secured by a mortgage.

Mortgagor's statement. The loan application form filed by a proposed borrower with the lending institution setting forth his or her assets, liabilities, income, and credit history for the review of the lending company.

MPS. Abbreviation for minimum property standards, an expression used in connection with FHA insured loans and also VA loans.

Muniments of title. Title deeds and documents showing the chain of title on a property.

Mutual consent. The complete agreement of all parties to a contract regarding the terms of that contract.

Mutual water company. A non-profit company formed to provide water to its stockholders who control its operation for their joint benefit.

NAHB. Abbreviation for National Association of Home Builders.

NAR. Abbreviation for National Association of Realtors®.

Naturalized citizen. A person who has been made a citizen of the United States under an act of Congress.

Negative amortization. When monthly payments on a mortgage are less than required to meet interest rate obligations, the result is negative amortization. The principal amount due increases or escalates until it is reversed by higher payments, payoffs, or refinancing.

Negotiable instrument. A promissory note or check that can be transferred by endorsement and that meets certain legal requirements.

Net earnings. Receipt from operating sources after deducting direct expenses but before depreciation, mortgage retirement, and financing charges.

Net income. *See* Net earnings.

Net lease. A lease wherein the landlord pays all expenses directly chargeable to the property, such as taxes and insurance.

Net listing. A listing agreement with a broker whose fee is determined by the amount he or she can obtain in excess of the seller's net figure. These listings have many problems and are frowned upon by many real estate boards and companies.

Net-net-net lease. A lease where the lessee pays a pro-rata share of direct expenses, such as taxes and insurance, and the lessor is assured of receiving a fixed income.

Notary public. A person authorized by law to take acknowledgments and oaths from individuals.

Note. *See* Promissory note.

Notice of abandonment. The notice that is filed when work is discontinued on an unfinished building job.

Notice of appeal. A notice filed to indicate that a court decision will be appealed to a higher court.

Notice of cessation. A *notice of abandonment.*

Notice of completion. Notice filed when all work has been completed upon a building according to contract specifications.

Notice of intended sale. A notice recorded when a business is sold, to give public and creditors knowledge of the transaction.

Notice of non-responsibility. A notice, which, when properly recorded and posted on the property, relieves the owner from the effect of mechanics' liens, under certain specified conditions.

Notice of default. A notice filed by a lender or trustee advising the borrower he or she is in default; starts the time running for foreclosure proceedings.

Notice to quit. A three-day notice required by law before a tenant delinquent in rental payments can be evicted by suit.

Obsolescence. *See* Depreciation, Functional obsolescence, and Social obsolescence.

Occupancy agreement. An interim agreement with a buyer to permit occupancy of the premises until the escrow can be closed and on specific terms and conditions.

Offset statement. A statement from a lender or lien holder as to the status of the lien, the balance due, and any other requirements.

Off-site improvements. In reference to subdivisions, these are improvements other than those physically on the lots involved and include streets, sewers, storm drains, and the like.

Open-end mortgage. A mortgage that permits the borrower to make improvements and obtain additional amounts to cover them without drawing new mortgages or creating additional costs.

Open listing. A non-exclusive listing given to one or more real estate agents; any agent can sell the property if he or she procures the buyer accepted by the owner, but the owner can also find his or her own buyer without paying any commission.

Open question. A question designed to open the response. It cannot be answered Yes or No and never suggests an answer.

Option. A written contract granting a proposed buyer or lessee a specific period of time in which to complete the agreement or forfeit the option deposit.

Optionee. The one obtaining the option right.

Optionor. The one granting the option to another.

Outlawed claim. A claim that is nullified because the person making it waited beyond the legal limits provided for exercising the claim.

Overbuilding. The construction of too many properties of a similar nature in a given market area, creating a surplus condition and reducing the price of all properties as a result.

Over-improved. A property that has received greater investment than its surrounding neighbors, when such cannot be easily regained upon sale, is considered over-improved.

Parol contract. A verbal contract or oral agreement.

Partial release clause. A clause in a land purchase contract and subsequent mortgage instruments which provides for the release of a parcel of land from the blanket mortgage when a specified, pro-rata sum has been paid to the holder of the mortgage or land owner. Subdividers use this procedure in order to develop land in sections while owner still holds an interest in the mortgage on the balance of the land involved.

Partial reconveyance. Same as partial release clause.

Partition. The dividing of an estate among its common owners.

Party wall. A dividing wall that separates two or more properties and to which each abutting owner has equal rights of use.

Par value. Market value. In reference to loan discount, no costs are involved when quoted at par, since this is 100¢ on the dollar.

Patent. An original conveyance of real estate from the federal government to a private owner.

Payee. The one receiving the sum due on a note.

Payor. The one paying the sum due on a note.

Payment guarantee. In trade-in housing programs, a guarantee to advance monthly payments and holding costs for a property owned by buyers, in order to give them time to sell and complete their other purchase.

Payoff penalty. *See* Prepayment penalty.

Pedestrian count. A tally of the number of persons passing a given location. Used for appraising business property.

Perceived value. A phrase used to depict what a buyer perceives or understands as value in terms of the investment or costs to be incurred for purchasing property.

Percentage lease. A lease that fixes the tenant's rent as a percentage of his or her gross monthly or annual business receipt.

Perfect escrow. The status of an escrow when all the monies, documents, and instructions necessary to close the transaction have been received by the escrow holder.

Periodic tenancy. Tenancy of property for an indefinite period; can be terminated by either party with proper notice.

Personal property. That which is essentially movable, or not affixed to real property; chattel.

Petition. An instrument presented to a court or legal body requesting action on a matter.

Physical depreciation. Any loss to property values caused by normal wear and tear or usage. Also includes such things as termite damage and dry-rot.

Piscary rights. The right to fish in the waters where such rights exist.

Plaintiff. The person commencing a lawsuit.

Planning commission. A government agency of city, town, or county which recommends certain zoning and property use for the benefit of the local citizens and whose actions are subject to the approval of elected officials as a rule.

Plat. A map or plan of a subdivision.

Pledge. A deposit of personal property used to secure a debt.

Pledgee. The person who receives a pledge.

Pledgor. The person making or giving a pledge.

Plottage value. The increased value enjoyed by a parcel when it can be acquired or used in connection with adjacent parcels.

Points. A term used to describe loan discounts collected by mortgage lenders as a means of increasing their yield on real estate loans.

Police power. A state government's power to enact and enforce laws that are for the public welfare.

Potential value. A value based on possible future circumstances, which must occur before the value exists.

Power of attorney. The instrument used to make one person an attorney-in-fact for another.

Power of sale. The right of a trustee or mortgagee to sell a property when the terms of the loan have not been met.

Pre-emption. The act of buying something before another person can do so.

Preliminary title report. A brief title report issued quickly to disclose any existing defects or problems, before completing the transaction.

Prepayment penalty. The penalty inflicted on mortgagors when they elect to pay the balance of the loan before it is due. Such payoff penalties vary greatly from one loan to another and should be checked before determining any given situation.

Prescription. Obtaining an easement on the property of another by adverse use for a number of years.

Prima facie. Literally, "on its face," or evident by its contents.

Principal. One who employs an agent or becomes a participant in a real estate transaction as owner, buyer, etc.

Privity. Mutuality of relationship or closeness.

Probate court. A court that has authority over the property of deceased persons and others incapable of managing their properties.

Procuring cause. The person responsible for bringing property and buyers together or introducing the facts to those who ultimately act upon them.

Profit-sharing guarantee. In trade-in housing, a contract that permits the seller and the guarantee company to share the profit generated above a certain fixed figure if more can be obtained.

Promissory note. A written promise to pay a certain sum of money at a definite date in the future.

Property management. A real estate specialty that includes the care, leasing, and maintenance of property for a fee. Property management is becoming an increasingly important service in all metropolitan areas.

Property settlement agreement. Agreements between divorcing man and wife as to the disposition of property they own jointly.

Proration. Division proportionately among the parties involved based on a fixed rate of computations.

Publication date. In foreclosure proceedings, the date when the notice of sale was first published as prescribed by law.

Public report. As pertains to subdivisions, a report issued by the real estate commissioner (or equivalent person) setting forth the known facts about a proposed subdivision; the report must be given to each buyer before he or she signs a purchase agreement.

P.U.D. Abbreviation for planned unit development: A zoning term for a land development plan based on density and use. Criteria established by planning authorities that permit the developer freedom to file a conforming master plan that balances open space, density of housing units and types of housing and related uses.

P.U.E. Abbreviation for public utilities easements.

Purchase-money mortgage. Any mortgage originated with the sale of property as part of the purchase price; in some states, any mortgage held by the seller of property as part of the purchase price.

Quasi. As, as if, or of similar nature to.

Quiet title. An action taken to remove clouds from a title by lawsuit, or to determine true status of title.

Quitclaim deed. A deed by which the grantor transfers any interest in a parcel of real estate he or she might have, but without any warranties.

Range. A strip of land running north and south, six miles wide, as established by U.S. Government Survey.

Ratification. Unqualified acceptance of a contract or agreement.

Real estate board. An organization of Realtors® and their associate salespeople, operating to improve their knowledge and the professional conduct of the real estate business.

Real property. Land and everything that is attached thereto.

Realtor®. The name applied to one who is a member in good standing of the National Association of Realtors®, which exclusively owns the rights to this title.

Recapture clause. A clause in an agreement, permitting the lessor to recover posession.

Receiver. One appointed to manage and dispose of the property of a bankrupt.

Reconveyance. Return to the original owner, as in the case of a trust deed that has been satisfied; the trustee signs a deed of conveyance.

Recovery fund. A fund established from the proceeds of licensing fees in some states for paying the claims of investors who have been injured by the acts of real estate professionals.

Redemption. The reacquisition of foreclosed property by the original owner during the prescribed time period.

Refinance. To restructure the financing on an existing property or to change the basic refinancing terms for a property already under financing.

Release clause. *See* Partial release clause.

Reliction. The gaining of land by the gradual receding of water from the usual water mark.

Remainder. The right to future possession after the termination of a life estate.

Remainderman. The one receiving the remainder.

Renegotiable mortgage. A mortgage that has a short-term rate that is adjusted at predetermined intervals (such as three to five years) and is renegotiated at the end of the short-term period according to rates then prevailing or according to previously agreed-upon terms.

Reproduction appraisal. A method of appraising based on computing the costs to reproduce a structure plus the value of the land involved.

Request for notice of default. An instrument anyone can file to request notification of any foreclosure action by a specific lien holder.

Rescission of contract. The nullifying of a contract by mutual consent or court decision.

Reservation. The temporary withholding of a property from the market to one buyer until he or she can confirm a decision.

Resident manager. One who lives on the premises of an income-producing building and manages the units in a limited fashion.

Restriction. A limitation on the use of property, imposed by the previous grantor or subdivider.

Retainer. An amount paid to retain the services of any professional, such as a lawyer.

Revenue stamps. The government documentary stamps, which are affixed to all deeds and transfer documents to verify payment of tax.

Reverse annuity mortgage. A mortgage in which regular payments are made to the mortgagor from the appraised equity of the property, to help supplement the mortgagor's income. The debt is repaid from the sale of the property or the estate upon the death of the owner. Occasionally, this is tied to a life insurance policy.

Reverse finance guarantee. A trade-in tool used to assure the seller of property that the funds necessary to liquidate the buyer's property will be available at a specified time.

Reverse trade-in guarantee. In trade-in housing, the transferring of a trade-in property to the seller of the first property with a back-up guarantee from the trade-in company to assure sale of said parcel.

Reversionary interest. The remaining right to an estate or the residue when the life estate is terminated.

Right of survivorship. The right, contained in a joint tenancy deed, for the surviving tenants to acquire the interest of the deceased tenant.

Right of way. An easement that grants to its receiver the right to pass over or maintain use of a parcel of property belonging to another.

Riparian rights. The rights of an owner to use the water that is on, under, or adjacent to his or her land.

Running with the land. An expression used to identify any right in property that continues despite the sequence of ownership.

Sale and leaseback agreement. *See* Leaseback agreement.

Sales and use tax. A levy on retail sales collected from the vendor by the state or city in which he or she operates.

Sandwich lease. The remaining interest of the original lessee after real estate has been subleased to another tenant.

Satisfaction of mortgage. An instrument recorded to verify that the mortgagor has satisfied his or her debt.

Seal. The legal identification of corporations and political entities used to attest to their actions.

Second deed of trust. *See* Second mortgage.

Second mortgage. A mortgage second in rank and subordinate to a first mortgage. In the event of foreclosure, the first mortgage is paid off before the second, or junior, mortgage.

Secondary financing. Junior liens created to help finance the acquisition of property or to secure additional indebtedness.

Secondary mortgage market. The outlet for primary mortgages to those who buy them for investment after the original lender has completed the purchase of the loans. Fannie Mae is a prime factor in the secondary mortgage market.

Section. Pertaining to land, a standard measurement containing 640 acres and equal to one square mile.

Security. Any stock, note, treasury stock, debenture, or other evidence of indebtedness that can be used to secure the interest named.

Separate property. Property of either spouse that is not part of the community estate.

Setback line. The building line established by local authorities who control where buildings may be placed on a given lot.

Severance damage. The loss in value to a property as a result of a partial condemnation or acquisition by another of a part of the original parcel. Compensation should be paid for the lowered remaining value after severance.

Shared appreciation mortgage (SAM). A mortgage in which the lender offers the borrower a below-market interest rate in exchange for a share in the equity appreciation of the property as determined at a specified future date. Sometimes the third party invests the down payment or underwrites the mortgage to the prime lender for the equity participation privilege.

Sheriff's deed. A deed given when property is sold by order of the court for payment of a debt.

Sinking fund. A method of handling depreciation by setting aside certain amounts from the income of the property to offset the replacement costs when they are needed.

Site economics. The analysis of a given building site for commercial purposes which relates cost to productivity and the efficiency of the site in terms of related amenities.

Social obsolescence. Depreciation in value due to external rather than internal influences, such as a change in the neighborhood or similar factors.

Soffit. The enclosed portion of the space bordering the room at ceiling level, normally above cabinets.

Special assessment. A levy against property for improvements which are designed to benefit that property particularly.

Specific lien. A lien that applies to one property in particular, as compared to a general lien, which applies to all property of the individual involved.

Specific performance. A court order requiring a person to do what he or she has previously agreed to do.

Specific risk guarantee. In trade-in housing, a guarantee that obligates someone to carry a specific amount of any loss that might result from the trade.

Spendable income. Money left from rent proceeds after paying mortgages, taxes, and other expenses, which gives the owner funds to use for other purposes.

Squatter's rights. The right to occupy land by virtue of undisputed and undisturbed usage, but without legal title to such property. *See* Adverse possession.

S.R.A. Abbreviation for "Society of Residential Appraisers."

Standard title policy. The title policy usually issued to a buyer of real property; insures against all defects of record, but excludes physical inspection of the premises and other important items. *See* A.T.A. policy.

Statement of conditions. *See* Mortgagor's statement.

Statement of identity. A questionnaire used by title companies to help identify a person when the records indicate confusion due to many persons having similar names.

Statute of frauds. Law that requires certain types of contracts to be in writing.

Statute of limitations. State law limiting the time in which certain actions may be introduced in a court of law. When expired, the action is said to have outlawed.

Statutory dedication. The enforced granting to city, state, county, etc. of land by an individual for certain specific uses, such as streets. Subdividers must frequently dedicate their completed streets to the municipality in which they subdivide.

Staybonds. A bond issued to cover a judgment while the judgment is on appeal to a higher court.

Step-up lease. A lease that provides for increased amounts of rent over succeeding periods.

Straight-line depreciation. Setting aside or allowing a fixed sum of money each year to offset replacement or improvements when needed.

Straight note. An unamortized note that is all due and payable at one time in one sum.

Subcontractor. One who accepts an assignment of work from another contractor, who is known as the general contractor.

Subdivision. Definition of a subdivision varies by state. In many, it is any parcel divided into five or more parcels for sale or lease. A subdivision map is usually required for filing within the county recorder's office of the area where project is located.

"Subject to" clause. In real estate contracts, such a clause acknowledges a condition or debt but does not necessarily make the purchaser liable for it. Also, any "subject to" condition of a contract becomes a contingency, which makes the entire contract void if not completed according to written terms.

Sublease. The letting of property to another under the terms of an existing primary lease.

Subordination clause. A clause in a mortgage or trust deed which provides that this debt and security be secondary to other obligations that the mortgagor intends to incur and that are usually specified in the agreement to subordinate.

Subpoena. A judicial writ requiring a person to appear in court at a particular time and for a particular matter.

Subrogation. The act of substituting one person in the place of another with reference to a claim or right.

Succession. The process of receiving property as the result of some subsequent event, such as the death of a spouse.

Successor's liability. The liability of the new owner of a business for the unpaid taxes of the former owner if they have not been satisfied.

Surety bond. A bond guaranteeing performance of a specified act or payment of the amount required to complete the act.

Surface-water rights. The right to use the water that is on the surface of the ground.

Sweat equity. Obtaining title to property or earning the down payment to purchase property by performing certain items of work for a predetermined value.

Tandem plan. A financing package that combines FHA and VA financing.

Tangible property. That which has material existence and is susceptible to the senses, such as land, buildings, and furnishings.

Tax abatement. A reduction or deduction in taxes generally resulting from an appeal to the Board of Equalization when one thinks he or she has been unfairly taxed.

Taxable value. *See* Assessed value.

Tax deed. The deed given when property is sold for a tax delinquency.

Tax penalty. A levy for failure to pay taxes on time.

Tax sale. The sale of property by the state at auction to settle delinquent taxes.

Tax-service fee. A fee paid to an independent company for searching the tax records annually to assure the lender that the taxes and other assessments are current or to report any delinquencies.

Tenancy. An estate less than freehold; a leasehold estate.

Tenancy at sufferance. The continued occupancy of a property by a tenant after the lease has expired, with the owner permitting this arrangement on a temporary basis.

Tenancy in common. Ownership by two or more persons who hold undivided interest, not necessarily equal, without any right of survivorship.

Tender. An unconditional offer of payment of a debt or an offer of performance.

Tenements. All rights in land that are conveyed when the land is conveyed.

Tentative map. The map produced by a subdivider for submission to governmental agencies and bodies for approval before finalization.

Tenure in land. The manner and nature in which land is held. Also, a period of time.

Testament. A will.

Testate. Leaving a will upon death.

Testator. Man who makes a will.

Testatrix. Woman who makes a will.

Tide lands. Property covered from time to time (if not permanently) by ocean or lake waters.

"Time is of the essence" clause. A clause that specifies that time is an essential ingredient in the contract concerned and that failure to meet time for performance will be considered a violation of the contract.

Title insurance. Protection to a property owner against loss through special insurance purchased when property is acquired or financed.

Titles. Evidences of ownership and lawful possession of property.

Topography. The general nature of the surface of land.

Tort. A wrongful or harmful act that violates legal rights.

Township. A unit of land six miles square (36 square miles) that is established by government survey.

Trust deed. A form of mortgage instrument used in lieu of a mortgage in many states. There are three parties to a trust deed: the trustor (borrower), the trustee (interim title holder), and the beneficiary (the lender). It has many advantages to both lender and borrower, and is gaining in popularity for that reason.

Trust fund. A fund or impound collected from the mortgagor to meet his or her tax and insurance payments when due. Many lenders require this monthly collection in order to assure having sufficient amounts on hand when obligations are due.

Trustee. A person or corporation that holds title in trust until a debt has been repaid or a service performed. Under trust deeds, the trustee holds title for the beneficiary until the obligation is paid.

Trustor. A person who borrows money under a deed of trust.

Truth-in-lending law. A federal law of the civil code (Section 226.10) that requires full disclosure of the costs of borrowing money in advertisements and promotional literature. The annual percentage rate must be accurately expressed in terms of all costs incurred in mortgage financing. Failure to include the words "annual percentage rate" or "A.P.R." in an ad that mentions interest rate is a violation of the truth-in-lending law.

Unbalanced improvement. An improvement to real property which is not the one best suited for the site on which it is placed.

Under-improvement. Construction of improvements on land which are less expensive and smaller than required for that land to produce highest use.

Undivided interest. An interest that cannot be separated from the interests in that property which others may have and that gives the holder an equal right to the use of the premises.

Undue influence. Taking any advantage of another by playing on his or her weaknesses or distress.

Unilateral contract. A contract that imposes an obligation on only one party to the contract.

Unimproved land. Land upon which no buildings have been constructed.

Unities. The essentials to a joint tenancy deed; the unities of time, title, interest, and possession.

Unlawful detainer action. A legal action to lawfully remove a tenant from a building after he or she has defaulted and been notified to move.

Unmarried. The status of one who has been married but is now divorced or widowed.

Unsecured. Not protected by assets or security instruments.

U.L.I. Abbreviation for Urban Land Institute—an association of organizations and individuals devoted to community planning and improvement of land-use concepts.

Urban property. Property located within the core of a city.

Urban renewal. Program to improve substandard areas and buildings in metropolitan cities.

Use tax. A sales tax on goods purchased out of state.

Usury. Charging a higher rate of interest than the law allows.

VA. Abbreviation for Veterans Administration.

Vacancy factor. The percentage of nonoccupancies in a building or a type of unit, as related to the total available.

Valid. Legally enforceable; binding.

Valuation. An estimate of worth or price.

Variable interest rate mortgage (VIRM). A mortgage that fluctuates in interest rates as the mortgage market changes in availability and cost of mortgage money. Such changes affect the monthly payments on VIRMs, usually within prescribed limits of change over specific periods of time.

Vehicular traffic. The number of cars or vehicles that pass a given point.

Vendee. A buyer.

Vendor. A seller.

Venue. The place where an acknowledgment is taken, or an action held.

Verification. A confirmation of the facts as sworn by written statement.

Verification of deposit. A document used by FHA and VA to verify the amount of cash assets held by the buyer or the buyer's trustees for performance of the purchase agreement.

Verification of employment. A document used by FHA and VA to verify the current and past history of employment for an applicant for a loan.

Vest. To bestow upon or grant, as title to property.

Veteran's exemption. In some states, veteran property owners are given a tax exemption on a portion of their tax bill.

Void. Not valid at law; not binding.

Voidable. May be declared void in the future, but is not actually void until so judged by a court of law.

Voluntary lien. A lien placed on the property with the consent of the owner, such as a mortgage.

Waive. To abandon, forgo, or relinquish a right.

Warranty deed. A deed that recites certain specified warranties, commonly used in most states, except California where the grant deed has replaced it.

Waste. In real estate, the abuse of property by a tenant or someone having a temporary interest in the property, resulting in loss to the owner.

Water table. The depth underground of the natural waters as measured from the surface.

Wraparound mortgages. The wraparound or all-inclusive mortgage combines existing mortgages plus additional financing into one comprehensive mortgage. The new mortgage thus incorporates older ones, although the sequence of senior to junior lien rights is unaffected.

Writ of execution. A court order that property must be sold to pay a debt.

Yield. The return for invested money anticipated by the investor. It is computed based on three factors: interest, term, and discount.

Yield guides. Tables for computing the various yields one can receive from investments such as mortgages and second deeds of trust.

Zero-lot-line housing. A zoning arrangement that permits the builder to design and build a residential structure abutting one or more of the boundaries of the lot. This concept is typically associated with planned unit developments or as a variation in condominium projects. Such housing is also known as: patio homes, garden homes, and cluster homes.

Zoning. The control of land usage by city, county, or state authorities with power to limit the property use to these standards.